Traveler's Language Guides:
Italian

Developed by
Raffaella Marini

All inquiries should be addressed to:
Barron's Educational Series, Inc.
250 Wireless Boulevard
Hauppauge, NY 11788
http://www.barronseduc.com

ISBN-13: 978-0-764-1320-70
ISBN-10: 0-7641-3207-5
Library of Congress Control Number 2005921554

Photo Credits
National Self-help Association for the Physically Handicapped,
Krautheim: 73; Cycleurope, Bergisch-Gladback: 58; ENIT (Italian
National Tourist Office), Frankfurt: 11, 29, 121; Ford Motor
Company, Inc.: 56; H. Geissel, Stuttgart: 15, 47, 77, 111, 133; HB
Publishing, S. Feldhoff and A.C. Martin: 139, HB Publishing, G.
Krewitt: 175; U. Messelhäuser, Salem: 69, 87, 164; M. Sucha, Prag:
19; Wolpert Photo Design, Stuttgart: 38-39, 96-102, 145

Cover: Tiophoto (Frank Chmura, Nisse Peterson, Torleif Svensson
Translated from the German by Eric A. Bye, M.A.

Printed in China
9 8 7 6 5 4 3 2 1

In general, Italian is pronounced just as it is written. In most words of more than one syllable, the emphasis falls on the next-to-the-last one: ristorante, venire, giornale. In this travel book exceptions will be indicated by a dot under the accented vowel (piccolo, giovane).

Pronunciation Details

- Double consonants are both sounded: bel-lo
- When two vowels fall together they are sounded individually: E-uropa

c, cc	like an English hard *c* or *k* sound (not aspirated) before consonants and before the vowels *a, o, u*	classe banco casa
	like the English *ch* sound in *chair* before the vowels *e, i*	accento dieci
ch, cch	like the English hard *c* or *k* (not aspirated)	che, pacchi
ci, cci	like the English *ch* sound in *chair:* before *a, o, u*	ciao! cioccolata
g, gg	like the English hard *g* sound before consonants and before *a ,o, u* [sic]	grande gondola
	as in *gentle* (soft *g*): before *e, i*	gente oggi
gh	like an English hard *g*	ghiaccio
gi, ggi	as in the English word *gentle* (soft *g*)	mangiare
gl	like the middle sound in *million*	figlio
gn	as in *cognac*	bagno
h	is never pronounced	ho
qu	as in the English word *quality*	acqua
r	trilled or rolled	mare
s	a soft *s* sound as in *house* and *case*: at the start of a word	sole sera
	a *z* sound as in *rose*: between two vowels	rosa

sc	as in *scale*: before consonants and before *a, o, u*	scrivere scusi
	like the final sound in *wash*: before *a, o, u*; the *i* is mute in this instance	pesce, uscita
sp	as in *wasp*	sport
st	as in *stand*	stato
v	as in *video*	vespa

Nouns that end in –*o* are masculine; nouns that end in -*a* are feminine. Only in the case of exceptions to this rule (**mano**, *f* hand) and with other endings (**canzone** *f* song) will the gender of nouns be indicated.

The Italian Alphabet

A	a	[ah]	J	j	[jeh loongah]	S	s	[éhsseh]
B	b	[beh]	K	k	[káhpah]	T	t	[teh]
C	c	[cheh]	L	l	[éhlleh]	U	u	[oo]
D	d	[deh]	M	m	[éhmmeh]	V	v	[veh]
E	e	[eh]	N	n	[éhnneh]	W	w	[dóhpeeah veh]
F	f	[éffeh]	O	o	[oh]	X	x	[eeks]
G	g	[jeh]	P	p	[peh]	Y	y	[yípseelohn]
H	h	[ákkah]	Q	q	[koo]	Z	z	[zeh]
I	i	[ee]	R	r	[éhrreh]			

acc	Accusative (direct object)	accusativo
adj	Adjective	aggettivo
adv	Adverb	avverbio
conj	Conjunction	congiunzione
dat	Dative (indirect object)	dativo
el	Electricity	elettricità
f	Feminine	femminile
m	Masculine	maschile
mech	Mechanics	meccanica
med	Medicine	medicina
pers prn	Personal Pronoun	pronome personale
pl	Plural	plurale
poss adj	Possessive Adjective	pronome possessivo
prn	Pronoun	pronome
prp	Preposition	preposizione
qc	Something	qualcosa
qd	Someone	qualcuno
refl prn	Reflexive Pronoun	pronome riflessivo
rel prn	Relative Pronoun	pronome relativo
sing	Singular	singolare
sn	Someone	a qualcuno
sth	Something	qualcosa
tele	Telecommunications	telecomunicazione

General Abbreviations

a.	arrivo	Arrival
a.C.	avanti Cristo	BC
ACI	Automobile Club Italiano	Italian Automobile Club
CIT	Compagnia Italiana Turismo	Italian Touring Club
D	diretto	Express Train
d.C.	dopo Cristo	AD
DD	direttissimo	Fast Train
dott.	dottore	Doctor
ecc.	eccetera	etc.
ENIT	Ente Nazionale Italiano per il Turismo	National Tourist Office
F.S.	Ferrovie dello Stato	National Railway

IVA	imposta sul valore aggiunto	Value Added Tax
m.	monte / metro	Mountain / Meter
mq.	metro quadrato	Square meter
p.	pagina	Page
part.	partenza	Departure
p. es.	per esempio	e.g., for example
P. S.	Pubblica Sicurezza	Public Security Police
rag.	ragioniere	Academic title (graduate of a professional training school)
RAI	Radio Audizioni Italiane	Italian Radio and Television Ital. Corporation
Sig.	signor	Mr.
Sig.na	signorina	Miss
Sig.ra	signora	Mrs.
s.p.a.	società per azioni	Corporation
s. r. l.	società a responsabilità limitata	Limited Liability Corporation
Ue	Unione europea	European Union
UME	Unione Monetaria Europea	European Union Currency

Different Countries, Different Customs

Cross-Cultural Tips

Direct Address

In Italy people commonly address one another in familiar terms, especially when the people are about the same age. People who have things in common change from formal to familiar terms quite quickly. Even colleagues at work often speak to each other with the familiar form of address.

Titles

Men are addressed as **signor** plus the family name (if known). Women are addressed as **signora**, and younger ladies as **signorina**, often without the family name. In Italy the salutation **signorina** definitely is the norm.

In formal dealings, titles are extremely important. Titles and professional designations are placed before the name. So for example, attorney Rossi will usually be introduced as **l'avvocato** Rossi. One frequent title is **dottore/dottoressa**, which people who have a college education can use. Except for elementary school teachers, all teachers and professors are addressed as **professore/professoressa**. One also frequently hears the terms **ragioniere/ragioniera** and **ingegnere** (for accountant and engineer, respectively).

Greetings

In formal situations people greet one another with a brief, firm handshake. In private, men also greet one another with a handshake; there is also the **bacino**, a kiss on each cheek.

People say **buon giorno** until the middle of the day, and **buona sera** thereafter. **Buona notte** is very familiar and is used in the late evening before going to bed.

Ciao is used to greet good friends and acquaintances with whom you use the familiar form of address.

Saying Good-bye

The official expression for good-bye is **arrivederci** or **arrivederLa**, if you want to be particularly respectful of an individual.

Ciao is used to say good-bye to good friends. **Ci vediamo**, *we'll see each other*, is yet another colloquial way in which acquaintances say good-bye to one another.

When a person leaves a shop, a restaurant, or a bar, it's also possible to say **buon giorno** or **buona sera**, depending on the time of day, instead of **arrivederci**.

Courtesy

Strangers are addressed politely using **scusi** (*excuse me*), or with **senta scusi** if you merely want to get someone's attention. **Mi dispiace** (I'm sorry) can be used to comment on a significant mishap.

Please

Italian has several expressions for *please:* **per favore, per piacere, per cortesia,** and **prego**. The first three expressions are used to request something or to ask for a favor, as in **Per me, per piacere, un caffè. Prego** is used to respond to **grazie** or when one offers something, as in **Ecco la birra, prego!**

Mi raccomando also means *please*, but it is used to place a special emphasis on a request: **Una birra, ma fredda, mi raccomando!** (*A beer, but make it a cold one!*)

If you want to ask someone for a favor, you begin the sentence with **scusi** or with **abbia pazienza, potrebbe aiutarmi a sistemare la valigia?** Translated literally: Would you have the patience, could you help me to move the suitcase?

If someone is standing in the way, you say **permesso!**—*May I?*

Eating and Drinking

Breakfast in Italy is not particularly substantial. It usually consists of only **caffè** and a couple of **biscotti** (biscuits) or **cereali** (cereals), less commonly of **pane, burro e marmellata** (bread, butter, and jelly). Many people have breakfast in a **bar** and quickly drink while standing. They drink a **cappuccino, caffè,** or **caffè marchiato** and eat a **brioscia**, a brioche or type of sweet roll.

The noon and evening meals consist of a **primo** and a **secondo piatto** (the appetizer and main course). The **primo** may be pasta, **riso** (a rice dish), or a **minestra** (soup); the **secondo, carne** (meat) or **pesce** (fish) with side dishes. The meal concludes with a **dolce** (a sweet) or **frutta** (fruit) and the nearly mandatory **caffè**.

Pizza is a main course and even in Italy is eaten without side dishes; most usually drink beer with it.

At the table, people wish each other **Buon appetito!** (Enjoy your meal!), and answer with **Grazie, altrettanto**—*thanks, same to you*. When people drink something together, they say **Alla salute, Cin cin,** or even **Prosit**.

Bars and Restaurants

When people go out with friends in Italy, they pay the bill together and then divide it up. That is referred to as **pagare alla romana**, paying in the Roman way. In a small group just one person takes care of the bill. The amount of the bill is not rounded up, as we often do, but rather people wait until the waiter returns with the change, and then the tip is left on the table.

It is considered impolite to sit at a table already occupied by people you don't know, even if there are empty seats. However in pizzerias that is becoming more accepted.

Invitations

In Italy it is customary to decline the first invitation politely; you can allow yourself to be convinced by the second invitation.

Gifts and compliments play an important role in Italy and are observed as rituals. Statements like **Ma non dovevi scomodarti!** or **Ma non occorreva!** *(You shouldn't have!)* are common. When you get an invitation, sweets and pastries from a confectioner's shop or a small gift are welcome. Flowers are rarely given, however.

Using the Telephone

Most Italians answer the telephone with the word **pronto**; that is, you don't immediately say your name. The other person then may respond with **pronto** and say who is calling.

Travel Preparations

> **When You Take a Trip...**
> You can find out all kinds of information about your
> destination by searching online under the place name. In
> addition, you can find information about
> • daily updates on travel news and interesting reports
> • regular theme specials and contests
> • mini-guides that can be printed out.

Booking a Hotel by E-mail

Vorrei prenotare una camera singola/matrimoniale/doppia per
due notti dal 24 al 25 giugno. Vi prego di informarmi sulle Vs.
disponibilità e sulle tariffe per il pernottamento e la mezza
pensione.
Distinti saluti.

Dear Sir or Madam:
I would like to reserve a single/double/room with a double bed
for two nights on June 24 and 25. Please let me know if you
have any vacancies and the total cost per night (including
dinner).
Sincerely,

Renting a Car by E-mail

Vorrei noleggiare un'automobile di piccola
(un'utilitaria)/media/grossa cilindrata/un minibus a 7 posti dal
20 al 25 luglio all'aeroporto di Firenze e restituirla all'aeroporto
di Linate/Milano dal quale ripartirò. Vi prego di mandarmi
informazioni sulle tariffe e sui documenti necessari.
Distinti saluti.

Dear Sir or Madam:
I would like to rent a small / mid-size / full size car / van from
July 20-25 from the Florence airport. I depart from Linate /
Milano, so I wish to drop off the car there. Please tell me your
rates and what documents I will need.
Sincerely,

General Questions

I plan to spend my vacation in... Could you please give me some information about accommodations in the area?
Ho intenzione di passare le vacanze a ... Potrebbe darmi informazioni sulle possibilità di alloggio nei dintorni?

What type of lodgings did you have in mind?
A quale tipo di alloggio aveva pensato?

Hotel
albergo
Pension
pensione
Tourist room
sistemazione in famiglia
Vacation apartment
appartamento (per le vacanze)

Questions about Lodging

Hotel—Pension—Bed and Breakfast

I'm looking for a hotel, but it mustn't be too expensive—in the medium price range.
Cerco un albergo, ma non troppo caro, a prezzo moderato.

I'm looking for a hotel with an indoor swimming pool / golf course / tennis courts.
Cerco un albergo con piscina coperta/ campo da golf/ campi da tennis.

For how many people?
Per quante persone?

Are dogs permitted?
Sono ammessi i cani lì?

Is it possible to add another bed to a room?
Potrebbe aggiungere un altro letto in una delle camere?

How much does it cost per week?
Quanto costa alla settimana?

Vacation Houses and Apartments

I'm looking for a vacation apartment or a bungalow.
Cerco un appartamento o un bungalow per le vacanze.

Is there...?
C'è ...?

a child's bed
un lettino

a high chair
un seggiolotto

a television
la televisione

a telephone
il telefono

a washing machine
la lavatrice

a dishwasher
la lavastoviglie

a microwave
il microonde

Is the cost of electricity included?
La corrente è inclusa?

Are there sheets and towels?
Ci sono la biancheria e gli asciugamani?

How much is the deposit and when is it due?
Quant'è la caparra e quando va pagata?

Where and when may I pick up the keys?
Dove e quando posso ritirare le chiavi?

Camping

I am looking for a small campground on the southern coast. Can you recommend something?
Cerco un piccolo campeggio sulla costa meridionale. Potrebbe raccomandarmi qualcosa?

Italy—Land of Longing?

Italy is the land of antiquity and modernity, of painting and sculpture, architecture, modern design, and the opera. Italy—the land of noise and silence of fast cars and traffic jams, of fashion, soccer, and commercial television. The land of good food, the best coffees and ice cream, Latin lovers and sunglasses, the land of "Mamma" and the momma's boy. Italy—the land of the changing government, the center of the Catholic Church and the cradle of European communism, the land of Don Camillo and Peppone, friendship and nepotism, revolution and conformity, of individualists and patriots, the land of communication. Get into communication in a big way! Have fun as you meet Italy, the Italians, and the Italian language!

The Essentials in Brief

Yes.
Sì.

No.
No.

Please.
Per favore.

Thank you!
Grazie!

Thanks a lot!
Grazie tante!

Thank you, same to you!
Grazie, altrettanto!

You're welcome. / Don't mention it.
Prego! Non c'è di che!

You're welcome.
Di niente!

Pardon me?
Come dice?

Of course!
Certo!

Agreed!
D'accordo!

OK!
Okay!

Fine!
Va bene!

Excuse me!
Scusi!

Just a moment, please!
Un momento, prego!

That's enough!
Ora/Adesso basta!

Help!
Aiuto!

Who?
Chi?

What?
Che cosa?

Which one?
Quale?

To whom?
A chi?

Whom?
Chi?

Where?
Dove?

Where is... / Where are...?
Dov'è ...? / Dove sono ...?

How much?
Quanto?

How long?
Quanto/Per quanto (tempo)?

When?
Quando?

At what time?
A che ora?

I would like...
Vorrei ...

Is there / Are there...?
C'è/Ci sono ...?

0	zero
1	uno
2	due
3	tre
4	quattro
5	cinque
6	sei
7	sette
8	otto
9	nove
10	dieci
11	undici
12	dodici
13	tredici
14	quattordici
15	quindici
16	sedici
17	diciassette
18	diciotto
19	diciannove
20	venti
21	ventuno
22	ventidue
23	ventitré
24	ventiquattro
25	venticinque
26	ventisei
27	ventisette
28	ventotto
29	ventinove
30	trenta
31	trentuno
32	trentadue
40	quaranta
50	cinquanta
60	sessanta
70	settanta
80	ottanta
90	novanta
100	cento
101	centouno
200	duecento
300	trecento
1000	mille

2 000	....	duemila
3 000	....	tremila
10 000	....	diecimila
100 000	....	centomila
1 000 000	....	un milione
1st	....	primo
2nd	....	secondo
3rd	....	terzo
4th	....	quarto
5th	....	quinto
6th	....	sesto
7th	....	settimo
8th	....	ottavo
9th	....	nono
10th	....	decimo
1/2	....	un mezzo
1/3	....	un terzo
1/4	....	un quarto
3/4	....	tre quarti
3,5 %	....	tre virgola cinque per cento
27 °C	....	ventisette gradi
–5 °C	....	cinque gradi sotto zero
1999	....	millenovecentonovantanove
2003	....	duemilatre
millimeter	....	millimetro
centimeter	....	centimetro
meter	....	metro
kilometer	....	chilometro
nautical mile	....	miglio marino
square meter	....	metro quadrato
square kilometer	....	chilometro quadrato
liter	....	litro
gram	....	grammo
100 grams	....	un etto
pound	....	mezzo chilo
kilo	....	chilogrammo

Telling Time

Clock Time

What time is it, please?
Che ore sono/Che ora è per favore?

It is exactly...
Sono le/È l' ... in punto.

23

It's about...
Sono circa ...

  three o'clock.
  le tre.

  five past three.
  le tre e cinque.

  ten past three.
  le tre e dieci.

  quarter past three.
  le tre e un quarto.

  three-thirty.
  le tre e mezza.

  quarter of four.
  le quattro meno un quarto.

  five to four.
  le quattro meno cinque.

It's one o'clock.
È l'una.

It's twelve noon / midnight.
È mezzogiorno/mezzanotte.

At what time? / When?
A che ora?/Quando?

At one o'clock.
All'una.

At two o'clock
Alle due.

Around four o'clock.
Verso le quattro.

In an hour.
Fra un'ora.

In two hours.
Fra due ore.

Not before nine o'clock in the morning.
Non prima delle nove del mattino.

After eight o'clock in the evening.
Dopo le otto di sera.

Between three and four o'clock.
Tra le tre e le quattro.

How long?
Per quanto tempo?

Two hours.
Per due ore.

24

From 10 to 11.
Dalle dięci alle ųndici.

Up till five o'clock
Fino alle cįnque.

Since what time?
Da quando?

Since 8:00 A.M. in the morning.
Dalle otto del mattino.

For (= since) a half hour.
Da mezz'ora.

For (=since) a week.
Da una settimana.

around noon	verso mezzogiorno
at night	la notte
at noontime	a mezzogiorno
the day after tomorrow	dopo domani
the day before yesterday	l'altro ieri
during the day	il giorno
early	presto
every day	ogni giorno
every day	tutti i giorni
every hour	ogni ora
from time to time	di tanto in tanto
in a week	fra una settimana
in the afternoon	il pomeriggio
in the evening	la sera
in the morning	la mattina
in two weeks	fra quindici giorni
last Monday	lunedì scorso
late	tardi
later	più tardi
next year	l'anno prossimo
now	ora, adesso
on Sunday	domenica
on the weekend	il fine settimana
recently	recentemente
sometimes	a volte
soon	presto
ten minutes ago	dieci minuti fa
this morning / this evening	stamattina/stasera
this week	questa settimana
today	oggi
tomorrow	domani
tomorrow morning/	domattina/domani sera

tomorrow evening

within a week .... entro una settimana
yesterday .... ieri

The Days of the Week

Monday .... lunedì
Tuesday .... martedì
Wednesday .... mercoledì
Thursday .... giovedì
Friday .... venerdì
Saturday .... sabato
Sunday .... domenica

The Months

January .... gennaio
February .... febbraio
March .... marzo
April .... aprile
May .... maggio
June .... giugno
July .... luglio
August .... agosto
September .... settembre
October .... ottobre
November .... novembre
December .... dicembre

The Seasons

Spring .... la primavera
Summer .... l'estate f
Fall .... l'autunno
Winter .... l'inverno

Holidays

New Year's .... Capodanno
Easter .... Pasqua
Easter Monday .... Lunedì dell'Angelo
April 25 (Liberation from ... Liberazione
Fascism)
May 1 (Workers' Day) ..... Festa del lavoro
June 2 (Founding of the ... Festa della Repubblica
  Italian Republic)
Assumption .... Assunzione, Ferragosto
All Saints' Day (Nov. 1) .... Ognissanti

December 8 (Immaculate . Immacolata Concezione
Conception)
Christmas Day . . . . Il giorno di Natale
Boxing Day . . . . Santo Stefano

The Date

What's today's date?
Quanti ne abbiamo oggi?

Today is May first.
Oggi è il primo maggio.

> **Primo, due, tre...**
> The Italians always use the cardinal numbers when giving the
> date; only for the first of each month do they use the ordinal
> number *primo*.

Weather

What great/awful weather!
Che tempo splendido/da cani.

It is very cold/hot/humid.
Fa molto freddo/caldo/è afoso.

It is foggy/windy.
C'è nebbia/vento.

The weather will remain nice/bad.
Rimane bello/brutto.

It's going to become warmer/colder.
Sta diventando più caldo/freddo.

It's going to rain/snow
Pioverà. / Nevicherà.

The roads are slippery.
Le strade sono ghiacciate.

Visibility is only 20 m / less than 50 m.
C'è una visibilità di soli 20 metri / inferiore ai 50 metri.

Chains are required.
Ci vogliono le catene.

air . . . . aria
calm . . . . bonaccia
cloud . . . . nuvola
cloudy . . . . nuvoloso
cold . . . . freddo

27

damp	bagnato
fog	nebbia
frost	gelo
gust of wind	raffica di vento
heat	caldo
heat wave	ondata di caldo
high tide	alta marea
hot	caldo, bollente
humid	afoso
ice	ghiaccio
lightning	il fulmine
low tide	bassa marea
rain	pioggia
rainstorm	gli scrosci di pioggia
rainy	piovoso
snow	la neve
sun	il sole
sunny	soleggiato
temperature	temperatura
thunder	tuono
variable	variabile
warm	caldo
weather	tempo
weather forecast	le previsioni metereologiche
weather report	bollettino meteorologico
wind	vento
wind speed	intensità del vento

Colors

beige	beige
black	nero
blue	blu
brown	marrone
colored	a colori
gold	color oro
gray	grigio
green	verde
orange	arancione
pink	rosa
purple	lilla
red	rosso
silver	color argento
single color	a tinta unita
turquoise	turchese
violet	viola

A Good Chat...

There is always a chance for a little chat in Italy—whether on the piazza or in front of the house, in a bar, or in front of the church, people meet up or stop by briefly for a chat; the onomatopoetic term for that in Italian is *chiacchierare*. The cell phone is always at hand, whether in the line at the supermarket checkout, on the beach while sunbathing, or during a pleasant evening meal with the family.

Saying Hello and Good-bye

Greetings

Good day!
Buon giorno.

Good morning!
Buon giorno.

Good evening!
Buona sera.

Buon giorno is used up until the midday meal; after the midday meal *buona sera* is used.

Hi! Howdy!
Ciạo!

Kisses

Friends, good acquaintances, and relatives greet one another with a kiss on each cheek.

What is your name?
Come si chiama?

What is your name?
Come ti chiami?

My name is...
Mi chiamo ...

How are you?
Come sta?

How's it going?
Come va?

Fine, thanks. How about you?
Bene, grazie. E Lei/tu?

May I make an introduction? This is...
Le posso presentare ... Questa / Questo è ...

Mrs. X / Miss X / Mr. X.
la signora X / la signorina X / il signor X.

my husband/son
mio marito/figlio.

my wife/ daughter
mia moglie/figlia.

my friend/good friend (m.)
il mio amico/ragazzo.

my friend/good friend (f.)
la mia amica/ragazza.

my partner (m. or f.)
il mio compagno /la mia compagna.

Pleased to meet you!
Piacere! / Molto lieto/a!

Professor
In Italy the use of titles and professional designations is obligatory; thus, for example, the attorney Conte will usually be introduced as *l'avvocato Conte.* A common title is *dottore/dottoressa,* which everyone can use who has completed a college education. Except for elementary school teachers all teachers and professors are addressed as *professore/professoressa.* Even the form of address *ragioniere/ragioniera* (accountant) is not uncommon.

Saying Good-bye

When a person leaves a shop, a restaurant, a bar, and so forth, instead of saying *arrivederci/arrrivederLa,* it is also possible to say *buon giorno* or *buona sera,* depending on the time of day.

INTERPERSONAL MATTERS

31

Good-bye
Arrivederci! / ArrivederLa!

See you soon!
A presto!

See you later!
A più tardi!

See you tomorrow!
A domani!

All the best!
Stammi bene!

See you soon!
Ci vediamo!

Good night!
Buona notte!

So long!
Ciao!

Have a good trip!
Buon viaggio!

Courtesy

Please and Thank You

Please.
Per favore.

Yes, please.
Sì, grazie.

No, thanks!
No, grazie.

May I?
Permette?

Can you please help me?
Mi può aiutare, per favore?

Thank you!
Grazie!

Thank you, very gladly!
Grazie, molto volentieri!

That's very nice, thank you!
Molto gentile, grazie!

You're welcome / Don't mention it!
Prego! / Non c'è di che!

Excuse me!
Scusi!

I'm very sorry!
Mi dispiace molto!

I didn't mean it that way.
Non volevo.

Don't mention it / Not at all.
Niente! / Non fa niente!

I'm afraid that's not possible.
Purtroppo non è possibile.

Congratulations!
Auguri!

Happy Birthday!
Tanti auguri per il compleanno.

Best wishes for success!
Buon lavoro!

Good luck!
Buona fortuna!

Good luck!
In bocca al lupo!

Bless you! (after a sneeze)
Salute!

Get well!
Buona guarigione!

Agreement and Keeping a Conversation Going

Good.
Bene.

Right.
Giusto.

Agreed!
D'accordo!

That's fine!
A posto! / Va bene!

OK
O.K./Va bene!

Precisely.
Preciso./Esatto.

Ah!
Ah! / Oh!

I see!
Ah, ecco! Ora capisco!

Really?
Davvero?

Interesting!
Interessante!

Great!
Che bello!

I understand.
Capisco.

That's the way it is.
Purtroppo è così.

I agree entirely.
Sono perfettamente d'accordo.

True.
È vero.

Good (great) idea.
Buona (ottima) idea.

Gladly!
Con piacere!

Declining

I don't want to.
Non voglio.

I don't feel like it.
Non ne ho voglia.

I don't agree.
Non sono d'accordo.

That's out of the question!
Non se ne parla neanche!

No way!
In nessun caso!

Not with me!
Non contate su di me!

I don't like that at all!
Non mi piace affatto.

Preferences

I like that. / I don't like that.
(Non) mi piace.

I would rather...
Preferisco ...

What I would like best ...
Più di tutto mi piacerebbe ...

Saying You Don't Know

I don't know.
Non lo so.

No idea.
Non ho idea. / Boh!

Indecision

It doesn't matter to me.
Non mi importa.

I don't know yet.
Non lo so ancora.

Maybe.
Forse.

Probably.
Probabilmente.

35

Happiness—Enthusiasm

Great!
Eccellente!

Wonderful!
Magnifico!

Neat!
Fantastico!

Super!
Super!

Wild!
Eccezionale!

Astonishment—Surprise

Oh!
Ah ecco!

Really?
Davvero? / Veramente?

Amazing!
Ma che sta succedendo?

Incredible!
Incredibile!

Relief

Fortunately...
Fortunatamente ...

Thank God!
Grazie a Dio!

Finally!
Finalmente!

Composure

Calm down!
Calma!

Don't worry!
Non si preoccupi!

Irritation

How annoying.
Però è una seccatura!

What a nuisance!
È un pasticcio!

That's enough!
Adesso basta!

That gets on my nerves / drives me up the wall.
... mi da sui nervi/ ... mi rompe.

That's shameful!
È una vergogna! / È una sfacciataggine!

That can't be true!
Ma è possibile!

Reprimand

What's gotten into you?
Cosa Le viene in mente!

Stay away from me!
Guai se mi tocca!

That's out of the question.
Nemmeno per sogno!

Regret / Disappointment

Oh my God!
O Dio! / Mamma mia!

I'm sorry.
Mi dispiace tanto.

I'm very sorry about...
mi dispiace davvero per ...

What a shame!
Peccato!

You can't trust him.

Great!

So what can I do about it?

Be so kind.

I don't care.

Are you pulling my leg?

Enough!

Of course!

What do you want?

Watch out!

Careful; they're in cahoots.

Yummy!

Compliments

Great!
Che bello!

That's wonderful!
È meraviglioso!

That's very kind of you!
Che bel pensiero da parte Sua / tua!

I think you are very nice!
La trovo molto simpatico, -a/carino, -a.

It's really wonderful here!
È veramente un incanto qui.

That looks very good!
Ti / Le sta proprio bene!

The dress looks good on you.
Il vestito Le / ti sta bene.

You speak very good Italian / English.
Lei lo parla molto bene l'italiano / l'inglese.

The meal was excellent!
Il mangiare era ottimo!

We have rarely eaten as well as we did at your house.
Non abbiamo mai mangiato così bene come da Lei.

We have been very happy at your house.
Ci siamo trovati molto bene da Lei.

beautiful	bello
delicious	squisito, gustoso
excellent	ottimo
friendly	gentile, cortese
impressive	impressionante
likeable	gentile, affabile
pleasant	comodo, confortevole; piacevole
pretty	carino, grazioso
splendid	magnifico

Personal Information

How old are you?
Quanti anni ha / hai?

I am 39.
Ho trentanove anni.

What kind of work do you do?
Qual è la Sua / tua professione?

I am...
Sono ...

I work for...
Lavoro presso ...

I am retired.
Sono pensionato/a.

I'm still in school.
Vado ancora a scuola.

I am a college student.
Sono studente/essa universitạrio/a.

Origin and Residence

Where are you from?
Di dov'è Lei? / Di dove sei tu?

I am from Minneapolis.
Sono di Minneapolis.

Have you been here for a long time?
È / Sei qui da molto?

I have been here since...
Sono qui da ...

How long are you staying?
Quanto si ferma / ti fermi?

Is this your first time here?
È / Sei qui per la prima volta?

How do you like it?
Che cosa ne pensa?

Are you married?
È sposato/sposata?

Do you have children?
Ha figli?

Yes, but they are already grown.
Sì, ma sono già grandi.

How old are your children?
Quanti anni hanno i suoi figli?

My daughter is eight (years old) and my son is five (years old).
Mia figlia ha 8 anni e mio figlio ne ha 5.

➤ also Active and Creative Vacations

Do you have a hobby?
Ha / Hai un hobby?

I spend a lot of time with my children.
Passo molto tempo con i miei figli.

I really enjoy reading.
Mi piace molto leggere.

I like to work in the garden.
Mi piace il lavoro in giardino.

I paint some.
Dipingo un po'.

I collect antiques / stamps.
Faccio la collezione di antichità/francobolli.

What are you interested in?
Di che cosa si interessa?

I'm interested in...
Mi interesso di ...

I belong to...
Appartengo a ...

... is one of my favorite activities.
... è una delle mie attività preferite.

to cook	cucinare
to do handcrafts	fare bricolage
to do pottery	lavorare la terracotta
to draw	disegnare

to learn languages . . . . studiare lingue
to listen to music . . . . ascoltare musica
to paint . . . . dipingere
to play music . . . . fare della musica
to read . . . . leggere
to relax . . . . rilassarsi
to travel . . . . viaggiare
to work in the garden . . . . . lavorare in giardino

Fitness

➢ also Active Vacations

How do you stay in shape?
Come si tiene in forma?

I jog / swim / cycle.
Faccio jogging. / Nuoto. / Vado in bicicletta.

I play tennis / volleyball once a week.
Una volta alla settimana gioco a tennis/a pallavolo.

I go to the gym fairly regularly.
Vado abbastanza regolarmente in palestra.

What sport do you do?
Quale sport pratica Lei?

I play...
Io gioco a ...

I'm a fan of...
Sono appassionato di ...

I like to go...
Mi piace andare a...

May I play?
Posso giocare anch'io?

Appointments

Do you have any plans for tomorrow evening?
Ha / Hai già un impegno domani?

Shall we go together?
Ci andiamo insieme?

Shall we go out together tonight?
Vogliamo uscire insieme stasera?

May I invite you to dinner tomorrow evening?
La / Ti posso invitare domani a cena?

When shall we meet?
A che ora ci incontriamo?

Let's meet at 9:00 in front of ... / at the...
Ci incontriamo alle 9 davanti a ... /nel ...

I'll pick you up.
La/Ti vengo a prendere.

May I see you again?
La/Ti posso rivedere?

This was really a nice evening!
È stata veramente una bella serata!

Familiar or formal?
In Italy people address one another in familiar terms quite soon, especially with people of comparable age. If you have something in common such as a hobby or children, people begin speaking in familiar forms of address after just a few sentences. Young people even address one another familiarly in purely business situations, for example in a pizzeria (waiter and diner) and in a shoe store (sales person and customer).

Flirting

You have beautiful eyes.
Hai degli occhi meravigliosi.

I like the way you laugh.
Mi piace come ridi.

I like you.
Mi piaci.

I like you.
Ti voglio bene.

I think you're great!
Ti trovo splendida!

I love you!
Ti amo!

Do you have a boyfriend / girlfriend?
Hai un ragazzo fisso / una ragazza fissa?

Are you living with anyone?
Convivi con qualcuno?

Are you married?
Sei sposato/a?

I am divorced. / We are separated.
Sono divorziata. / Siamo separati.

Would you like to come to my place?
Vuoi venire da me?

No, this is too soon.
No, ti stai allargando!

We can cuddle.
Possiamo accarezzarci.

Go away!
Adesso vai per favore!

Leave me alone!
Mi lasci in pace, per favore!

Stop that right now!
La smetta subito!

Pappagalli

The *pappagalli,* the Italian *machos,* still exist, but with Italian young people it's more important to be *cool.* And the modern, emancipated Italian women don't care so much for the *pappagalli* any more.

How do you know a *pappagallo* when you see one? He is deeply tanned, muscular, not always handsome, and wears sunglasses—even in a discotheque. They usually come two or three together and wander from one group of girls to another until they find an appropriate victim. Here's one simple rule for dealing with the *pappagalli:* if you don't want to have anything to do with them, don't get involved even in the most harmless conversation, otherwise you're lost. It's best just to pretend they don't even exist. How do the Italian women handle them? They first fend off the attacks and then wait to see if the suitor really is a tough fighter.

Communication Difficulties

Pardon me?
Come dice? *(Sie)* / Come dici? *(du)*

I don't understand you.
Non La capisco.

Would you please repeat that?
Potrebbe ripęterlo, per favore?

Could you please speak more slowly?
Per favore, parli più piano.

Yes, I understand.
Sì, capisco.

Do you speak...
Parla/Parli ...

German?
tedesco?

English?
inglese?

Italian?
italiano?

I speak only a little...
Parlo solo un po' di ...

Could you write that down for me, please?
Potrebbe scrįvermelo, per favore!

Italy: the Land of Fast Cars and Chaotic Traffic

The thing that makes foreign drivers in Italy pull their hair out the most is the way the Italians drive. The Italian traffic rules are like many other countries', but they are usually interpreted by the Italians as *discretionary* regulations and are adapted to individual situations.

So you will see Italian drivers who line up at a red light in the turn lane and nevertheless drive straight ahead just because they know there's enough room there for two cars; the only thing that counts is that the traffic keeps moving and nobody has to wait unnecessarily. And at three in the morning there is no taboo against driving through a red light at an intersection if there are no cars visible anywhere.

Even pedestrians don't necessarily obey red lights and crosswalks; instead, people check out the cars and look for a favorable moment to cross the street. So the first rule for drivers is to always watch out for pedestrians and other cars! Venture calmly into a pedestrian crossing—in spite of the stream of traffic that doesn't want to be interrupted, as soon as you set foot onto the road, you will see the cars come to a halt. It's more important to watch the driving and the behavior of the other drivers and react appropriately than it is to obey the traffic regulations.

Asking Directions

Directions

across from	di fronte a
after	dopo
behind	dietro
beside	vicino a
close	vicino
curve	curva
far	lontano
here	qui
in front of	prima di
intersection	incrocio
left	a sinistra
right	a destra
straight ahead	diritto
street	strada, via

street corner	angolo della strada
there	là
traffic light	semaforo

> Another tip for drivers: In Italy the traffic lights turn a little differently from green to red: the green-yellow-red phase is very long, so you still have time to make it through. But when it's red you really have to stop!

Giving Directions

Excuse me, how do I get to...?
Senta, scusi, per andare a ...?

Straight ahead until...
Sempre diritto fino a ...

Then turn left/right at the traffic light.
Poi al semaforo svolti a sinistra/destra.

Follow the signs.
Segua le indicazioni.

How far is it?
Quanti chilometri sono?

It's quite close to here.
È vicinissimo.

Pardon me, is this the road to...?
Scusi, è questa la strada per ...?

Excuse me, sir, miss, Madame, would you please tell me where ... is?
Scusi signore/signora/signorina, dov'è ...?

I'm sorry, I don't know.
Mi dispiace, non lo so.

Go straight ahead / turn left / right.
Vada diritto / a sinistra / a destra.

The first/second street on the left/right.
La prima/seconda strada a sinistra /a destra.

Cross...
Attraversi ...
  the bridge.
  il ponte.
  the square.
  la piazza.
  the street.

la strada.

It's best to take the bus number...
Il meglio è prendere la linea N° ...

At the Border

Passport Inspection

Your passport, please!
Il Suo passaporto, per favore!

Do you have a visa?
Ha il visto?

Can I get the visa here?
Mi potete rilasciare qui il visto?

Customs Inspection

Do you have anything to declare?
Ha niente da dichiarare?

Please go to the right / left!
Si metta lì a destra / a sinistra!

Please open up the trunk / this suitcase!
Apra, per favore, il bagagliaio / questa valigia!

Do I need to declare that?
Devo sdoganare questo?

Particulars

Date of birth . . . . data di nascita
Family name . . . . il cognome
First name . . . . il nome
Maiden name . . . . il nome da ragazza
Marital status . . . . stato di famiglia
  married . . . . *(man)* sposato; *(woman)* sposata
  single . . . . *(man)* celibe; *(woman)* nubile
  widowed . . . . *(man)* vedovo; *(woman)* vedova
Nationality . . . . nazionalità
Place of birth . . . . luogo di nascita
Residence . . . . domicilio

Border

border . . . . frontiera
border crossing . . . . frontiera, il confine
citizen of the European Union cittadino unitario
customs . . . . dogana

customs duties	le tariffe doganali
departure, exit	passaggio di confine
driver's license	la patente
duty free	esente da dazio doganale
entry	entrata (in territorio straniero)
green insurance card	carta verde
ID card	carta d'identità
international vaccination ..	certificato internazionale di
record	vaccinazione
license plate	targa
national ID plate	targa di nazionalità
passport	passaporto
passport inspection	controllo dei passaporti
subject to duties	soggetto a dazio doganale
valid	valido
visa	visto

Car and Motorcycle

Travel Routes and Regulations

blood alcohol level	il limite (massimo consentito) di alcol nel sangue
fast lane	superstrada
fine	ammenda
highway	autostrada
highway tolls	pedaggio autostradale

Modern "Highway Robbery"

Highways in Italy are toll roads. In order to get through the toll stations quicker, you should get a **Viacard** at a gas station shortly after crossing the border; this is a debit card from which the tolls are deducted at every toll booth. If you have a credit card, you don't need a **Viacard**. In either case, line up in the appropriate lane according to the signs.

hitchhike	viaggiare in autostop
hitchhiker	l'autostoppista m/f
main road	strada principale
radar speed control	controllo radar
rest area	piazzola di sosta
road use fee	pedaggio
secondary road	strada maestra
service area	la stazione di servizio, l'autogrill m

51

side road	strada secondaria
signpost	il segnavia
toll booth	casello
traffic jam	ingorgo

Signs and Information

en cadena	Pileup
Attenzione	Careful
Bambini	Children
Cambio corsia	Change lanes
Cantiere edile	Construction
Circonvallazione	Bypass
Curva pericolosa	Dangerous curve
Dare la precedenza	Yield right of way
Deviazione	Detour
Discesa pericolosa	Steep hill
Disco orario	Parking disk
Divieto di sorpasso	No passing
Divieto di sosta	No stopping
Ingorgo	Traffic jam
Lavori in corso	Construction
Limite di velocità	Speed limit
Mettersi in fila	Fall into line
Ospedale	Hospital
Parcheggio	Parking
Passaggio a livello incustodito	Unguarded crossing
Passaggio pedonale	Crosswalk
Pericolo	Danger
Pista ciclabile	Bicycle path
Ponte	Bridge
Principiante	Beginner
Rallentare	Slow down
Scuola	School
Senso unico	One-way street
Sottopassaggio	Pedestrian underpass
Strada sdrucciolevole	Slippery road
Tamponamento	Collision
Tenere la destra	Keep right
Tenere libero l'accesso	Do not block access
Uscita	Exit
Vietato al traffico	Closed to traffic
Vietato l'accesso	No entry
Zona a disco orario	Short-term parking (Parking disk)
Zona pedonale	Pedestrian zone

At the Gas Station

> ➢ also Repair Shop

Where is the nearest gas station, please?
Dov'è la prossima stazione di servizio, per favore?

I would like ... liters.
Vorrei ... litri di ...

Regular gas
benzina normale.

Super
super.

Diesel
gasolio.

Blend
miscela.

Unleaded / .... Octane
senza piombo(verde) / a ... ottani.

... euros of super, please.
Super, per favore, per ... euro.

Fill it up, please!
Il pieno, per favore!

Would you please check the oil?
Scusi, potrebbe controllare il livello dell'olio?

I would like a roadmap of this area.
Vorrei una carta stradale di questa zona.

Parking

Excuse me, is there any parking around here?
Scusi, prego, c'è un parcheggio qui vicino?

Can I leave the car here?
Posso lasciare la macchina qui?

Could you please give me change for the parking meter?
Mi può cambiare i soldi in moneta per il parchimetro, per favore?

Is the parking area supervised?
Il parcheggio è custodito?

How much per hour is the parking?
Qual è la tariffa per un'ora?

Is the parking garage open all night?
Il parcheggio è aperto tutta la notte?

A Breakdown

I've had a breakdown.
Ho un guasto / una panne.

Is there a repair shop in the area?
Scusi signore/signora/signorina, c'è un'officina qui vicino?

Could you please call roadside service for me?
Potrebbe telefonare al soccorso stradale?

Could you please send me a mechanic / a tow truck?
Mi potrebbe mandare un meccanico / un carro-attrezzi?

Could you give me a little gas?
Mi potrebbe dare un po' di benzina?

Could you help me change the tire?
Mi potrebbe aiutare a cambiare la ruota?

Could you take me to the nearest repair shop?
Mi potrebbe dare un passaggio fino alla prossima officina?

breakdown	guasto, panne
breakdown service	autosoccorso; soccorso stradale
emergency flashers	i lampeggiatori d'emergenza
emergency telephone	telefono d'emergenza
flat tire	gomma a terra
gas can	lattina, tanica
jack	il cric
jumper cable	cavo ausiliario per la messa in moto
spare tire	ruota di scorta
tool	l'utensile *m*, attrezzo
to tow	rimorchiare, trainare
towing cable	cavo da rimorchio
warning triangle	triangolo
wrecker, tow truck	carro attrezzi

In the Repair Shop

My car doesn't start.
La macchina non parte.

Something is wrong with the motor.
Il motore non va bene.

... isn't / aren't working.
... è/sono difettoso/difettosi.

The car is leaking oil.
La macchina perde olio.

Can you please take a look?
Scusi, ci potrebbe dare un'occhiata, per favore?

Please change the spark plugs.
Cambi le candele, per favore.

Please do only the necessary repairs.
Faccia soltanto le riparazioni indispensabili, per favore.

When will the car/motorcycle be ready?
Quando sarà pronta la macchina / la motocicletta?

About how much will that cost?
Quanto costerà su per giù?

air filter	filtro dell'aria
alarm system	il sistema d'allarme
alternator	la dinamo
antifreeze	antigelo
auto repair shop	autofficina
automatic transmission	cambio automatico
backup lights	fanalino posteriore
blinker	il lampeggiatore, la freccia
bolt	la vite
brake	freno
brake fluid	olio per freni
brake lights	le luci di arresto
bumper	il paraurti
clutch	la frizione
coolant	acqua di raffreddamento
defect	difetto
electronic start protection	antifurto elettronico
emergency brake	freno a mano
exhaust pipe	scappamento, tubo di scarico
gas pedal	l'acceleratore m
gas pump	pompa della benzina
gas tank	serbatoio
headlight	faro
high beams	i fari abbaglianti
hood	cofano
horn	il clacson
ignition	l'accensione f
low beams	le luci anabbaglianti
motor	il motore
oil	olio
oil change	cambio dell'olio
parking lights	le luci di posizione
radiator	il radiatore
rearview mirror	specchietto retrovisore
seat belt	cintura di sicurezza

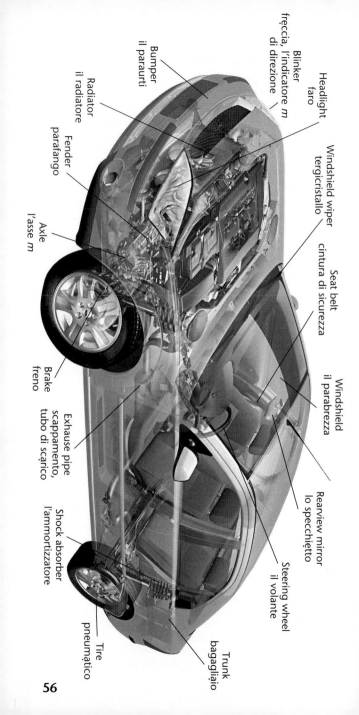

Headlight
faro

Blinker
freccia, l'indicatore *m*
di direzione

Bumper
il paraurti

Radiator
il radiatore

Fender
parafango

Axle
l'asse *m*

Brake
freno

Exhause pipe
scappamento,
tubo di scarico

Shock absorber
l'ammortizzatore

Tire
pneumatico

Trunk
bagagliaio

Steering wheel
il volante

Rearview mirror
lo specchietto

Windshield
il parabrezza

Seat belt
cintura di sicurezza

Windshield wiper
tergicristallo

56

short circuit	corto circuito
snow tires	gli pneumatici da neve
spark plug	candela
speed	marcia
first	la prima
neutral	la folle
reverse	marcia indietro
starter	motorino d'avviamento
tachometer	tachimetro
tire	pneumatico
transmission	cambio
trunk	bagagliaio
wheel	ruota
windshield	il parabrezza
windshield wiper	tergicristallo

Accidents

There has been an accident.
C'è stato un incidente!

Please call... quickly.
Chiami subito ...

  an ambulance
  un'autoambulanza!

  the police
  la polizia!

  the fire station
  i vigili del fuoco!

> ### Traffic Police Times Two
> In Italy, the traffic police are not just traffic police: the **polizia stradale** with blue cars and uniforms are responsible for the roads outside a city; the vigili control the traffic inside the city. Their uniform may vary from area to area, but they usually wear a black (or white in the summer) uniform with a white hat and white gloves.

Do you have a first-aid kit?
Ha materiale di pronto soccorso?

You didn't...
Lei ...

  respect the right of way.
  non ha rispettato la precedenza.

  signal.
  non ha messo la freccia.

Reckless drivers have been in for it ever since July of 2003. As in other countries, there is a point system for traffic violations. In addition, there is now a law that requires using the headlights while driving during the day.

You...
Lei ...

were driving too fast.
andava troppo forte.

went through a red light.
è passato col rosso.

Give me your name and address, please.
Mi dia il Suo nome e indirizzo.

Thanks a lot for your help!
Grazie dell'aiuto!

Renting a Car, Motorcycle, or Bicycle

Saddle — sella
Gear lever — cambio
Handlebar — manubrio *m*
Air pump — pompa d'aria
Headlight — il fanale anteriore
Taillight — riflettore *m* posteriore
Brake — freno
Inner tube — camera d'aria
Tire — pneumatico
Chain — catena
Pedal — il pedale
Wheel — ruota
Spoke — raggio
Hub — mozzo

I would like to rent ... for two days / a week.
Vorrei noleggiare per due giorni / una settimana ...

a car
una macchina.

a four-wheel drive vehicle
un fuoristrada.

a motorcycle
un motociclo.

a motor scooter
una motoretta / uno scooter.

a moped
un motorino.

a bicycle
una bicicletta.

In large cities you can get around best with a maneuverable small car or with a two-wheeled vehicle; that allows you to take advantage of gaps and slip through the endless lines of cars. But be careful, because many drivers signal with their arm rather than their blinkers, and sometimes they don't signal at all for a right turn.

How much is that per day / week?
Qual è il forfait giornaliero/settimanale?

With unlimited mileage?
È a chilometri illimitati?

What's the cost per kilometer?
Quanto si paga per ogni chilometro percorso?

Is the vehicle covered by comprehensive insurance?
Il veicolo è assicurato contro tutti i rischi?

Is it possible to return the vehicle in ...?
È possibile lasciare la macchina a ...?

child seat	seggiolino auto (per bambini)
comprehensive insurance . .	l'assicurazione f parziale per tutti i rischi
deposit	la cauzione
driver's license	la patente
full-coverage insurance	forfait (forfé) per il fine settimana
green insurance card	carta verde
helmet	casco
ignition key	chiavetta di accensione
kidney belt	fascia coprireni
to leave, drop off	depositare
papers	i documenti
sunroof	tetto apribile
weekend rate	l'assicurazione f di totale copertura

Booking a Flight

Could you please tell me when the next flight to... is?
Saprebbe dirmi, quando parte il prossimo aereo per ...?

Are there still seats available?
Ci sono ancora posti liberi?

I would like a one-way ticket to...
Vorrei prenotare un volo di sola andata per ...

I would like a round-trip plane ticket to...
Vorrei prenotare un volo di andata e ritorno per ...

How much is the flight for tourist / first class?
Scusi, quanto costa un volo per la classe turistica / per la prima classe?

Smoking or non-smoking?
Fumatori o non fumatori?

I would like...
Per favore vorrei ...

  a window seat.
  un posto al finestrino.

  an aisle seat.
  un posto al corridoio.

I would like to cancel this flight.
Vorrei annullare questo volo.

I would like to change this flight.
Vorrei prendere un altro volo.

At the Airport

Where is the desk for ... Airlines, please?
Saprebbe dirmi dove trovare lo sportello della compagnia aerea ...?

May I see your ticket, please?
Potrei vedere il Suo biglietto?

Can I take this on as carry-on baggage?
Posso portare appresso il bagaglio a mano?

On Board

Could you please bring me a glass of water?
Potrebbe portarmi un bicchiere d'acqua?

Could I please have another pillow / a blanket?
Potrei avere anche un cuscino / una coperta?

Would you mind changing places with me?
Le dispiacerebbe se cambiassimo i posti?

Arrival
➢ also Lost and Found

My baggage has been lost.
Il mio bagaglio è stato smarrito.

My suitcase is damaged.
La mia valigia è stata danneggiata.

Where does the bus to... leave from?
Da dove parte il bus in direzione ...?

➢ also Rail Travel

airline	compagnia aerea
airport	aeroporto
airport bus	collegamento pullman con l'aeroporto
airport taxes	i diritti aeroportuali
arrival	arrivo
arrival time	orario d'arrivo
baggage	bagaglio
baggage cart	il vagone bagagli
baggage check-in	la spedizione bagagli
baggage pick-up	consegna del bagaglio
boarding pass	carta d'imbarco
to cancel	annullare
to change the reservation . .	cambiare il biglietto
check-in	fare il check-in
connection	coincidenza
delay	ritardo
departure, takeoff	decollo
domestic flight	volo nazionale
duty-free shop	spaccio porto-franco
emergency exit	uscita d'emergenza
emergency landing	atterraggio di fortuna
evacuation slide	scivolo d'emergenza
exceeds the weight limit . .	supera il peso consentito

61

flight	volo
flotation vest	giubbetto di salvataggio
gate	sala d'attesa passeggeri
international flight	volo internazionale
landing	atterraggio
passenger	passeggero
pilot	il pilota
scheduled flight	volo regolare
seat belt	tassa per controlli di sicurezza
security check	controllo di sicurezza
steward	lo steward, l'assistente m/f di bordo / l'hostess f
stopover	scalo
terminal	l'air terminal m

Train Travel

Buying Tickets

Two one-way tickets to... , please.
Due biglietti per..., solo andata, per favore.

tourist class / first class
2a classe / 1a classe

non-smoking / smoking
non fumatori / fumatori

A round-trip ticket to ..., please.
Vorrei un biglietto di andata e ritorno per...

Are there any discounts for children, students, senior citizens?
C'è una riduzione per bambini/studenti/pensionati?

> Tickets for local trains must be cancelled on the platforms in
> automatic machines – **convalidare**. If you neglect to do that, as
> soon as you get on the train you should report to the
> conductor.

I would like to reserve to non-smoking seats, please:
Vorrei prenotare due posti per non fumatori:

in the EC to...
nell'EC per ...
on... at... o'clock
per il/l' ... alle ...
in the couchette car
in cuccetta
in the sleeper car
in vagone letto

Is there a motorail train?
C'è un treno-traghetto per ...?

What time is my connection for... in...?
A che ora ho la coincidenza per... a ...

How many times do I have to change?
Quante volte devo cambiare?

> The schedule changes in June! Don't rely blindly on the
> published schedule; it's better to play it safe and ask an
> employee of the railroad.

In the Railroad Station

I would like to send this suitcase as registered baggage.
Vorrei spedire questa valigia come bagaglio appresso.

Where can I check in my bicycle?
Dove posso consegnare la mia bicicletta per la spedizione?

Excuse me, what platform does the train to ... leave from?
Senta, scusi, da quale binario parte il treno per ...?

When does the train to... leave?
Quando parte il treno per ...?

The IC coming from ... is expected to arrive ten minutes late.
L'IC proveniente da ... arriverà probabilmente con 10 minuti di
ritardo.

Notices and Information

Ai binari	To the Platforms
Arrivi	Arrival
Deposito bagagli	Baggage Check-in
Deposito a cassette	Baggage Locker
Informazioni	Information
Orario	Schedule
Partenze	Departure
Posto di pronto soccorso	First Aid Station
Rinfreschi	Refreshments
Sala d'aspetto	Waiting Room
Signore	Ladies
Signori	Gentlemen
Sottopassaggio	Underpass
Sportello biglietti	Ticket Window
Toilette	Toilets
Uscita	Exit

ON THE MOVE

63

On the Train

Is this seat taken?
Scusi, è libero questo posto?

May I please open / close the window?
Scusi, potrei aprire/chiudere il finestrino?

Excuse me; I think that's my seat. Here is my reservation.
Scusi, ma questo è il mio posto, credo! È prenotato.

➢ also Airplane

aisle	corridoio
arrival	arrivo
baggage	bagaglio
baggage check-in	sportello accettazione bagagli
baggage consignment	deposito bagagli
baggage locker	deposito a cassette
car number	numero del vagone
child's ticket	biglietto per ragazzi
companion	l'accompagnatore, m, (-trice), f
compartment	scompartimento
conductor	conduttore/-trice
departure	partenza
dining car	il vagone ristorante
discount	la riduzione
EC (Euro City)	EuroCity
to get off	scendere
to get on	salire
head conductor	il/la principale
IC (Inter City)	IC (InterCity)
Interrail	l'interrail m
main railroad station	la stazione centrale
minibar	il minibar
motorail train	treno traghetto
non-smoking section	scompartimento per non fumatori
open car	il grande vagone
person in a wheelchair	il/la disabile in sedia a rotelle
railroad station	la stazione
reservation	la prenotazione
reserved seat	la prenotazione
round-trip ticket	biglietto di andata e ritorno
schedule	orario
severely handicapped person	invalido/a
smoking section	scompartimento per fumatori
staff	il personale viaggiante

stop	fermata
surcharge	supplemento
ticket	biglietto
ticket control	controllo dei biglietti
ticket price	prezzo del biglietto
ticket window	biglietteria
track	binario
train	treno
waiting room	sala d'aspetto
window seat	posto al finestrino

Boat Travel

In the summer months, reserve your place on the ferry to the islands in advance; otherwise you may have to spend a couple of days on a stopover on the mainland.

Information

Could you please tell me when the next boat / ferry to... leaves?
Scusi, saprebbe dirmi quando parte la prossima nave / il prossimo traghetto per ...?

How long does the crossing take?
Quanto dura la traversata?

When do we arrive in...?
Quando attracchiamo a ...?

How long is the stopover in...?
Quanto ci fermiamo a ...?

I would like...
Vorrei ... per favore.

a ticket to...
un biglietto per ...

first class
di prima classe

tourist class
di classe turistica

a private cabin
una cabina singola

a cabin with two beds.
una cabina doppia

I would like a ticket for the tour at ... o'clock.
Vorrei un biglietto per il giro delle ...

On Board

Where is the dining room / the lounge, please?
Dov'è la sala da pranzo / il salone, per favore?

I don't feel well.
Non mi sento bene.

Would you please call the doctor on board?
Per favore, chiami il medico di bordo!

Could you please give me some medicine for seasickness?
Per favore, mi dia un rimedio contro il mal di mare.

cabin	cabina
captain	capitano
coast	costa
cruise	crociera
deck	coperta
dock	banchina
ferry	traghetto
car ferry	autotraghetto
hovercraft	l'hovercraft *m*
hydrofoil	aliscafo
land excursion	l'escursione *f* a terra
life vest	giubbetto di salvataggio
lifeboat	scialuppa di salvataggio
lifesaver	il salvagente
mainland	terraferma
port, harbor	porto
reservation	la prenotazione
sea conditions	moto ondoso
to be seasick	avere il mal di mare
steamer	piroscafo, la nave a vapore
to have a stopover in	far scalo/attraccare a
ticket	biglietto
tour	giro

Where is the nearest...
Dov'è la prossima ...

bus stop?
fermata dell'autobus?

streetcar stop?
fermata del tram?

subway station?
stazione della metropolitana?

Which line goes to..., please?
Qual è la linea che va a ...?

When does the first / last subway leave for...?
Quando parte la prima / l'ultima metropolitana per ...?

Excuse me, is this the bus to...?
Scusi, è questo l'autobus per ...?

How many stops are there?
Quante fermate ci sono?

Pardon me, where do I have to get off / change?
Scusi, dove devo scendere/cambiare?

Would you please let me know when I have to get off?
Senta, scusi, potrebbe avvertirmi quando devo scendere?

One ticket to..., please.
Un biglietto per ..., per favore.

The ticket machine is out of order.
L'automatico dei biglietti é rotto/guasto.

The ticket machine doesn't accept bills.
L'automatico non prende le banconote.

automatic ticket machine	il distributore automatico di biglietti
bus	l'autobus *m*
bus station	la stazione degli autobus
to cancel	convalidare
city bus	l'autobus *m* urbano
coach	l'autobus *m* interurbano
cog railway	cremagliera
conductor	il controllore
day ticket	biglietto giornaliero
departure	partenza
direction	la direzione
to get on / in	salire
itinerary	orario
local train	treno locale
multiple ride ticket	biglietto a più obliterazioni

ON THE MOVE

67

stop, station	fermata
streetcar	il tram
subway	metropolitana
terminal	il capolinea
ticket	biglietto
ticket inspector	il controllore
ticket price	prezzo del biglietto
ticket puncher	l'obliteratore *m*
trolley	il filobus
weekly ticket	abbonamento settimanale

Taxi

Excuse me, where is the nearest taxi stand?
Senta, scusi, c'è un posteggio di tassì qui vicino?

To the railroad station, please.
Alla stazione, prego.

To the... Hotel, please.
All'albergo, prego.

To ... Street, please.
In via ..., prego.

To..., please.
A ..., prego.

How much does it cost to get to...?
Quanto costa andare a ...?

Would you please stop here?
Potrebbe fermarsi qui, per favore?

Would you give me a receipt, please?
Potrebbe rilasciarmi una ricevuta, per favore?

This is for you.
Questo è per Lei.

flat rate	prezzo forfettario
to fasten the seatbelt	mettere la cintura
house number	numero civico
price per kilometer	prezzo per chilometro
receipt	ricevuta
seatbelt	cintura di sicurezza
to stop	fermars
taxi driver (m. and f.)	il/la tassista
taxi stand	posteggio di taxi
tip	mancia

Children are Welcome

Traveling with small and older children is no problem in Italy. Even though many places don't have conveniences like changing tables and bottle warmers (many auto service areas have micro-wave ovens, however), children are welcome guests everywhere and generally can move about freely. That's one reason why there are relatively few and modestly equipped playgrounds in Italy—the whole country is a playground!

The best choice for a swimming vacation with children is one of the numerous private beaches, for they are kept very clean. But be careful! People don't always appreciate seeing little children run around naked—but there are more and more daycare and children's programs available for that.

Useful Questions

Is there a childcare facility here?
C'è un servizio baby-sitter qui?

Starting with what age?
A partire da quale età?

Do you know anyone who could babysit at our place?
Conosce qualcuno che potrebbe farci da baby-sitter?

Do you have an intercom for the baby?
Ha un babyfon?

Are there also performances for children?
Ci sono anche degli spettacoli per bambini?

Are there discounts for children?
Ci sono delle riduzioni per bambini?

On the Move

We are traveling with children. Could we get seats near the front?
Viaggiamo con bambini. Potremmo avere un posto nelle prime file?

Would you have any crayons and paper / a coloring book?
Ha per caso matite e fogli di carta / un libro da colorare?

Do you rent children's car seats?
Noleggia dei seggiolini auto (per bambini)?

Children's Safety in Traffic

Safety measures in traffic hardly correspond to our ideas: you will rarely see a child wearing a bicycle helmet, and more commonly will see children standing up as passengers on mopeds and motor scooters. Your children surely will find that amusing; maybe you will allow them as an exception to take a spin on a borrowed Vespa (motor scooter) around a parking lot or on the access road to a private beach, preferably around midday or in the afternoon when automobile drivers are taking their siesta.

In a Restaurant

Would you please bring us a child's seat?
Scusi, potrebbe portarci un seggiolone?

Are there child-size portions?
Avete anche porzioni per bambini?

Could you please warm up this bottle for me?
Abbia pazienza potrebbe riscaldarmi il biberon?

Is there a changing table here?
C'è un fasciatoio qui?

Can you please tell me where I can go to nurse?
Scusi,c'e un posto qui dove potrei allattare?

amusement park	parco dei divertimenti
baby bathtub	piscina per bambini
baby bottle	il biberon
baby car seat	seggiolino auto per bebè
baby food	l'alimentazione f infantile
baby intercom	il babyfon
babysitter	il/la baby-sitter
bottle	bottiglia
bottle warmer	lo scaldabiberon
cap	berretto con visiera
changing table	fasciatoio
child's bed	lettino (per bambini)
child's bicycle seat	seggiolino per la bicicletta
child's car cushion	il sedile auto per bambini
child's car seat	seggiolino auto
child's discount	la riduzione per bambini
childcare	assistenza ai bambini
children's clothing	abbigliamento per bambini
coloring book	libro da colorare
diapers	i pannolini

lifesaver	il salvagente
mini-club	il mini-club
nipple	ciuccio, succhietto
pacifier	succhietto, tettarella
playground	parco giochi
sand castle	castello di sabbia
sandbox	recinto con la sabbia
sunscreen	la protezione solare
swimming lessons	corso di nuoto
toys	i giocattoli
wading pool	piscina/vasca per bambini
water wings	i bracciali salvagente

Health

Can you please tell me if there is a children's doctor here?
Saprebbe dirmi se c'è un pediatra qui vicino?

My son / daughter has...
Mio/a figlio/a ha ...

He / she is allergic to...
È allergico/a a ...

He / she threw up.
Ha vomitato.

He / she has diarrhea.
Ha la diarrea.

He / she has been stung.
È stato/a punto/a.

allergy	allergia
chicken pox	varicella
childhood illness	malattia infantile
children's hospital	l'ospedale *m* pediatrico
constipation	la costipazione
electrolyte solution	la soluzione elettrolitica
fever	la febbre
flu	il raffreddore
German measles	rosolia
inner ear infection	l'otite *f*
measles	morbillo
medicinal food	alimento curativo
mumps	gli orecchioni
mycosis	la micosi
rash	l'eruzione *f* cutanea, l'esantema *m*
scarlet fever	scarlattina
vaccination record	libretto di vaccinazione

Travel for Handicapped People

Good Planning

As with individual travelers who are not handicapped, this motto applies: the better the planning, the better the trip. Especially in northern Italy, where there are many associations for handicapped people that can help you with your preparations.

I am...
Sono ...
  physically handicapped.
  handicappato (fisico), disạbile.
  visually impaired.
  ipovedente.

I have ...
Soffro ...
  difficulty walking.
  non deambulante.
  multiple sclerosis.
  di sclerosi mụltipla.

On the Move

Can I take my own folding wheelchair on the plane?
Posso portare in aẹreo la mia propria carrozzella pieghẹvole?

Is there a wheelchair available on departure from / arrival at the airport?
Ci sono carrozzelle disponịbili all'aeroporto di partenza/destinazione?

Are there handicap toilets?
C'è una toilette per handicappati?

Is there a handicap washroom?
C'è un lavatọio per handicappati?

Public Transportation for Handicapped People

There are a few easy-access buses only in large cities. Many cities offer a driving service for people in a wheelchair. The bus stops serviced by buses for handicapped people are indicated by the international handicap sign.

Around 150 Italian train stations offer aid for handicapped people; you must make a reservation 24 hours before departure. This includes help with ticket purchase (seats for handicapped people can be reserved), escort service in your own wheelchair or one belonging to the train station, and help getting on and off the train.

Are there access ramps on the platforms for people in wheelchairs?
Ci sono delle rampe sulle quali una persona in carrozzella può
accędere ai binari?

Can someone help me change trains?
Mi potrebbe aiutare qualcuno a cambiare?

Are there cars with hand controls for handicapped people?
Ci sono delle automobili a nolęggio per handicappati fisici con
acceleratore a mano?

Accommodations

**Could you please send me information on the hotels in... that
are set up for handicapped people?**
La/Vi prego di inviarmi informazioni su alberghi idọnei per
handicappati in carrozzella a ...

**Which hotels and campgrounds are set up for handicapped
people?**
Mi saprebbe dire quali alberghi e campeggi dispọngono di
appọsiti impianti per handicappati?

Museums, Tourist Sites, Theater...

Is the exhibition accessible by elevator for handicapped people?
I non deambulanti possono accędere alla mostra con ascensori?

Are there stairs at the entrances?
Le entrate sono senza gradini?

Are there special tours/city tours for the hearing impaired?
Esịstono vịsite guidate / giri turịstici della città appositamente
concịpiti per non udenti (sordi).

**Are there museum tours/theater performances for deaf-
mutes/blind people?**
Ci sono vịsite guidate nei musei/rappresentazioni per
sordomuti/ciechi?

access ramp	rampa
accessibility	accessibilità
assistance service	servịzio assistenza
association for handicapped	associazione *m* handicappati/
people	svantaggiati
at ground level	a livello del suolo
automatic door opener	apriporta automạtico
banister	corrimano, il mancorrente
barrier-free	senza barriere architettọniche
blind person	cieco/a
cane (of blind person)	il bastone per ciechi

crutch	gruccia, stampella
deaf	sordo, non udente
deaf mute	sordomuto
disabled	non deambulante
elevator platform, lift	l'elevatore *m*
epilepsy	epilessia
escort (m. and f.)	l'accompagnatore *m*
hand controls (car)	l'acceleratore *m* a mano
hand hold	sostegno, maniglia
handicap ID	tesserino di riconoscimento per portatori di handicap
handicapped toilet	il bagno/la toilette per handicappati
handrail	rampa
headset, headphones	cuffia
hearing impaired	sordastro
height	altezza
in need of care	bisognoso di cure
lift seat	banco l'elevatore *m*
mentally handicapped	minorato mentalmente
mobile medical station	il day hospital
mute	muto
paraplegic	paraplegico
parking place for handicapped people	posteggio per handicappati
passable	viabile
person in a wheelchair	persona in carrozzella
person with restricted mobility	menomato/a nella mobilità
physical handicap	l'handicap *m* fisico
seeing-eye dog	il cane guida per ciechi
set up for handicapped people	idoneo per / a misura degli handicappati
severely handicapped person	gravemente handicappata/o
sight-impaired	menomato nella vista
sign language	linguaggio mimico / a segni
slope	salita
social assistance services	servizio assistenza sociale
steering wheel knob (car)	manopola sul volante
step	gradino; scalino
step (of bus, train, etc.)	i presidi ortopedici
transportation service	servizio di trasporto
walker	bicicletta per disabili
walker	carrello
wheelchair	carrozzella, sedia a rotelle
wheelchair-accessible	adatto/idoneo per carrozzelle
width	larghezza

Accommodations

Information

Could you please recommend...
Scusi signora/signorina/signore, potrebbe consigliarmi ...

a good hotel
un buon albergo?

a modest hotel
un albergo non troppo caro?

a guest house
una pensione?

Is it in the center / in a quiet area / near the beach?
Si trova in centro / in una posizione tranquilla / vicino al mare?

Is there also...
C'è/Ci sono anche... qui?

a campground
un campeggio

a youth hostel
un ostello della gioventù?

Hotel—Guest House—Private Room

At the Registration Desk

I·have a room reserved. My name is...
Ho prenotato una camera. Il mio nome è ...

Do you still have rooms available?
Ha camere libere?

...for one night
... per una notte.

...for two days
... per due giorni.

...for a week
... per una settimana.

78

No, I'm afraid not.
No, purtroppo no.

Yes, what kind of room do you want?
Sì, che tipo di camera desidera?

I would like …
Vorrei

a single room
una singola

a double room
una matrimoniale

a quiet room
una camera tranquilla

with a shower
con doccia

with a bath
con bagno

with a balcony / terrace
con balcone / con terrazza

with an ocean view
con vista sul mare

on the inner courtyard
che dà sul cortile

May I see the room?
Posso vedere la camera?

I don't like this room. May I please see another one?
Questa camera non mi piace. Potrei vederne un'altra?

I'll take this room.
Prendo questa camera.

Can you put in a third bed / a child's bed?
Può aggiungere un altro letto / un lettino (per bambini)?

My bed is too soft, would you have a different one / a different mattress / a board to put underneath?
Il mio letto è troppo morbido, potrei averne un altro / avere un altro materasso / una tavola?

How much is the room including…
Quanto verrebbe a costare la camera con…?

breakfast?
la prima colazione

half-board?
la mezza pensione

full board?
la pensione completa

Would you please fill out the registration form?
Vuole riempire, per favore, il modulo d'accettazione?

May I see your passport / ID card?
Potrebbe farmi vedere il Suo passaporto / La Sua carta
d'identità?

Could you have my baggage brought to my room?
Potrebbe farmi portare i bagagli in camera?

Where can I leave the car?
Dove posso lasciare la macchina?

In our garage.
Nel nostro garage.

In our parking lot.
Nel nostro parcheggio.

Questions and Requests
➢ also Breakfast

When is breakfast?
Da che ora si può fare colazione?

What times are meals served?
Quali sono gli orari per i pasti?

Where is ...
Dov'è ...
  the dining room?
  la sala da pranzo?
  the breakfast room?
  la sala per la colazione?

Can you wake me up at 7:00 A.M. tomorrow morning, please?
Potrebbe svegliarmi domattina alle sette..., per favore?

Could you please bring me...
Potrebbe portarmi ..., per favore?
  a bath towel
  un telo da bagno
  another blanket
  un'altra coperta

How does ... work?
Come funziona ...?

Is there any mail for me?
C'è posta per me?

Where can I ...
Dove posso ...
  get something to drink here?
  bere qualcosa qui?

80

rent a car?
noleggiare una mạcchina?
make a phone call?
telefonare qui?

Can I leave my valuables in your safe?
Posso lasciare i miei valori in depọsito nella vostra cassaforte?

Can I leave my baggage here?
Posso lasciarli qui i bagagli?

Complaints

My room has not been cleaned today.
La cạmera non è stata pulita oggi.

The air conditioning doesn't work.
L'ạria condizionata non funziona.

The faucet drips.
Il rubinetto perde.

There is no (warm) water.
Non c'è ạcqua (calda).

The toilet / the sink is plugged up.
Il gabinetto / Il lavandino è intasato.

I would like another room, please.
Vorrẹi un'altra cạmera.

Departure

I am leaving this evening / tomorrow at … o'clock.
Parto stasera/domani alle …

When do I have to vacate the room?
Per quando devo liberare la stanza?

Could you prepare the bill for me, please?
Potrebbe prepararmi il il conto?

Could you call a taxi for me?
Potrebbe chiamarmi un tassì?

Thanks for everything! Good-bye!
Grạzie di tutto. Arrivederci!

air conditioning	ạria condizionata
armchair	sẹdia
ashtray	il portacẹnere
balcony	il balcone
bath towel	telo da bagno
bathroom	bagno
bathtub	vasca da bagno
bed	letto

81

bidet	il bidet
blanket	coperta
breakfast	la colazione
breakfast buffet	il buffet della colazione
breakfast room	sala per la colazione
busy season	alta stagione *f*
chair	sedia
change of linen	cambio biancheria
to clean	pulire
cleaning lady	cameriera
combination (for room door)	il codice per la porta della camera
cupboard / wardrobe	armadio
dining room	sala da pranzo
dinner	cena
elevator	l'ascensore *m*
extra week	settimana supplementare
faucet	rubinetto
floor/story	piano
full pension	la pensione completa
garage	il garage
glass	il bicchiere
guest house	la pensione
half pension	la mezzapensione
hand towel	asciugamano
hanger	gruccia (per i panni)
heating	riscaldamento
key	la chiave
lamp	lampada
light	la luce
lightbulb	lampadina (ad incandescenza)
light switch	l'interruttore *m*
living room	il soggiorno
lunch	pranzo, il desinare
mattress	materasso
mini-bar	il minibar
mirror	specchio
motel	il motel
multi-plug adaptor	spina di adattamento
night lamp	lampada del comodino
night table	comodino
off-season	bassa stagione *f*
overnight	pernottamento
parking space	parcheggio
pillow	cuscino
place setting *(for breakfast)* .	coperto(per la colazione)
plug	spina
porter, concierge	il portiere

pre-season	bassa stagione *f*
radio	la radio
reception	la reception
reception hall	la hall
reception room	l'accettazione *f*
to repair	riparare
reservation	la prenotazione
room	camera
room telephone	telefono in camera
safe (box)	la cassaforte
sheets, bed linens	biancheria da letto
shower	doccia
shower attachment	doccia
shower curtain / sliding door	tenda per doccia/la scorrevole
shower head	doccia
shuttle bus	servizio pulman
sink	lavandino
stationery	carta da scrivere
table	tavolo
television	il televisore
terrace	terrazza
toilet	gabinetto
toilet paper	carta igienica
TV room	stanza della televisione
ventilator	il ventilatore
wall socket/ plug	presa
wastebasket	pattumiera
water	acqua
cold water	acqua fredda
hot water	acqua calda
water glass	il bicchiere da acqua
window	finestra
wool blanket	coperta di lana

Vacation Houses and Vacation Rentals

Find out if the apartments are rented on a weekly or on a monthly basis, and if bed linens, towels, and place settings are provided.

Are electricity and water included in the rent?
La luce / L'acqua è compresa nel prezzo d'affitto?

Are there place settings, towels, and bed linens?
Ci sono le posate / gli asciugamani / C'è la biancheria?

Are pets allowed?
Si possono portare animali?

Where are the trash bins?
Dov'è il bidone delle immondizie?

Do we have to do the final cleaning ourselves?
Spetta a noi il lavoro di pulizia finale?

Farm Vacations and Agrotourism
Many farms—**aziende agrituristiche**—accept guests; most are
located in Tuscany, Umbria, South Tyrol, and Apulia. You can
even find quaint farms in Sicily. Many are organic food farms
that sell their produce directly—**agrispaccio.**

➢ **also Hotel—Guest House—Private Room**

apartment	appartamento
arrival day	giorno d'arrivo
bedroom	camera da letto
bungalow	il bungalow
bunk bed	letto a castello
central heat	riscaldamento centrale
charges	le spese (accessorie)
coffee maker *(American)*	macchina del caffè americana
(Italian)	macchinetta per il caffè
dishes	le stoviglie, i piatti
dishtowel	canovaccio per asciugare i piatti
dishwasher	la lavastoviglie
electric current	la corrente
electricity cost	prezzo forfettario per la corrente
farm	fattoria
farm vacation	agriturismo
final cleaning	pulizia finale
key return	consegna delle chiavi
kitchenette	cucinino, cucinotto
living room	soggiorno
microwave	microonda
owner	il padrone di casa
pets	gli animali domestici
refrigerator	frigorifero
rent	affitto, noleggio
sleeper couch	divano letto
stove	cucina
electric stove	cucina elettrica
gas stove	cucina a gas
studio	studio

to rent	affittare, noleggiare
toaster	il tostapane
trash/garbage	immondizia
vacation center	centro vacanze
vacation/country home	casa per le vacanze
voltage	voltaggio
washing machine	la lavatrice
water consumption	consumo d'acqua

Camping

Campgrounds are usually well equipped and are often situated in more beautiful locations than many luxury hotels. You can get information from the Italian Tourist Bureau (ENIT) and online.

Could you tell me if there is a campground near here?
Saprebbe dirmi, se qui vicino c'è un campeggio?

Do you have a spot for a trailer / tent?
C'è ancora posto per una roulotte / una tenda?

What is the charge per day and per person?
Quanto si paga al giorno a persona?

How much is it for...
Quanto si paga per ...

the car?
l'auto?
the trailer?
la roulotte?
the camper?
il camper?
the tent?
la tenda?

Do you rent camping trailers?
Si possono affittare roulottes?

We are staying... days/weeks.
Rimaniamo ... giorni/settimane.

Where are...
Dove sono ...

the toilets?
i servizi igienici?
the washrooms?
i lavandini?

the showers?
le docce?

Is there an electrical hookup here?
C'è una presa di corrente?

Where can I change gas cylinders?
Dove posso cambiare le bombole di gas?

Is the campground guarded at night?
Il campeggio è sorvegliato la notte?

camp director	guida dei campeggi
camper	il camper
campground	camping *m*, campeggio
to go camping	campeggiare
camping permit	tessera di campeggio
campsite	campeggio
clothes dryer	l'asciugatrice *f*
drinking water	acqua potabile
drying rack	stendibiancheria;
electric current	la corrente
gas cartridge	cartuccia del gas
gas cylinder	bombola di gas
gas stove	fornello a gas
kerosene lamp	lampada a petrolio
plug	spina
propane	propano
reservation	preavviso
RV	la roulotte
sink for dirty dishes	lavandino per i piatti
stove	fornello
tent	tenda
tent pole	palo da tenda
tent rope	laccio da tenda
tent stake	picchetto
wall plug	presa di corrente
wall socket	presa
washroom	stanzino da bagno
water	acqua
water can	tanica, latta

There are about fifty youth hostels in Italy. Many of them are in fortresses or villas that date from the Middle Ages. You can get complete information on the Internet at www.ostellionline.org (Ostelli per la Gioventù—Associazione italiana alberghi per la gioventù).

**Gastronomy
(Culinary Customs)**

Buon appetito!

There are many kinds of restaurants in Italy:

osteria—a wine bar where people drink mainly wines produced in the area. Sometimes you can also get something to eat there.

trattoria—a small, inexpensive restaurant—usually it's a family business. In large cities, expensive restaurants where the food is not necessarily good hide behind the label **trattoria**. The best idea is to ask locals to recommend a good restaurant.

ristorante—a restaurant with an extensive menu. A complete meal consists of a noodle or rice dish or soup (= *primo*), a meat or fish dish (= *secondo*), and fruit, cheese, or a dessert. If you want to eat only a plate of spaghetti or just a *secondo*, it's best to go to a

tavola calda—a self-service restaurant. Here you have to pay extra for the *coperto*, the place setting.

bar—a café to which Italians go at any time of the day to drink their *espresso, macchiato, cappuccino,* or an aperitif and eat snacks at the counter or table.

Some bars also offer *tavola calda* ("warm table"). Usually you first have to get a *scontrino* (ticket) at the cash register and then get the drink at the counter. The prices listed in the menu (*listino prezzi*) apply only to consumption at the counter.

Bars are also a meeting place. People meet informally, talk, watch television, play cards, foosball, pool, or a video game. For many Italians, the bar is like a second living room.

paninoteca—a restaurant in which you can get hot and cold sandwiches. This type of restaurant is frequented especially by young people.

Going Out to Eat

Excuse me, could you recommend...
Scusi, mi potrebbe indicare ...

a good restaurant?
un buon ristorante?

a reasonably priced restaurant?
un ristorante a buon mercato?

a snack bar?
una tavola calda / rosticceria?

Where can one go to eat around here without spending too much?
Dove si può andare a mangiare qui nelle vicinanze senza spendere molto?

In the Restaurant

Could you reserve a table for four people this evening?
Può riservarci per stasera un tavolo per quattro persone?

Is this table available, please?
È libero questo tavolo/posto?

A table for two / three people, please.
Per favore, un tavolo per due/tre persone.

Where are the restrooms, please?
Scusi, dov'è il bagno?

May I smoke?
Posso fumare?

Ordering

Waiter
Cameriere, …,
  A menu, please.
  il menù,
  The beverage list, please.
  la lista delle bevande, per favore.

> In pizzerias, drinking beer is considered "in." Beer from the tap is served in wine carafes with wine glasses and not very much foam.

What do you recommend?
Che cosa mi raccomanda?

Do you have vegetarian dishes / foods for special diets?
Avete piatti vegetariani / cibo dietetico?

Are there children's servings?
Fate anche porzioni per i bambini?

Have you decided?
Ha già scelto?

I'll have…
Prendo …

As an appetizer / main course / dessert, I'll have…
Per antipasto/dessert/secondo prendo …

I don't want an appetizer, thanks.
L'antipasto non lo prendo, grazie.

Unfortunately we have no (more)…
Purtroppo il/la… è finito.

We serve this meal only on special order.
Questo piatto lo serviamo solo su ordinazione.

Could I have … instead of …?
Al posto di … protrei avere …?

I can't eat … Could you prepare the dish without …
Non tollero il,lo,l',la/i,gli,le …. Potrebbe preparare il piatto senza …?

How do you want your steak cooked?
Come vuole la carne?

Well done
ben cotta

Medium
non troppo cotta

Rare
all' inglese / al sangue

What would you like to drink?
Che cosa desidera da bere?

A glass of…, please.
Per favore, un bicchiere di …

A bottle / a half-bottle of…, please.
Per favore, una/mezza bottiglia di …

With ice, please.
Con ghiaccio, per favore.

Enjoy your meal!
Buon appetito!

Here's to your health!
Salute!

Would you like anything else?
Desidera altro?

Please bring us…
Ci porti, per favore …

Could you please bring us some more bread / water / wine?
Ci può portare un altro po' di pane / d'acqua / di vino?

Complaints

I don't have a...
Manca ...

Have you forgotten my...?
Ha dimenticato il mio / la mia ...?

This is not what I ordered.
Non ho ordinato questo.

The soup is cold / too salty.
La minestra è fredda / troppo salata.

This meat is tough / too fatty.
La carne è dura/troppo grassa.

The fish is not fresh.
Il pesce non è fresco.

Please take this back.
Lo porti indietro, per favore.

Please get the manager.
Mi chiami per favore il direttore / il proprietario!

The Bill

The check, please.
Il conto/Pagare, per favore.

All together, please.
Tutto insieme.

Separate checks, please.
Conti separati, per favore.

Is service included?
È compreso il servizio?

I don't think the bill is correct.
Il conto non mi pare esatto.

I didn't have this. I had...
Non ho mangiato questo. Ho mangiato ...

Did you like it?
Era di Suo gradimento?

The meal was excellent.
Il mangiare era eccellente.

This is for you.
Questo è per Lei.

Keep the change.
Il resto è per Lei.

Ice Cream Parlors

Ice cream Time

It is reported that ice cream has been made in Italy since the seventeenth century. In many large Italian cities, from Milan to Palermo, there are traditional ice cream parlors that were founded at the end of the nineteenth century. Every good ice cream place makes its own ice cream (*produzione propria, produzione artigiana*): for milk-based ice cream, the main ingredients are eggs, sugar, and milk; for fruit ice cream, fruit pulp, egg whites, and sugar.

A good Italian ice cream parlor has fifteen to twenty flavors, and many have even more. Every ice cream parlor has a specialty that sometimes turns into a national fad, e.g., the Smurf ice cream (*gelato puffi*) of several years ago, which was as blue as the skin of the Smurfs. The flavors *bacio* and *gianduia* owe their names to famous Italian chocolates. Nowadays you can also find "healthy" kinds such as frozen yogurt, soy ice cream, and soy sprout ice cream.

In addition to the hard ice cream, there is also soft ice cream (*semifreddo*). These may include the types stored in the coolers such as *cassata* (made from chocolate, cream, and triangular candied fruits) and *zuccotto* (made from cream, chocolate, and cocktail cherries with round, thin biscuits soaked in liqueur), plus ice creams that are better known as desserts such as *zuppa inglese* and *tiramisu.*

I would like one scoop / two scoops of ice cream.
Vorrei una pallina / due palline di gelato.

One chocolate and one vanilla.
Una al cioccolato e una alla crema.

I would like an ice cream for one euro sixty.
Vorrei un gelato da 1 euro e sessanta.

In a cone or a dish?
Nel cono o nel bicchierino?

A mixed ice cream with cream.
Un gelato misto con panna.

A dish of ... but without cream, please.
Una coppa ..., ma senza panna, per favore.

alcohol-free	analcolico
appetizer	antipasto
ashtray	il portacenere
bone	osso
breakfast	prima colazione
child's portion	la mezza porzione
chili oil	olio e peperóncino
cook (m. and f.)	cuoco
corkscrew	il cavatappi
course	pietanza; portata
cup	tazza
saucer	piattino
daily menu	il menù del giorno
daily special	piatto del giorno
dessert	il dessert, il dolce
diabetic	diabetico
dinner	cena
dish	terrina, insalatiera
drink	bevanda
dry (wine)	(vino) secco
first course	primo
fishbone	spina, lisca
fork	forchetta
from the tap	alla spina
glass	il bicchiere
water glass	il bicchiere da acqua
wine glass	il bicchiere da vino
grill	griglia, graticola
homemade	fatto in casa
hot	caldo, bollente
to be hungry	aver fame
ketchup	il ketchup
knife	coltello
lunch	pranzo, il desinare
main course	secondo
mayonnaise	la maionese
mellow / smooth (wine)	amabile
menu	lista delle vivande, il menu
mustard	la senape
napkin	tovagliolo
oil	olio
order	l'ordinazione f
pepper	il pepe
pepper shaker	peparola, pepaiola

pitcher	caraffa
place setting	coperto
place settings	le posate
plate	piatto
portion	la porzione
salad bar	il buffet delle insalate
salt	il sale
saltshaker	spargisale *m*, saliera
sauce	salsa
slice	fetta
to season	condire, drogare
soup	minestra
soup bowl	piatto fondo, scodella
special diet	cibo dietetico
specialty	specialità
spice	le spezie
spoon	cucchiaio
teaspoon	cucchiaino
spot	macchia
stir-fry	piatto al tegame
straw	cannuccia
sugar	zucchero
sweetener (artificial)	l'edulcorante *m*, dolcificante *m*
tablecloth	tovaglia
tip	mancia
toothpick	lo stuzzicadenti
tough	duro
vegetarian	vegetariano
vinegar	aceto
waiter	cameriere *m*
waiter / waitress	il cameriere / la cameriera
water	acqua

Preparation

au gratin	gratinare
boiled	bollito, cotto
braised	brasato; stufato
cooked	cotto
fried	fritto
juicy	succoso
lean	magro
raw	crudo
roast	arrostito
from the grill	alla griglia
in a frying pan	al tegame
on a spit	allo spiedo

roasted	tostato, arrostito
smoked	affumicato
soft	tenero, morbido
sour	agro, aspro
spicy	piccante
steamed	cotto a vapore
stuffed	ripieno
sweet	dolce
tender	tenero
tough	duro
well done	ben cotto

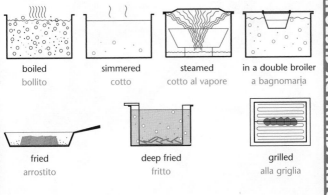

boiled
bollito

simmered
cotto

steamed
cotto al vapore

in a double broiler
a bagnomaria

fried
arrostito

deep fried
fritto

grilled
alla griglia

I would like ...
Vorrei ...

Ginger zenzero

Garlic
aglio

Onion
cipolla

Dill
aneto

Bay leaf
alloro

Rosemary
rosmarino

Majoram / oregano
maggiorana/origano

Coriander
coriandolo

Parsley
prezzemolo

Basil
basilico

98

Nutmeg la noce moscat

Chili pepper
peperoncino

Hot pepper
peperoncini verdi

Chives
erba cipollina

Sage
salvia

Chervil
cerfoglio

Thyme
timo

Savory
sautoreggia

Lovage
appio montano

I would like ...
Vorrei ...

I would like ...
Vorrei ...

Menù   ## Menu

Colazione   ### Breakfast

caffè·amaro .... black coffee
caffellatte .... coffee with milk
caffè decaffeinizzato .... decaffeinated coffee
tè al latte / al limone ...... tea with milk / lemon
tisana .... herbal tea
camomilla .... chamomile tea
cioccolata .... chocolate
succo di frutta / spremuta .... fruit juice / freshly squeezed fruit juice
uovo à la coque .... soft-boiled egg
uova strapazzate .... scrambled eggs
uova con lo speck .... eggs and bacon
il pane .... bread
i panini .... roll
il pane tostato .... toast
cornetto .... croissant
burro .... butter
formaggio .... cheese
i biscotti .... biscuits
prosciutto .... ham
il miele .... honey
marmellata .... jelly / jam
il müesli .... cereal
lo iogurt .... yogurt
la frutta .... fruit

Antipasti   ### Appetizers

antipasto caldo di mare ...... hot seafood appetizer
antipasto misto di terra/di mare assorted appetizers (without fish) / assorted fish appetizers
bresaola, rucola e parmigiano . roast beef, rucola and parmesan
bruschetta .... toasted slices of white bread with pieces of fresh tomato and garlic
insalata caprese .... tomatoes, mozzarella cheese, and basil
insalata di frutti di mare ..... seafood salad
insalata di gamberetti .... shrimp cocktail
melanzane alla parmigiana .... eggplant in tomato sauce, baked with cheese
prosciutto e melone .... Parma ham with melon

rucola e parmigiano	salad containing rucola and parmesan
tonno con fagioli	tuna salad with white beans
vitello tonnato	cold veal slices in tuna sauce

Minestre	**Soups**
ravioli in brodo	ravioli in meat broth
crema di pomodori	cream of tomato
minestrone	hearty vegetable soup
pasta e fagioli	hearty soup with beans and noodles
pastina in brodo	meat broth with noodles
stracciatella	soup with egg added
zuppa di pesce	fish soup
zuppa pavese	meat soup with toast and egg

Primi Piatti	**Noodles and Rice Dishes**
spaghetti, penne, rigatoni	spaghetti, pointed hollow noodles, hollow noodles
– al burro / in bianco	—with butter
– alla napoletana / al pomodoro	—with tomato sauce (no meat)
– alla bolognese / al ragù	—with tomato sauce (with meat)
– alle vongole	—with small mussels
– alla carbonara	—with egg and bacon
– al pesto	—with a sauce made of basil, pine nuts, olive oil, garlic, and sheep's milk cheese
– alla puttanesca	—with tomato sauce, olives, and strong spices
gnocchi	small potato noodles
gnocchi alla romana	gnocchi baked with cheese
polenta (alla valdostana)	cornmeal mash (with melted cheese)
agnolotti/ravioli/ tortellini	stuffed pasta pockets
cannelloni	cylindrical noodles stuffed with meat or vegetables
fettuccine / tagliatelle	flat noodles
lasagne al forno	baked, layered sheets of pasta with meat and béchamel sauce
tagliatelle verdi	green flat noodles
maccheroni	macaroni

vermicelli	thin spaghetti
risotto alla milanese	rice dish with saffron
risotto con funghi	rice dish with mushrooms

Carni	Meat Dishes
abbacchio	roast lamb *(Roman specialty)*
agnello	lamb
anitra	duck
arrosto di vitello	roast veal
bistecca ai ferri	grilled steak
bollito misto	assorted cooked meats
capretto	young goat
cervello	brain
coniglio	rabbit
cotoletta alla milanese	breaded veal cutlet
cotoletta di maiale	pork chop
fegato	liver
fesa di vitello	veal cutlet
lepre	hare
lingua	tongue
maiale	pork
lombata di vitello	veal loin
manzo / bue	beef
montone	mutton
faraona farcita	stuffed guinea hen
ossobuco	veal with sauce
petti di pollo	chicken breast
piccione	pigeon, dove
pollo	chicken
pollo arrosto	roast chicken
polpette (svizzere)	hamburger
rognoni	kidneys
saltimbocca alla romana	small veal cutlet with ham and sage
scaloppine di vitello	small veal cutlet
spezzatino	goulash with tomatoes
stufato	pot roast
tacchino	turkey
trippa	tripe
vitello	veal
zampone	stuffed pig's foot

Pesce	Fish
anguilla	eel
aragosta	lobster

calamari	squid
cozze / vongole	mussels
datteri di mare	sea dates
fritto di pesce	fried small fishes
branzino	sea perch
gambero, granchio	crab
pesce spada	swordfish
salmone	salmon
scampi fritti	fried small sea crabs
sgombro	mackerel
sogliola	sole
triglia	mullet
tonno	tuna
trota	trout

Verdura e contorni — Vegetables and Side Dishes

asparagi	asparagus
bietola	beet
broccoli	broccoli
carciofi	artichokes
carote	carrots
cavolfiore	cauliflower
cicoria	chicory
fagioli	white beans
fagiolini	green beans
finocchi	fennel
funghi	mushrooms
lenticchie	lentils
melanzane	eggplants
patate	potatoes
patatine fritte	french fries
peperoni	chili peppers
piselli	peas
pomodori	tomatoes
purè di patate	mashed potatoes
ravanelli	radishes
sedano	celery
spinaci	spinach
zucchini	zucchini

Insalate — Salads

insalata mista	mixed salad
insalata russa	Italian salad
insalata verde	green salad
radicchio	red lettuce salad

Uova — Egg Dishes

frittata	omelet
uova al tegame	fried eggs
uova sode	hard-boiled egg
uova strapazzate	scrambled eggs

Formaggi — Cheese

bel paese	mild, soft cheese
gorgonzola	spicy soft cheese with green mold
gruviera	Emmentaler cheese
mozzarella	fresh buffalo cheese
parmigiano / grana	parmesan cheese
pecorino	sheep's milk cheese
provolone (affumicato)	buffalo cheese, spicy (and smoked)
ricotta	mild soft cheese made from sheep's or cow's milk
stracchino	mild cheese spread
taleggio	white soft cheese

Dolci e frutta — Desserts and Fruits

> also ice cream parlors

bongo	small cream puff with cream filling and chocolate sauce
creme caramel	caramel pudding
cassata	ice cream with candied fruits
frutta cotta	fruit compote
gelato	ice cream
macedonia	fruit salad
sorbetto	lemon sherbet
tiramisu	sweet dessert made from a sweet fresh cheese and biscuits soaked in coffee
zabaione	eggs, Marsala wine, whipped cream
zuppa inglese	sweet made from various cream layers and bottom layer of biscuits soaked in liqueur
albicocca	apricots
ananas	pineapple
arancia	orange
ciliegie	cherries
cocomero / anguria	watermelon
fichi	figs
fragole	strawberries

frutti di bosco	cranberries
lamponi	raspberries
mela	apple
melone	melon
mirtilli	blueberries
pera	pear
pesca	peach
pompelmo	grapefruit
prugna / susina	plum
uva	grape

Gelati, granite e frappè — Ice Creams and Milkshakes

amarena	vanilla ice cream with hard, black cherries
bacio	nougat ice cream with pieces of hazelnuts
cioccolata	chocolate ice cream
coppa assortita	assorted ice cream dish
coppa con panna	dish of ice cream with cream
fior di latte	creamy ice cream
frappè alla fragola	strawberry shake
germi di soia	soy sprout ice cream
granita alla menta/ al limone ecc.	crushed ice with peppermint / lemon syrup (and others)
lampone	raspberry ice cream
limone	lemon ice cream
menta	mint ice cream
mirtilli	blueberry ice cream
nocciola	hazelnut ice cream
tartufo	vanilla or chocolate ice cream with chocolate syrup
torrone	almond ice cream with candied fruits
vaniglia / crema	vanilla ice cream

Lista delle bevande — Beverage Menu

Vini — Wine

Asti spumante	a usually delightful sparkling wine from the Piedmont
Barbera	dry, fruity Piedmont red wine
Bardolino	red table wine from the area around Lake Garda

Brunello di Montalcino	heavier, noble wine from Tuscany
Chianti	the best-known wine from Tuscany
Frascati	dry white wine from the "Castelli" around Rome
Grignolino	tangy Piedmont red wine
Làcrima Christi	somewhat sour, heavy red wine from the Naples region
Lambrusco	somewhat sparkling red wine from the Modena-Bologna area
Marino	dry sparkling wine from Friaul
Marsala	heavy sweet wine from Sicily
Pinot Grigio	dry white wine from Friaul or Trentino
Orvieto	fine, delightful or tangy white wine
Ruffino	Tuscan red wine that is still bottled in the typical Chianti basket-covered bottles
Valpolicella	a light red wine from Verona

Birre	**Beers**
birra scura, bruna	dark beer
birra chiara, bionda	light beer
birra alla spina	beer on tap

Bevande analcoliche	**Non-alcoholic Drinks**
acqua minerale	mineral water
gassata/non gassata	with / without carbonation
aranciata	orangeade
cedrata	mineral water with cedar juice
gassosa	mineral water
lemonsoda / oransoda	mineral water with pulp from lemons / oranges
spremuta d'arancia/ di pompelmo	freshly squeezed orange / grapefruit juice
succo di frutta	fruit juice
succo di pesca	peach juice
succo di pomodoro	tomato juice
succo di pera	pear juice

Liquori — Spirits and Liquors

amaro	bitters
amaretto	almond liqueur
grappa	marc wine
Limoncello	lemon liqueur
sambuca	liqueur with anise taste
Vecchia Romagna	Italian cognac
vinsanto, vin santo	white liqueur wine

Caffetteria — Drinks in a Bar

caffè, espresso	small, strong coffee without milk
caffè corretto	small, strong coffee with schnapps
caffè macchiato caldo/ freddo	small, strong coffee with warm / cold milk
caffè doppio	two *espressi* in a single cup
caffè lungo/corto	small, strong coffee with a little more / a little less water
cappuccino	coffee with milk beaten to a froth
camomilla	chamomile tea
tè al latte / limone	tea with milk / lemon
cioccolata con panna	hot chocolate with whipped cream

Take a look!

Over forty percent of the world's cultural heritage is located in Italy. Accordingly, there are many worthwhile sites to visit. In fact, all of Italy is a unique open-air museum: you can visit all periods of culture, including early history (the *Nuraghen* on Sardinia—fortress towers that were erected between the Bronze and Iron ages, i.e., 2000-1000 BC), classical antiquity (*Pompeii and Herculaneum, the Roman Forum in Rome, the Segesta Temple* in Sicily), the Middle Ages with its Romanesque *Piazza dei Miracoli*, leaning tower in Pisa, and San Ambrogio in Milan. You can also see Byzantine influences (including the famous Mosaics of Ravenna and *San Marco* in Venice), Gothic influences (The Milan Cathedral, the Cathedral in Orvieto), the Renaissance, with its magnificent buildings (e.g., the Cathedral of *Santa Maria dei Fiore* and the *Palazzo Vecchio* in Florence), and the Baroque age—with their purity of style and their homogeneity, the churches of Lecce in Apulia are highly recommended. For people who are interested in art and cultural history, Apulia is a real treasure trove, for nearly all eras are represented here, including modern times, with splendid Art Nouveau buildings such as the *Galleria Vittorio Emanuele II* in Milan (a sumptuous shopping mall), modern, and post-modern buildings. The architects Rossi and Pier Paolo Portoghesi, who built the controversial mosque in Rome, are among the most important adherents of this architectural style.

At the Tourist Office

I would like a map of…
Vorrei una pianta di …

Do you have multiple visit tickets for the museums in the city?
Vendete i biglietti cumulativi per i musei della città?

Are there city tours?
Ci sono giri turistici della città?

Do you have a schedule of performances for this week?
Ha un programma delle manifestazioni di questa settimana?

L'Italia in Miniatura
In Viserba, near Rimini, you have an opportunity to visit all of Italy in a single day: "Italy in Miniature" is the name of the amusement park where you can get an overview of the most appealing buildings in Italy in an area of about 102,000 square yards (85,000 square meters) in a scale of 1:25 to 1:50.

Sightseeing—Museums

The Uffizi Gallery *(Galleria degli Uffizi)* in Florence and the Vatican Museums are among the most significant museums in the world. The National Museum in Reggio Calabria holds a remarkable collection of remains from prehistoric times and antiquities from Calabria and ancient Greece. One of the most important collections of Egyptian art is found in the Egyptian Museum *(Museo Egizio)* in Turin, where, among other things, you can admire giant statues of pharaohs such as Ramses II and Tutankhamen.

In recent years, some Italian museums have been bringing art to children in a playful way. The Capitoline Museum in Rome has set up a multimedia tour for children ages seven and higher, where it is possible to display the history of the exhibited works on screens, along with lots of suggestions for games. The children can further develop the things they have seen and heard in a related experiential workshop. One of the most famous museums in Italy, the Museum of Capodimonte in Naples, has set up a workshop inside the museum in which children between the ages of four and ten have an opportunity to copy pieces on display while their parents walk around through the museum in peace.

Hours of Operation, Guided Tours, Tickets

Some museums are open until 10:00 P.M. in an effort to deal with the flood of visitors. In cities where lots of museums are concentrated, there is the possibility of buying cumulative tickets *(biglietti cumulativi)*. Ask about these at the tourist office.

Could you please tell me which monuments to see here?
Scusi, saprebbe indicarmi le cose da vedere qui?

You absolutely must visit...
Non deve assolutamente perdere ...

When is the museum open?
Quando è aperto il museo?

113

When does the tour begin?
Quando comincia la visita con la guida?

Does the guide also speak English?
La guida parla anche inglese?

Is photography allowed?
È permesso fare fotografie?

Two tickets, please.
Due biglietti, per favore!

Two adults and one child.
Due adulti e un bambino.

Is there a discount for...
Ci sono riduzioni per ...

  ... children?
  ... bambini?

  ... students?
  ... studenti?

  ... senior citizens?
  ... pensionati?

  ... groups?
  ... gruppi?

Are cumulative tickets for the museums?
Avete dei biglietti cumulativi per i musei?

Is there a catalog for the exposition?
Esiste un catalogo dell'esposizione?

What? When? Where?

Is this...
È questo il ...? / È questa la ...?

When was this building constructed / restored?
Quando fu costruito/restaurato questo palazzo?

Who painted this picture?
Chi ha dipinto questo quadro?

Is there a poster / postcard / slide of this picture?
Ha un poster / una cartolina / una diapositiva di questo quadro?

The rules of good manners dictate that people don't go into museums wearing just an undershirt, dangle their feet in the fountains, spread out picnic blankets and baskets in front of monuments and museums, or go into churches with shorts and bare arms.

General Information

alley	vicolo
archeological remains	i reperti archeologici
art	l'arte, *f*
birth city	città natale
changing of the guard	cambio della guardia
downtown	centro città
emblem	l'emblema *m*
emperor / empress	imperatore / imperatrice
guided city tour	giro turistico della città
guided tour	visita guidata
history	storia
house	casa
king / queen	re / regina
market	mercato
material	il materiale
monument protection	tutela dei monumenti
multiple-visit ticket	biglietto cumulativo
museum	museo
museum of folk art	museo di tradizioni popolari
outskirts, suburbs	sobborgo
park	parco
pedestrian zone	zona pedonale
precinct	il quartiere
to reconstruct	ricostruire
to restore	restaurare
religion	la religione
remains	i resti
street	strada, via
things to see, monuments	le cose da vedersi, i monumenti
tourist guide	guida turistica, il cicerone
visit / tour	visita

Architecture

abbey	abbazia
altar	l'altare *m*
amphitheater	anfiteatro
arcades	i portici
arch	arco
arch of triumph	arco di trionfo
archeology	archeologia
architect	architetto
architecture	architettura
arena	arena
bridge	il ponte
building	edificio, la costruzione
castle	castello

cathedral	duomo; la cattedrale
ceiling	soffitto
cemetery	cimitero
chapel	cappella
château	fortezza
church	chiesa
church tower	il campanile
city walls	le mura della città
cloister	chiostro
column	colonna
convent / monastery	convento, monastero
crypt	cripta
cupola / dome	cupola
excavations	gli scavi
façade	facciata
fortress	fortezza
fountain	fontana
gate	il portone
grave	tomba
inner courtyard	il cortile interno
inscription	l'iscrizione f, l'epigrafe f
marketplace	mercato coperto
mausoleum	mausoleo
memorial	monumento commemorativo
menhir	le nuraghe
monument	monumento
obelisk	obelisco
old city	centro storico
opera	opera
palace	palazzo
pediment	timpano
pilgrimage museum	santuario
place	piazza
portal	il portale
pulpit	pulpito
to reconstruct	ricostruire
roof	tetto
ruin	rovina
temple	tempio
theater	teatro
tomb	monumento sepolcrale
tower	la torre
town hall	municipio
treasure chamber	tesoreria
university	università

vault	volta
wall	muro
window	finestra
wing	ala

Fine Arts

bronze	bronzo
carpet	tappeto
ceramics	ceramica
copperplate engraving	l'incisione f su rame, calcografia
copy	copia
cross	la croce
crucifix	crocifisso
decorative arts	artigianato
design	disegno
display piece	pezzo d'esposizione
etching	l'acquaforte f
exposition	mostra, l'esposizione f
figurative arts	l'arti figurative
gallery	galleria (d'arte)
goldsmith's art	l'arte f orafa
graphic art	l'arte f grafica
ink	inchiostro, china
lithography	litografia
model	modello
mosaic	mosaico
mosaic worker	il mosaicista
nude	atto
original	l'originale m
painter	pittore / pittrice
painting	dipinto; pittura; quadro
painting on glass	pittura su vetro, vetrocromia
photograph	fotografia
porcelain	porcellana
portrait	ritratto
poster	manifesto
pottery	l'arte f di vasaio
sculptor	lo scultore
sculpture	scultura
silkscreen	serigrafia
statue	statua
still life	natura morta
terra-cotta	terracotta
torso	torso
vase	vaso

watercolor	acquerello
woodcarving	intaglio
woodcut	silografia

Styles and Eras

after Giotto	giottesco
antique	antico
antiquity	antichità
Art nouveau	Art Nouveau
baroque	barocco
Bronze Age	età del bronzo
Byzantine	bizantino
Celtic	celtico
century	secolo

> **Designating centuries** the history of art and culture: *il Quattrocento*—the fifteenth century; *il Cinquecento*—the sixteenth century, and so forth.

Christianity	cristianesimo
Classicism	classicismo
contemporary art	arte contemporanea
Cubism	cubismo
dynasty	dinastia
epoch	epoca
Expressionism	espressionismo
Gothic	gotico
Greek	greco
high point	periodo aureo
Impressionism	impressionismo
Iron Age	età del ferro
Macchiaioli	macchiaioli *pl*
(painting movement)	
Mannerism	manierismo
Middle Ages	Medioevo
Modern	moderno
Norman	normanno
Ostrogoth	ostrogoto
pagan	pagano
prehistoric	preistorico
prehistory	preistoria
Raphaelite	raffaellesco
Renaissance	rinascimento
Risorgimento	risorgimento
Rococo	rococò
Romanesque Art	l'arte *f* romanica

118

Romanticism	romanticismo
Stone age	età della pietra
style	lo stile
Surrealism	surrealismo

Tours

Where do we meet?
Dov'è il punto d'incontro?

When shall we meet?
Quando ci incontriamo?

Will we go by the ...?
Passiamo da ...?

Will we also visit ...?
Andiamo anche a vedere ...?

When do we return?
Quando torniamo?

amusement park	parco divertimenti
backcountry	il retroterra
bird sanctuary	zona di protezione degli uccelli
botanical garden	giardino botanico
cave	grotta, caverna
cave with stalactites and stalagmites	grotta con stalattiti e stalagmiti
coast	il litorale
countryside	paesaggio
day trip	gita di un giorno
fishing port	porto di pesca
fishing village	villaggio di pescatori
forest	bosco, foresta
forest fire	incendio forestale
gorge	gola
grotto	grotta
high plains	altopiano
island tour	giro dell'isola
lake	lago
lava	lava
lighthouse	faro
market	mercato
mountain	il monte
mountain pass	passo
mountain town	villaggio di montagna
mountains	montagna
museum village	villaggio museale

national park	parco nazionale
nature preserve	parco nazionale
observatory	osservatorio astronomico
open-air museum	museo all'aperto

> Italy's greatest "open air museum" is surely **Venice**. Highlights include St. Mark's Square (*Piazza San Marco*), the palace of the Doges (*Palazzo Ducale*), and the Rialto Bridge (*Ponte di Rialto*).

overlook	il belvedere
pilgrimage site	luogo di pellegrinaggio
reef	scoglio
river	il fiume
round trip	giro
spring	la sorgente, la fonte
summit	cima
surroundings	i dintorni
swamp	la palude
swampy coast	maremma
tour, excursion	gita, l'escursione *f*
valley	la valle
volcano	vulcano
waterfall	cascata
wildlife park	riserva di caccia
zoo	lo zoo

Active and Creative Vacations

Summer, Sun, and Beach
For many people, summer vacation in Italy means vacation by the sea. But be careful: in Italy there are private beaches, and the only way to get access to them is to rent an umbrella and a beach recliner. Topless sunbathing is always permitted, but topless bathers are less common. Pay attention to the practices of the local people.

Many private resorts—especially on the Adriatic, which has a long tradition of foreign tourism—offer sports and entertainment.

The *vu' cumprà*—usually illegal North African immigrants (also known as *extracomunitari* because they don't belong to the European community) live on the beaches and offer carpets, cigarette lighters, sunglasses, imitation designer pocketbooks, and other such things for sale without a sales permit. They are forced into these jobs by their escape helpers, have to pay a lot of money for their bunk in a ten-bed room, and give away the major portion of their income.

Swimming Vacation

Excuse me, is there a ...
Scusi, c'è qui ...

swimming pool?
una piscina?

an outdoor pool?
una piscina all'aperto?

an indoor pool?
una piscina coperta?

One ticket, please!
Un biglietto, per favore!

Could you tell me where the... are?
Scusi, dove sono le ...

showers
docce?

changing rooms
cabine?

122

People change clothes only in changing rooms or in the bathrooms. Some people who want to change on the beach have to cover themselves up with their towel, and that's not very easy to do. The unwritten rule is simple: adults don't appear totally naked at the beach, unless it's one of the rare nudist beaches.

Is the beach...
La spiaggia è ...
sandy?
sabbiosa?
rocky?
ghiaiosa?

Are there sea urchins / jellyfish / Is there seaweed?
Ci sono ricci/meduse/alghe?

Is the current strong?
È molto forte la corrente?

Can you tell me if it's dangerous for children?
Sa dirmi se è pericoloso per i bambini?

Per soli nuotatori!	For Swimmers Only!
Vietato tuffarsi!	No Diving!
Vietato bagnarsi!	No Swimming!

When is low tide / high tide?
Quando viene la bassa / l'alta marea?

I would like to rent...
Vorrei noleggiare ...
a beach chair.
una (sedia a) sdraio.
an umbrella.
un ombrellone.
a rowboat / pedal boat.
una barca a remi / un pedalò.
a pair of water skis.
un paio di sci nautici.

How much is it per hour / per day?
Quanto costa all'ora / al giorno?

air mattress	materasso pneumatico
beach volleyball	il beach-volley
free beach	spiaggia libera
jet-ski	lo scooter
kiddy pool	piscina/vasca per bambini
lifeguard	bagnino
non-swimmer	non nuotatore
nudist beach	spiaggia per nudisti
pedal boat	patino a pedali, pedalò
sunning lawn	prato per sdraiarsi
to swim	nuotare
swim fins	le pinne
swimmer	il nuotatore
swimming area	zona balneare
to go water skiing	andare su sci nautici
water skiing	gli sci nautici
water wings	i braccioli
windshield	frangivento

Active Vacations

What kinds of sports are available here?
Quali sport si possono praticare qui?

Is there ... here?
C'è ...

a golf course
un campo da golf?

a tennis court
un campo da tennis?

Excuse me, could you tell me where one can...
Scusi, saprebbe dirmi dove si può / possono ...?

go fishing?
pescare

take some good hikes?
fare delle belle escursioni

Where can I rent...
Dove posso noleggiare ...?

I would like to take a beginning / advanced course in...
Vorrei fare un corso di ... per principianti/avanzati.

Water Sports

boating *(houseboat)*	turismo sui corsi d'acqua
boating permit	la patente nautica
canoe	canoa
canoe, to paddle	canoa, andare in canoa
canyoning	il canyoning
house boat	la house boat
inflatable boat	canotto pneumatico
motorboat	motoscafo
oar	remo
regatta	regata
to row	remare
rowboat	barca a remi
sail, to sail	la vela, navigare a vela
sailboat	barca a vela
sailing cruise	veleggiata, gita in barca a vela
to surf	praticare il surfing
surfboard	tavola del wind-surf
wind conditions	la situazione termica
windsurfing, to wind surf	il windsurf; fare windsurf

Diving

deep-sea diving	immersione con le bombole
to dive	nuotare sott'acqua
diving equipment	attrezzatura da sub
diving goggles / face mask	la maschera da sub
harpoon	fiocina
oxygen tank	l'ossigenatore, *m*
snorkel	il respiratore di superficie, il snorkel
to go snorkeling	fare lo snorkeling
wet suit	la muta in neoprene

Fishing

closed season	periodo di divieto di caccia
deep sea fishing	pesca d'altura
to go fishing	pescare con l'amo
fishing license	licenza di pesca
fishing rod	canna da pesca
harbor master	capitaneria di porto

Ball Games

ball	palla
basketball	il Basketball, pallacanestro
goal *(apparatus)*	porta
(score)	il goal
goalie	il portiere
halftime	primo/secondo tempo
handball	palla a mano
net	la rete
rugby	il rugby
soccer ball	calcio
soccer field	terreno di gioco
soccer game	partita di calcio
team	squadra
volleyball	la pallavolo

Tennis and Badminton

badminton	il badminton, gioco del volano
doubles	doppio
floodlight	impianto di proiettori
racket	racchetta
shuttlecock	volano
singles	singolo
squash	lo squash
table tennis / ping-pong	il ping-pong
tennis	il tennis
tennis racket	racchetta

Fitness and Strength Training

aerobics	aerobica
bodybuilding	culturismo
conditioning	allenamento per migliorare la forma
fitness center	centro di fitness, palestra
gymnastics	ginnastica
gymnastics for the spinal column	ginnastica per la colonna vertebrale
jazzercise	ginnastica jazz
to jog	fare jogging
jogging	il jogging
stretching	lo stretching

Wellness

massage	massaggio
sauna	sauna
solarium	solario
steam bath	bagno turco
swimming pool	piscina
whirlpool	vasca per idromassaggio

Cycling

bicycle	bicicletta
bicycle path	percorso ciclabile
bicycle route	pista ciclabile, ciclopista
bicycle tour	itinerario in bici(cletta)
to go bike riding	andare in bicicletta
cycling	ciclismo
cycling helmet	casco di protezione
inner tube	camera d'aria
mountain bike	la mountain bike
pump	pompa d'aria
racing bicycle	bicicletta da corsa
rollers	monopattino
tire repair kit	gli accessori per la riparazione di forature
touring bike	bicicletta da turismo
trekking bike	bicicletta da trekking

Hiking and Mountain Climbing

I would like to take a hike in the mountains.
Vorrei fare una gita in montagna.

Can you show me an interesting route on the map?
Mi può indicare un itinerario interessante sulla carta?

day trip	marcia di un giorno
free climbing	il freeclimbing
hiking trail	sentiero (per escursioni)
hiking, to go hiking	il trekking, camminare / fare un'escursione
major trail	sentiero per escursioni a lunga distanza
mountain climbing	alpinismo
route	percorso, itinerario

ACTIVE AND CREATIVE VACATIONS

127

safety rope	corda di sicurezza
shelter	rifugio
trail map	mappa dei sentieri
trekking	il trekking

Horseback Riding

horse	cavallo
polo	polo
ride	cavalcata
to ride	cavalcare
riding school	scuola di equitazione
riding vacation	le vacanze a cavallo

Golf

18-hole course	campo con 18 buche
clubhouse	circolo, il club
day visitor	visitatore giornaliero
golf	il golf
golf club *(implement)*	mazza da golf
golf club *(organization)*	circolo golfistico
golfer	giocatore di golf
greens fee	greenfee
tee-off	il teeing-ground

Flying Kites, Hang-gliders, and Gliders

gliding	volo a vela
hang-glider	parapendio
hang-gliding	lo sport del deltaplano
landing strip	pista di decollo
paragliding	il paragliding
parasail	deltaplano dirigibile
parascending *(on beach)*	parapendio a motore trainante
sky-diving	paracadutismo
thermal	termica

Winter Vacation

A day pass, please.
Un (biglietto) giornaliero, per favore.

How many points does this lift cost?
Quanti punti costa lo ski-lift / l'impianto di risalita?

What time is the last trip up / down?
A che ora c'è l'ultima salita a monte / discesa a valle?

alpine skiing	lo sci alpino
cable car	funivia, la funicolare
chairlift	seggiovia
cross-country ski track	pista di fondo
cross-country skiing	lo sci di fondo
curling	il curling, l'eisschiessen
daily lift ticket	(abbonamento) giornaliero
halfway stop on ski lift	la stazione a mezza quota
ice hockey	l'hockey *m* su ghiaccio
ice skates	i pattini (per ghiaccio)
kiddy tow	l'impianto di risalita per bambini
lift loading area	la stazione a valle
powder snow	la neve farinosa
to skate	pattinare (sul ghiaccio)
skating	pattinaggio su ghiaccio
skating rink	pista per pattinaggio su ghiaccio
to ski	sciare
ski binding	attacco
ski goggles	gli occhiali da sci
ski instructor (m. and f.)	maestro/a di sci
ski lessons	corso di sci
ski poles	i bastoni da sci
ski tow	sciovia
skiing	lo sci
sled	slitta
to go sledding	andare in slitta
snow rafting	lo snowrafting
snowboard	lo snowboard
top of the lift	la stazione a monte
week's pass	abbonamento settimanale

Other Sports

base jumping	il basejumping
bocce	il gioco delle bocce
bowling	il bowling
bungee jumping	il bungeejumping
inline skating	pattinaggio sui rulli
to go inline skating	pattinare sui rulli

miniature golf	il minigolf
motorcycling	motociclismo
ninepins	gioco dei birilli
roller blades	i rollerblades
roller skate	i pattini a rotelle
to roller skate	andare sui pattini a rotelle
skateboard	lo skate-board
to skateboard	andare sullo skate
track and field	atletica leggera

Attending Sporting Events

Could you tell me what kinds of sporting events there are here?
Scusi, saprebbe dirmi quali manifestazioni sportive ci sono qui?

I would like to attend the soccer game.
Vorrei vedere la partita di calcio.

When / where does it take place?
Quando/Dove ha luogo?

How much does it cost to get in?
Quanto costa l'ingresso?

What's the score?
Come stanno?

Two to one.
2 a 1.

One to one.
uno a uno.

Foul!
Fallo!

Good shot!
Bel tiro!

Goal!
Goal!

athlete (m. and f.)	sportivo/sportiva
bicycle race	corsa ciclistica
cash register	cassa
championship	campionato
competition	gara
cross	il cross, il traversone
free shot	il calcio di punizione
game	partita
kickoff	calcio d'inizio
to lose	perdere

loss	sconfitta
offside	fuorigioco
pass	passaggio
penalty area	area di rigore
penalty kick	calcio di rigore
playing field	campo sportivo
program	il programma
race	corsa
referee	arbitro
stadium	stadio
ticket	biglietto d'ingresso
tie	pari
win	vittoria
to win	vincere

Creative Vacations

I would like to take ...
Mi interesserebbe fare ...

pottery lessons
un corso di ceramica.

an Italian course
un corso d'italiano.

for beginners
per principianti

for advanced students
per avanzati

How many hours per day is it?
Quante ore al giorno si lavora?

Is enrollment limited?
Il numero dei partecipanti è limitato?

Is any experience required?
Sono richieste delle conoscenze preliminari?

What's the registration deadline?
Fino a quando ci si deve iscrivere?

Are the materials costs included?
I costi per il materiale sono compresi?

What do we have to bring?
Cosa si deve portare?

belly dancing	danza del ventre
cooking	il cucinare, la cucina
course	corso
dance theater	teatro-danza

131

Theater—Concerts—Movies

La Scala in Milan was opened in 1778, and since that time it has been the world center of melodrama. The season always opens on December 7 and everybody snatches up the expensive tickets. The sale of 200 standing places *(posti in piedi)* always begins one hour before the start of the performance; however, you should get in line in the morning.

Could you please tell me what play is being presented tonight?
Scusi, saprebbe dirmi che pezzo danno oggi a teatro?

What's playing tomorrow evening at the movie?
Che cosa c'è al cinema domani sera?

Can you recommend a good play?
Mi può raccomandare un buon pièce teatrale?

At what time does the performance start?
Quando comincia lo spettacolo?

In most Italian movies the screenings don't begin at any specific hour, so you can go in at any time and stay as long as necessary to see the whole film. Since not everyone likes to see the end of a movie before the beginning, you can ask at the ticket window when the next showing begins.

Where does one get tickets?
Dove si comprano i biglietti?

Two tickets for this evening, please.
Due biglietti per stasera, per favore.

Two ...-euro seats, please.
Per favore due biglietti da ... Euro.

May I have a program, please?
Mi può dare un programma, per favore?

134

For the most famous music performances (opera in the arena at Verona, concerts in the *Caracalla* hot springs in Rome, the Ravello Music Festival, along the Amalfi coast, the *Maggio Musical Fiorentino* in Florence), it's advisable to get tickets well in advance.

advance sale	prevendita
festival	il féstival
intermission	intervallo
performance	spettacolo
program (booklet)	opúscolo del programma
ticket	biglietto
ticket window	biglietteria

Theater

act	atto
actor / actress	l'attore *m* / l'attrice *f*
ballet	balletto
box	palco
cabaret	il cabaret
comedy	commedia
dancer (m. and f.)	ballerino/a
direction	messa in scena
drama	il dramma
first / second row	prima/seconda fila di palchi
folkloric play	commedia popolare
Greek drama	teatro greco
musical comedy	il musical, commedia musicale
opera	opera
operetta	operetta
orchestra *(seating)*	platea
outdoor theater	teatro all'aperto
play	opera teatrale
premiere	prima
presentation	spettacolo
program	il programma
tragedy	tragedia
variety show	il varietà

Concerts

blues	il blues
choir	coro
classical music	musica classica
composer (m. and f.)	il compositore / la compositrice

135

concert	concerto
chamber music concert	concerto da camera
church concert	concerto di musica sacra
symphony orchestra concert	concerto sinfonico
folk	il folk
folk music	musica popolare
jazz	il jazz
orchestra	orchestra
orchestra conductor	il direttore / la direttrice d'orchestra
pop	il pop
rap	il rap
reggae	il reggae
rock	il rock
singer (m. and f.)	il/la cantante
soloist (m. and f.)	il/la solista
soul	il soul
techno	tecno

Movies

direction	regia
film	il film
action film	d'azione
animated film	a cartoni animati
black and white film	in bianco e nero
classic	classico
comedy	commedia
documentary	documentario
drama	tragedia
science fiction film	di fantascienza
short feature	a corto metraggio
thriller	thrilling
leading role	ruolo principale
movie	il cinema
art film	il cinema d'essai
outdoor movie	il cinema all'aperto
movie actor / actress	l'attore m/l'attrice f di cinema
original version	la versione originale
special effects	effetti speciali
subtitle	sottotitolo

Nightlife

What is there to do around here in the evening?
Cosa si può fare qui la sera?

Is there a pleasant bar around here?
C'è un locale simpatico da queste parti?

Where can you go dancing around here?
Dove si può andare a ballare?

Shall we have another dance?
Balliamo (ancora)?

band	complesso
bar	il night
casino	casinò
dance band	orchestra
dance, to	ballare
discotheque	discoteca
evening attire	abito da sera
folk dance evening	serata folcloristica
folklore	il folclore
game of chance	gioco d'azzardo
go out, to	uscire
live music	musica dal vivo
nightclub	il night-club
pub	il locale, il pub
show	lo show

Festivals and Functions

The *Palio di* Siena, the most famous medieval horse race, takes place twice a year. The word *palio* comes from the Latin *pallium* (victory ribbon), and is also the prize that's presented to the victor after three laps around the *Piazza del Campo* (main square of Siena). The competition is among the city precincts that enter a rider. For the residents of Siena, this festival is more than a traditional spectacle; for many it's the stuff of life. The oldest *palio*, which dates back to the year 1275, takes place every year on September 16 in Asti, Piemont.

Could you tell when the ... festival takes place?
Scusi, potrebbe dirmi quando avrà luogo il Festival ...

from the... to the ...
dal ... al ...

every year in August
ogni anno in agosto

every two years
ogni due anni

Can everyone participate?
Può partecipare chiunque?

annual fair . . . . fiera
band . . . . banda

The region with the most traditional celebrations is Umbria. The three most famous ones are *Il Calendimaggio, La Corsa dei Ceri,* and *La Quintana.* The *Calendimaggio* (May Festival) originated in the Renaissance era and takes place in Assisi between April 29 and May 1. The upper and lower city play against one another and the victor may then proclaim the *Madonna Primavera* (Lady of the Springtime). During the festival, the whole city adopts a Renaissance motif and everywhere you can see ladies and gentlemen in traditional dress.

La Corsa dei Ceri (Altar Candle Competition) dates from the Middle Ages and takes place on May 15 in Gubbio. Three teams from three sections of Gubbio carry the nearly fifteen-foot high wooden statue known as *Ceri* on their shoulders and race in breakneck fashion through Gubbio's narrow alleys on a hill, on top of which stands the Basilica of San Ubaldo.

Carnival . . . . il carnevale

Carnival in Venice is surely one of the most famous traditional festivals in Italy. Most of the figures and masks that are displayed on bridges and in squares for ten days leading up to carnival Tuesday (*martedi grasso*) come from the *Commedia dell'arte*, which dates back to the sixteenth century. In addition to the classical figures such as *Arlecchino, Pulcinella,* and *Colombina,* there are also fantasy figures that wander through Venice's alleyways. The carnival parades in Ronciglione (Viterbo Province) and in Viareggio (Lucca Province) are also worth seeing.

Carnival Tuesday . . . . martedì grasso
gentleman . . . . il cavaliere
Giro d'Italia . . . . Giro d'Italia
jousting . . . . giostra
lady . . . . madonna

La Quintana is similar to *La Giostra del Saracino* (The Saracen's Joust), which takes place in Arezzo in September; a medieval knight's game is repeated ever year on the second Sunday in September in Foligno.

May Day celebration . . . . . . Calendimaggio
medieval horse race . . . . . . palio
procession . . . . la processione

Shopping

Questions

I'm looking for...

Is someone helping you?
La servono già?

I would like...
Vorrei ...

Thanks, I'm just looking.
Grazie, vorrei solo dare un'occhiata.

Do you have...?
Ha ...?

Will there be anything else?
Altro?

Haggling and Purchasing

Even though it's becoming increasingly difficult, you should
always haggle in markets. You can also try it in retail stores,
but then you will have to pay cash, just as in the markets.

How much is that?
Quanto costa? Quanto viene?

140

That's expensive!
Ma è caro!

But you ought to give me a little break on the price!
Un po' di sconto me lo dovrebbe fare però!

Sorry, but our prices are firm.
Mi dispiace, ma abbiamo i prezzi fissi.

Do we have a deal if I give you...?
È d'accordo se Le lascio ...?

All right.
D'accordo.

Fine, I'll take it.
Bene, lo prendo.

Do you take credit cards?
Accetta carte di credito?

With every purchase you must be sure to get a cash register slip (*scontrino*), which you will have to show in case you get checked by the finance police. Such checks may occur about a hundred yards from the display area.

Shops

Excuse me, where can I find...
Scusi, dove potrei trovare ...?

Business hours—orari d'apertura

aperto . . . . open
chiuso . . . . closed
chiuso per ferie . . . . closed for vacation

Store business hours are flexible. At the ocean, the supermarkets are usually open from 8 A.M. to 9 P.M.; specialty shops often take a long midday break between 1:00 and 5:00 P.M., but many stay open until 11:00 P.M. In the cities, the department stores are usually open from 8:00 or 9:00 A.M.until 8:00 P.M. Specialty stores generally take a midday break between 1:00 and 4:00 P.M., and close between 7:30 and 8:00 P.M.

141

antique shop	negozio di antichità
art dealer	il commerciante in oggetti d'arte
bakery	panificio
bookstore	libreria
boutique	la boutique
butcher shop	macelleria
camera shop	gli articoli fotografici
caterer	negozio di prodotti dietetici
coin-operated laundromat	lavanderia a gettone
confectioner's shop	negozio di dolciumi
delicatessen	negozio di specialità gastronomiche
department store	il grande magazzino

There are not very many department stores in Italy, and they are only in the large cities.

dry cleaner's	agenzia viaggi
electrical appliances store	l'elettricista *m*, elettrodomestici
fish market	pescheria
flea market	mercato delle pulci
florist	fioraio
fruit and vegetable shop	fruttivendolo
grocery store	negozio di generi alimentari
hair stylist's	il parrucchiere
hardware store	negozio di ferramenta, mesticheria
health food shop	lavanderia a secco, tintoria
jewelry store	gioielleria
laundromat	lavanderia
leather goods	pelletteria
liquor store	rivendita di prodotti alcolici, bottiglieria
market	mercato

In the markets, you can buy clothing, leather goods, and household wares in addition to foods. The clothing stands include the names of some large companies. Sometimes there are items that have been selected from expensive boutiques. But oftentimes, they are simply cheap imitations.

medicinal herb shop	erboristeria
natural products shop	negozio di prodotti biodinamici
newspaper seller	giornalaio
optician	ottico
pastry shop	pasticceria
perfume shop	profumeria

pharmacy	farmacia
second-hand dealer	il rigattiere
shoe store	calzolaio
souvenir shop	negozio di souvenir
sporting goods store	gli articoli sportivi
stationery store	negozio di calzature
supermarket	supermercato
tailor / seamstress	cartoleria
tobacco shop	tabaccaio
toy shop	negozio di giocattoli
travel agency	sarto/sarta
watchmaker	orologiaio
wine shop	fiaschetteria

Books, Periodicals, and Writing Materials

I would like...
Vorrei ...

an American newspaper.
un giornale americano.

a magazine.
una rivista.

a visitors' guide.
una guida turistica.

a hiking map of the area.
una mappa dei sentieri di questa zona.

Books, Periodicals, and Newspapers

book	libro
comic book	fumetto
cookbook	libro di cucina
daily newspaper	quotidiano
detective novel	(romanzo) giallo
magazine	periodico
magazine	rivista, rotocalco
map	carta geografica
map of the city	pianta della città
newspaper	il giornale
novel	romanzo
pocket book	libro tascabile
road map	carta automobilistica
visitors' guide	guida turistica
women's magazine	rivista femminile

Writing Materials

ballpoint pen	la biro
colored pencil	matita colorata
coloring book	l'album *m* da colorare
envelope	busta
notepad	blocchetto per appunti
pad for letters	blocco (di carta)
paper	carta
pencil	il lapis
postcard	cartolina illustrata
stationery	carta da lettere

CD and Cassettes

> ➤ also *Electronics* and *Concerts*

Do you have CDs / cassettes by...?
Ha dei CD/delle cassette di ...?

I would like a CD of typically Italian music.
Vorrei un CD con musica tipica italiana.

Can I listen to a bit of it, please?
Scusi, potrei ascoltare un brano o due?

cassette	cassetta
CD (compact disc)	il CD (compact disc)
CD player	il lettore CD
portable CD player	il lettore CD portatile
DVD	DVD
headphones	cuffia
portable cassette player . . .	il walkman
speaker	l'altoparlante *m*

Drugstore Items

There are no drugstores in Italy. Drugstore items are found in supermarkets, perfume shops, pharmacies, and in stores for house and kitchen appliances (*mesticheria*). Baby items (including potties!) and cosmetics are found in pharmacies. The Italian *drogheria* is more like what we would call a grocery store or a general food store. Delicatessen items and spices are sold in such stores.

aftershave lotion	la lozione dopobarba
band aid	cerotto
brush	spazzola
comb	il pettine
condom	preservativo
cotton pad	il cotone idrofilo
cotton swab	i bastoncini igienici
cream	crema
dental floss	filo interdentale
deodorant	il deodorante
dish soap	detersivo per le stoviglie
dish towel	straccio per lavare i piatti
dishwashing brush	spazzolino per le stoviglie
elastic hair band	elastico per capelli
electric razor	rasoio
hair gel	il gel per capelli
hair setting lotion	la frizione
hairpins	le mollette (per capelli)
hand cream	crema per le mani
laundry detergent	detersivo
lip balm	l'emolliente (m) per le labbra
lipstick	rossetto
mascara	il mascara
mirror	specchio
moisturizing cream	crema idratante
nail clippers	le forbici per le unghie
nail polish	smalto
nail polish remover	l'acetone m, il solvente per smalto
night cream	crema da notte
panty liners	le assorbenti sottili, i proteggi-slip
paper tissues	i fazzoletti di carta
perfume	profumo
powder	(face) cipria; (dusting powder) borotalco
razor blades	la lametta
sanitary napkins	gli assorbenti
shampoo	lo shampoo
shaving brush	pennello da barba
shaving cream	schiuma da barba
shower gel	il gel per la doccia
soap	il sapone
sun protection factor (SPF)	il fattore protettivo
sunscreen	crema solare
suntan lotion	il latte solare
suntan oil	olio solare

tampons	i tamponi
mini / regular / super / super plus	mini/normale/super/superplus
tea tree oil	estratto di melaleuca
toilet paper	carta igienica
toothbrush	spazzolino da denti
toothpaste	dentifricio
toothpick	lo stuzzicadenti
tweezers	le pinzette
washcloth	guanto di spugna, manopola

Electrical Items

➤ also Photo Items and CDs and Cassettes

adapter	l'adattatore *m*
alarm clock	sveglia
battery	batteria
calculator	il calcolatore tascabile
extension cord	cavo di prolungamento, prolunga
hair dryer	il föhn
lightbulb	lampadina (ad incandescenza)
notebook	il notebook
organizer	l'organizer *m*
pager	il pager
plug	spina
recharger	apparecchio carica-batterie
wall socket	presa

Photo Items

➤ Film and Photography

I would like...
Vorrei ...

a roll of film for this camera.
una pellicola per questa macchina.

a roll of color film (for slides).
una pellicola a colori (per diapositive).

a roll of film with 36 / 20 / 12 exposures.
una pellicola da 36/20/12 fotografie.

... is not working.
... non funziona.

This is broken. Can you please repair it?
Questo non funziona, me lo può riparare per favore?

automatic shutter . . . . autoscatto
black and white film . . . . . . pellicola in bianco e nero
camcorder . . . . il videoregistratore
camcorder . . . . videocamera
camera with self-developing   macchina fotografica a sviluppo
  film   immediato
digital camera . . . . macchina fotografica digitale
DVD . . . . DVD
film speed . . . . sensibilità del film
flash . . . . il flash
lens . . . . la lente
light meter . . . . esposimetro
objective . . . . obiettivo
shutter release . . . . scatto
telephoto lens . . . . teleobiettivo
tripod . . . . il treppiedi
underwater camera . . . . macchina fotografica subacquea
video film . . . . il videofilm
videocamera . . . . videocamera
videocassette . . . . videocassetta
viewfinder . . . . mirino

At the Hairstylist's

Shampoo and blow-dry, please.
Shampoo e fon, per favore.

A haircut with / without shampoo, please.
Tagliare e/senza lavare, per favore.

I would like...
Vorrei ...

Just a trim.
Solo le punte.

Not too short / quite short / a little shorter, please.
Non troppo corti / Molto corti / Un po' più corti, per favore.

Above the ears / touching the ears.
Le orecchie devono essere scoperte/coperte.

A shave, please.
La barba, per favore.

Please trim my beard.
Mi spunti la barba, per favore.

148

Thanks a lot. It's fine.
Grazie. Va bene così.

bangs	frangetta
beard	barba
blond	biondo
curls	i ricci
dandruff	forfora
hair	i capelli
dry hair	i capelli secchi
oily hair	i capelli grassi
hair curler	i bigodini
hairdresser	il parrucchiere
hairpiece	il toupet
hairstyle	pettinatura
layer cut	taglio scalato
mustache	i baffi
part	riga
permanent	la permanente
shampoo	lo shampoo
sideburns	le basette
strands	i colpi di sole, le méches
tint	tingere
to blow dry	asciugare con il fon
to color	tingere
to comb	pettinare
to do one's hair	pettinare
to set	mettere in piega
wig	parrucca

Household Goods

aluminum foil	foglio di alluminio
bottle opener	l'apribottiglie m
can opener	l'apriscatole m
candles	le candele
charcoal	carbonella
clothesline	corda per stendere il bucato
clothespins	molletta (per stendere la biancheria)
corkscrew	il cavatappi
denatured alcohol	spirito industriale
fork	forchetta
freezer packet	piastra refrigerante
glass	il bicchiere

grill	griglia
insulated bag	borsa frigo
knife	coltello
paper napkins	i tovagliolini di carta
petroleum	petrolio
plastic bag	sacchetto di plastica
plastic cup	il bicchiere di plastica
plastic wrap	pellicola (per la conservazione dei cibi)
pocket knife	temperino, coltello tascabile
safety pin	spillo di sicurezza
scissors	forbici *(pl)*
solid fuel	il combustibile solido
spoon	cucchiaio
string	spago
thermos bottle	il termos
trash bag	sacco delle immondizie
wire	filo

Groceries

What would you like?
Cosa desidera?

Please give me...
Mi dia ..., per favore.

one kilo of...
un chilo di ...

ten slices of...
10 fette di ...

a piece of...
un pezzo di ...

a package of...
un pacco di ...

a glass of...
un vasetto di ...

a can of...
una scatola di ...

a bottle of...
una bottiglia di ...

a shopping bag.
un sacchetto, una sportina.

Will there be anything else?
È un po' di più, è lo stesso?

May I have a taste?
Ne posso assaggiare un po'?

No, thanks, that's all.
Nient'altro, grazie.

Fruits   La frutta

apples	le mele
apricots	le albicocche
bananas	le banane
blackberries	le more
blueberries	i mirtilli
cherries	le ciliegie
coconut	la noce di cocco
dates	i datteri
figs	i fichi
fruit	la frutta
gooseberries	uva spina
grapefruit	pompelmo
grapes	l'uva *f*
khaki fruit	il cachi
lemons	i limoni
mandarin oranges	i mandarini
medlars	le nespole
melon	il melone, il popone
oranges	le arance
peaches	le pesche
pears	le pere
pineapple	l'ananas *m*
plums	le prugne
prickly pear	fico d'India
raspberries	i lamponi
strawberries	le fragole
watermelon	anguria, cocomero

Vegetables   La verdura

artichoke shoots or thistles	i gobbi, i cardi
artichokes	i carciofi
asparagus	gli asparagi
avocado	l'avocado *m*
beans	i fagioli
green beans	i fagiolini
white beans	i fagioli bianchi
beet	bietola

cabbage	cavolo
carrots	le carote
cauliflower	il cavolfiore
celery	sedano
chickpeas	i ceci
corn	il mais, granturco
cucumber	cetriolo
eggplants	le melanzane
endive	indivia del Belgio
fennel	finocchio
garlic	aglio
greens	ortaggi
leek	porro
lentils	le lenticchie
olives	le olive
onions	le cipolle
peas	i piselli
potatoes	le patate
pumpkin	zucca
salad	insalata
lettuce	insalata verde, lattuga
spinach	gli spinaci
sweet pepper	il peperone
tomatoes	i pomodori
turnip greens	le rape
valerian	valeriana
vegetables	verdura

Baked Goods, Sweets   I dolci e dolciumi ...

bread	il pane
brown bread	il pane misto di segale e frumento
black bread	il pane nero
white bread	il pane bianco
cake	il dolce, torta
candy	le caramelle
chewing gum	gomma da masticare
chocolate	cioccolata
chocolate bar	dolcetto di cioccolata
cookies	i biscotti
ice cream	gelato
jelly	marmellata
muesli	il müesli
oatmeal	i fiocchi d'avena
pastries	i biscotti

152

roll	panino
sandwich	i panini imbottiti
sweets	i dolciumi
toast	il toast

Eggs and Milk Products

Le uova e i latticini

butter	burro
cheese	formaggio
goat's cheese	formaggio di capra
sheep's milk cheese	pecorino
cream	panna
cooking cream	panna da cucina
whipped cream	panna montata
eggs	le uova
milk	il latte
skim milk	il latte magro
whole milk	il latte intero
ricotta cheese made from sheep's milk	ricotta di pecora
yogurt	lo iogurt

Meats and Sausages

La carne ed i salumi

beef	la carne di manzo
chicken	pollo
cold pork	arista
cutlet	costoletta
goulash	spezzatino
ham	prosciutto
cooked ham	prosciutto cotto
Parma ham	prosciutto di Parma
uncooked ham	prosciutto crudo
hamburger	la carne macinata
lamb	la carne d'agnello
leg of beef	bresaola
meat	la carne
mortadella with/without pistachios	mortadella con/senza pistacchi
mutton	la carne di montone/castrato
pâté	pasticcio di fegato
pork	la carne di maiale
pork sausage	coppa
rabbit	coniglio

roast piglet	porchetta
salami	il salame
sausages	le salsicce
small sausages	i wurstel
veal	la carne di vitello
wild boar	il cinghiale

Fish and Seafood — Il pesce ed i frutti di mare

anchovies	le acciughe
clams	le vongole
crab	i granchi
cuttlefish	seppia, calamaro
dried cod	il baccalà
eel	anguilla
fish	il pesce
herring	aringa
mackerel	sgombro
mullet	triglia
mussels	i mitili, le cozze
ocean bass	branzino
octopus	polpo
oysters	le ostriche
perch	il pesce persico
sea bream	orata
shrimp	i gamberetti
sole	sogliola
sprat	sarda
swordfish	il pesce spada
tuna	tonno

Spices and Herbs — Le spezie e le erbe aromatiche

basil	basilico
bay leaf	alloro
borage	la borragine
chervil	cerfoglio
chili	peperoncino
chive	erba cipollina
cinnamon	cannella
clove	i chiodi di garofani
coriander	coriandolo
cumin	cumino
dill	aneto

garlic	aglio
ginger	zenzero
green pepper	peperoncini verdi
herbs	le erbette
marjoram	maggiorana
mint	menta
nutmeg	la noce moscata
onion	cipolla
oregano	origano
parsley	prezzemolo
pepper	il pepe
red pepper	(vegetable) il peperone; (spice) paprica
rosemary	rosmarino
saffron	zafferano
sage	salvia
salt	il sale
tarragon	dragoncello
thyme	timo

This and That — Un po' di tutto

almonds	le mandorle
bouillon cube	dado da brodo vegetale
butter	burro
flour	farina
honey	il miele
margarine	margarina
mayonnaise	la maionese
mustard	la senape, la mostarda
noodles	la pasta
spaghetti	gli spaghetti
nuts	le noci
oil	olio
olive oil	olio d'oliva
rice	riso
salt	il sale
sugar	zucchero
vinegar	aceto

Drinks — Le bevande

apple juice	succo di mele
beer	birra
non-alcoholic beer	birra analcolica

champagne	lo champagne
coffee	il caffè
decaffeinated coffee	il caffè decaffeinato
lemonade	limonata
mineral water	acqua minerale
carbonated/non-carbonated	naturale/frizzante
orange juice	succo d'arancia
tea	il tè
black tea	tè
chamomile tea	camomilla
fruit tea	tisana alla frutta
green tea	tè verde
herbal tea	tisana alle erbe
mint tea	tisana alla menta
rose hips tea	tisana di rosa canina
teabag	bustina di tè
wine	vino
red	vino rosso
rosé	vino rosato
white	vino bianco

Fashion

➢ Colors

Don't be alarmed!
When you buy clothes, you must remember that Italian sizes are different than ours. With women's clothing you have to add at least two sizes. Men's sizes are not so different from ours.

Clothing

Could you please show me...?
Scusi, potrebbe mostrarmi ...?

May I try it on?
Posso provarlo/-la/-li/-le?

What size are you?
Che taglia porta?

It is too... for me
Questo mi è troppo ...
  narrow / wide
  stretto/largo.
  short / long
  corto/lungo.
  small / large
  piccolo/grande.

This fits me. I'll take it.
Va bene. Lo prendo.

This is not exactly what I wanted.
Non è proprio quello che volevo.

bathing cap	cuffia
beach robe	accappatoio
bikini	il bikini
blazer	il blazer
blouse	camicetta
body	il body
bow tie	il papillon, farfalla
bra	reggiseno
cap	berretto
cardigan	giacca di lana, il golf
coat	cappotto, soprabito
cotton	il cotone
dress	vestito
gloves	i guanti
hat	cappello
sun hat	cappello da sole
jacket	giacca
jeans	i jeans
jogging pants	i calzoni della tuta
jogging suit	tuta da ginnastica
leggings	i fuseaux
linen	lino
necktie	cravatta
pants	i pantaloni, i calzoni
panty	lo slip
panty hose	il collant, calzamaglia
pullover	il pullover, il maglione
raincoat	l'impermeabile *m*
scarf	il foulard
shawl	lo scialle; sciarpa
shirt	camicia
shorts	i pantaloncini, gli shorts
silk	seta

silk stockings	le calze di seta
ski pants	i pantaloni da sci
skirt	gonna
sleeve	le maniche
socks	i calzini
stocking	le calze
suit	abito
swimming trunks	il costume da bagno
swimsuit	il costume da bagno
T-shirt	maglietta
umbrella	ombrello
underpants	le mutande
undershirt	maglietta, canottiera
underwear	biancheria intima
vest	il golf, il gilè
windbreaker	giacca a vento
wool	lana

Cleaning

I would like to have these things cleaned / washed.
Vorrei far lavare a secco / lavare questa roba.

When will they be ready?
Quando sarà pronta?

dry cleaning	lavare/pulire a secco
to iron	stirare
laundry (to be washed) . . .	bucato

Optician

Would you please repair these glasses / frames?
Mi potrebbe aggiustare, questi occhiali / la montatura, per favore?

I am nearsighted / farsighted.
Sono miope/presbite.

How is your vision?
Che capacità visiva ha?

Right eye..., left eye.
a destra ..., a sinistra ...

When can I pick up the glasses?
Quando posso venire a prendere gli occhiali?

I need ...
Ho bisogno di ...

contact lens soaking solution.
soluzione per la conservazione

cleaning solution.
soluzione detergente

hard / soft contact lenses.
per lenti a contatto rigide/morbide.

I'm looking for...
Vorrei ...

sunglasses.
un paio di occhiali da sole.

a pair of binoculars.
un cannocchiale.

Shoes and Leather Goods

I would like a pair of shoes.
Senta, vorrei un paio di scarpe da ...

My size is...
Ho il numero ...

These are too narrow.
Sono troppo strette.

They are too big.
Sono troppo larghe.

athletic shoes	le scarpe da ginnastica
backpack	zaino
bag	borsa
bathing shoes	le scarpe da bagno
beach shoes	le scarpe da spiaggia
belt	cintura
belt bag	marsupio
boots	gli stivali
fanny pack	borsa a tracolla
handbag	borsa
heel	tacco
leather coat	cappotto di pelle
leather jacket	giacca di pelle
leather pants	i calzoni di pelle

rubber boots	gli stivali di gomma
sandals	i sandali
shoe	scarpa
shoe brush	spazzola da scarpe
shoe polish	lucido per scarpe
shoelace	laccio/stringa per scarpe
ski boots	gli scarponi da sci
sole	suola
straps	tracolla
suitcase	valigia
travel bag	borsa da viaggio
wheeled suitcase	(valigia/borsa) trolley

Souvenirs

I would like...
Vorrei ...
   a nice souvenir.
   un bel ricordo.
   a souvenir typical of the area.
   un oggetto tipico della zona.

How much do you want to spend?
Quanto vuole spendere?

I would like something not too expensive.
Vorrei spendere il giusto.

Oh, that's nice.
Questo sì che è carino.

Thanks, but I haven't found anything (that I like).
Grazie, ma non ho trovato niente che mi piaccia.

alabaster piece	i lavori in alabastro
ceramic	ceramica
china	il vasellame
coral jewelry	i gioielli di corallo
embroidery	i ricami
fancy glassware	le conterie
Florentine hat	cappello fiorentino
folk shop	negozio con oggetti folkloristici
handmade	lavorato a mano
intaglio	intaglio
jewelry	i gioielli

knickknacks	il soprammobile
lucky charm	il portafortuna
marble work	i lavori in marmo
real	vero, puro
regional products/specialties	i prodotti / le specialità regionali
Sicilian cart	il carro siciliano
souvenir	regalino
stein	il boccale
straw-wrapped bottle	fiasco

Tobacco Products

Cigarettes are sold through cigarette machines and everywhere there is a sign with a large white "T" on a blue background. It hangs on tobacco shops, where they also sell stamps, bus tickets, and telephone calling cards. Bars and newspaper dealers also often have licenses for tobacco products and postage stamps

A package / a carton of...
Un pacchetto / Una stecca di ...

with / without filter, please.
con/senza filtro, per favore.

Ten cigars, / cigarillos, please.
Dieci sigari/sigaretti, per favore.

A pack / a package of tobacco for cigarettes / pipe.
Un pacchetto / Una scatola di tabacco per sigarette / per la pipa, per favore.

ashtray	il posacenere
cigar	sigaro
cigarette	sigaretta
cigarillo	sigaretto
lighter	accendino
matches	fiammiferi
pipe	pipa

Watches and Jewelry

bracelet	braccialetto
brooch	spilla
chain	collana, catena
costume jewelry	bigiotteria
crystal	cristallo
earring for pierced ears	orecchino a perno
earrings	gli orecchini
gold	oro
jewelry	gioiello
pearl	perla
pendant	ciondolo
ring	anello
silver	argento
tie tack	spillo da cravatta
travel alarm clock	sveglia da viaggio
waterproof watch	orologio waterproof
wristwatch	orologio da polso
for women / for men	da donna/ da uomo

Health

In the Drugstore

Could you please tell me where the nearest drugstore (with on-call service) is located?
Scusi, potrebbe dirmi dove si trova la farmacia (di turno) più vicina?

Could you please give me something for...?
Potrebbe darmi qualcosa contro ...

This medicine is by prescription.
Questo medicinale è soggetto a prescrizione medica.

➢ also A Visit to the Doctor

absorbent cotton	il cotone idrofilo
analgesics	le compresse contro il dolore
antibiotic	antibiotico
aspirin	aspirina
Band-aid	cerotto
bug bite medication	rimedio contro le punture d'insetto
burn ointment	pomata per le bruciature
condom	preservativo, profilattico
contraceptive	l'anticoncezionale *m*
contraceptive pill	le pillole anticoncezionali
cough syrup	sciroppo (contro la tosse)
disinfectant	il disinfettante
drops	le gocce
ear drops	le gocce per gli orecchi
elastic band	benda elastica
eye drops	le gocce per gli occhi, collirio
gauze	fascia di garza
headache pills	le compresse contro il mal di testa
insulin	insulina
laxative	lassativo

medication for the .... circulatory system	medicamento per disturbi circolatori
medicine	medicina, farmaco
powder	borotalco
prescription	ricetta
remedy	medicina, medicinale
salve	pomata
sedative	il calmante
sleeping pills	i sonniferi
sunburn	scottatura (solare)
sunburn cream	pomata per le scottature
suppository	supposta
tablet	compressa, pasticca, pillola
thermometer	termometro
throat tablets	le pastiglie per la gola
tincture of chamomile	tintura di camomilla
tincture of iodine	tintura di iodio
vitamin pills	compressa vitaminica

foglio illustrativo	Instruction Leaflet
la composizione	Formulation
le indicazioni terapeutiche	Indications
le controindicazioni	Contraindications
effetti collaterali	Side effects
le interazioni	Interactions
le precauzioni	Safety precautions
posologia:	Dispensing Instructions
... viene somministrato	Take... once / ... times
una/più volte al giorno	a day
1 compressa	1 tablet
20 gocce	20 drops
1 misurino	1 measure
prima dei pasti	before eating
dopo i pasti	after eating
a stomaco vuoto	on an empty stomach
viene somministrato con un po'	do not chew, but
di liquido senza masticare	swallow with a little water
diluire in acqua	dissolve in a little water
far sciogliere in bocca	let dissolve in the mouth
applicare uno strato sottile sulla	apply a thin layer onto the
pelle e frizionare	skin and rub in
i lattanti	infants
i bambini piccoli	toddlers
(fino a circa ... anni)	(up to the age of ...)
gli scolari	small children
gli adolescenti	youth
gli adulti	adults
Tenere fuori dalla portata	Keep out of the reach of
dei bambini!	children

HEALTH

165

A Visit to the Doctor

> ➤ also Traveling with Children

Could you recommend a good ...
Potrebbe raccomandarmi un buon ...

doctor (m. and f.)?
medico?

eye doctor?
oculista?

gynecologist?
ginecologo?

ear-nose-throat doctor?
otorinolaringoiatra?

dermatologist?
dermatologo?

children's doctor?
pediatra?

general practitioner?
medico generico?

urologist?
urologo?

dentist?
dentista?

Where is his/her office?
Dov'è il suo ambulatorio?

Complaints

What's wrong?
Che disturbi ha?

I have a fever.
Ho la febbre.

I often feel sick.
Spesso mi sento male/ho la nausea.

I frequently feel dizzy.
Spesso mi gira la testa.

I passed out.
Sono svenuto/a.

I have a bad cold.
Sono molto raffreddato/a.

I have a headache / sore throat.
Ho mal di testa / mal di gola.

I have a cough.
Ho la tosse.

I have been stung.
Sono stato punto/a.

I have been bitten.
Sono stato morso/a.

I have indigestion.
Ho fatto un'indigestione.

I have diarrhea.
Ho la diarrẹa.

I am constipated.
Soffro di stitichezza.

I have an upset stomach. / I can't stand the heat.
Digerisco male. / Non sopporto il caldo.

I hurt myself.
Mi sono fatto/a male.

I fell.
Sono caduto/a.

Can you please give me / prescribe something for…?
Mi può dare/prescrịvere qualcosa contro …?

Normally I take…
Di sọlito prendo …

I have high / low blood pressure.
Ho la pressione alta/bassa.

I am diabetic.
Sono diabẹtico/a.

I am pregnant.
Sono incinta.

A while ago I had…
Poco tempo fa ho …

Examination

What can I do for you?
Cosa posso fare per Lei?

Where does it hurt?
Dove fa male?

I have a pain here.
Ho dei dolori qui.

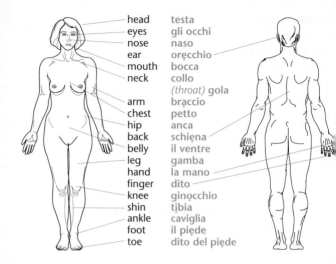

head	testa
eyes	gli occhi
nose	naso
ear	orecchio
mouth	bocca
neck	collo
	(throat) gola
arm	braccio
chest	petto
hip	anca
back	schiena
belly	il ventre
leg	gamba
hand	la mano
finger	dito
knee	ginocchio
shin	tibia
ankle	caviglia
foot	il piede
toe	dito del piede

Please undress / roll up your sleeve.
Si spogli, per favore. / Si scopra il braccio.

Take a deep breath. Hold your breath.
Respiri profondamente. Trattenga il respiro, per favore.

I need a blood / urine sample.
Ho bisogno dell'esame del sangue / dell'urina.

You should stay in bed for a couple of days.
Deve stare a letto per qualche giorno.

It's nothing serious.
Non è niente di grave.

Do you have a vaccination record?
Ha un certificato di vaccinazione?

I have been vaccinated for…
Sono vaccinato contro …

In the Hospital

How long do I have to stay here?
Per quanto tempo devo stare qui?

Give me ... please.
Potrebbe darmi per favore...

a glass of water
un bicchiere d'acqua.

a pain pill
delle compresse contro il dolore.

a sleeping pill
un sonnifero.

a hot water bottle
una borsa dell'acqua calda.

I can't go to sleep.
Non riesco ad addormentarmi.

When can I get up?
Quando potrò alzarmi?

Illnesses and Ailments

abscess	ascesso
AIDS	Aids
to be allergic to	essere allergico a ...
allergy	allergia
angina	angina
appendicitis	l'appendicite *f*
asthma	l'asma *m/f*
back pain	il dolore alla schiena
bleeding	emorragia
bloody nose	emorragia nasale
breathing difficulties	difficoltà di respirazione
broken	rotto
bronchitis	la bronchite
bruise	la contusione
burn	l'ustione *f*
cancer	cancro
cholera	il colera
circulatory problems	disturbi circolatori
cold	il raffreddore
colic	colica
concussion	la commozione cerebrale
constipation	la costipazione, stitichezza
contagious	contagioso
contusion	la contusione
cramp	crampo

cut	ferita da taglio
diabetes	il diabete
diarrhea	diarrea
diphtheria	la difterite
fainting fit	svenimento
fever	la febbre
flatulence	flatulenza
food poisoning	l'intossicazione *f* da alimenti
fracture	frattura
grippe	influenza
hay fever	il raffreddore da fieno
headaches	il mal di testa
heart attack	attacco cardiaco
heart defect	difetto cardiaco
heart trouble	i disturbi cardiaci
heartburn	acidità di stomaco
hemorrhoids	le emorroidi
hernia	l'ernia;
hoarse	avere la voce rauca
to hurt	fare male
hypertension	l'ipertensione, *f*
illness	malattia
impaired balance	disturbi dell'equilibrio
indigestion	l'indigestione *f*
infarction	infarto
infection	l'infezione *f*
inflammation	l'infiammazione *f*
to injure	ferire
injury	ferita
inner ear infection	il raffreddore
insomnia	insonnia
jaundice	itterizia
kidney inflammation	la nefrite
kidney stone	calcolo renale
lumbago	colpo della strega
malaria	malaria
migraine	emicrania
miscarriage	aborto
(muscle) pull	stiramento
nausea	nausea
pain in the side	le fitte al fianco
pains	i dolori
paralysis	la paralisi
pneumonia	la polmonite
poisoning	avvelenamento
polio	la polio(mielite)

rashes	l'eruzione *f* cutanea, l'esantema *m*
rheumatism	i reumatismi
ruptured tendon	strappo dei legamenti
sciatica	sciatica
seizure	colpo apoplettico
septicemia	setticemia
shivers	i brividi
sinusitis	la sinusite
smallpox	vaiolo
sore throat	mal di gola
sprained	slogato
stomachache	il mal di stomaco
stroke	apoplessia cerebrale
sunburn	scottatura (solare)
sunstroke	colpo di sole
swelling	il gonfiore, la tumefazione
swelling, tumor	il tumore
swollen	gonfio
swollen tonsils	la tonsillite
tachycardia	tachicardia
tetanus	tetano
typhoid	tifo
ulcer	ulcera
venereal disease	malattia venerea
vertigo	le vertigini
vision problems	disturbi della vista
whooping cough	la pertosse
wound	ferita
yellow fever	la febbre gialla

Body—Doctor—Hospital

anesthesia	anestesia
appendix	l'appendice *f*
bandage	benda
to bandage	fasciare
bladder	vescica
to bleed	sanguinare
blood	il sangue
blood pressure (*high/low*)	la pressione sanguigna (alta/bassa)
blood type	gruppo sanguigno
bone	osso
bowel movement	l'evacuazione *f*
brain	cervello
to breathe	respirare
bronchia	i bronchi
bypass	il bypass

cardiologist	cardiologo
certificate	certificato
clavicle	clavicola
cough	la tosse
diagnosis	la diagnosi
diet	il regime, la dieta
digestion	la digestione
disinfect	disinfettare
esophagus	esofago
examination	l'esame *m*
face	faccia
gallbladder	la cistifellea
genitals	gli organi genitali
health insurance	cassa malattia
hearing	udito
heart	il cuore
hospital	l'ospedale *m*
injection	*(syringe)* siringa; *(puncture)* l'iniezione *f*, puntura
insurance card	buono per le cure mediche
intestine	intestino
joint	l'articolazione *f*
kidney	il rene
lip	labbro
liver	fegato
lower abdomen	l'addome *m*
lung	il polmone
menstruation	la mestruazione
muscle	muscolo
nerve	nervo
nervous	nervoso
nurse	infermiera
office hours	orario di visita
operation	l'operazione *f*
pacemaker	il cardiostimolatore, il pacemaker
pregnancy	gravidanza
prescribe	prescrivere
prosthesis	la protesi
pulse	polso
pus	il pus
rib	costola
scar	la cicatrice
shoulder	spalla
sick	malato
skin	la pelle
specialist	lo specialista

spinal column	spina dorsale, colonna vertebrale
splint	stecca
station	reparto
stitch	punto; *(Einstich)* puntura
to stitch	cucire
stomach	stomaco
surgeon	chirurgo
to sweat	sudare
tongue	lingua
tonsils	le tonsille
transfusion	la fleboclisi
tympanum membrane	membrana del timpano
ultrasound test	l'esame *m* con ultrasuoni
unconscious	privo di sensi
urine	urina
vaccination	la vaccinazione
vaccination record	libretto di vaccinazione
virus	il virus
visiting hours	orario di visita
to vomit	vomitare
waiting room	sala d'aspetto
X-ray	radiografia
to X-ray	radiografare

At the Dentist's

I have a (bad) toothache.
Ho (un forte) mal di denti.

It's this tooth (top / bottom / front / back) that hurts.
Questo dente (di sopra / di sotto / davanti / in fondo) fa male.

I have lost a filling.
La piombatura è andata via.

I have broken a tooth.
Mi si è rotto un dente.

I will merely give you a temporary treatment.
Faccio soltanto un trattamento provvisorio.

Give me a shot, please.
Mi dia una puntura, prego.

Please don't give me a shot.
Non mi dia una puntura, per favore.

173

bridge	il ponte
cavity	buco
crown	corona
dentures	la prọtesi
filling	piombatura
gums	gengiva
incisor	incisivo
jaw	mascella
molar	il molare
to pull	estrarre
tooth	il dente
toothache	il mal di denti
wisdom tooth	il dente del giudịzio

Exchange Offices

When exchanging money, you often have to present personal identification and give your vacation address. In many banks you have to deposit all metal objects in a locker; otherwise the front door won't open. A recorded voice message directs you to the lockers. Banks are open for three to four hours in the mornings, and usually just one hour in the afternoons. Banks are closed on Saturdays, Sundays, and holidays, but you can get money out of ATMs that display the EC symbol.

Bank

Can you please tell me where there's a bank around here?
Scusi, saprebbe dirmi se c'è una banca qui vicino?

I would like to change...dollars into euros.
Vorrei cambiare ...dollari americani in euro.

What is today's exchange rate, please?
Quant'è oggi il cambio, scusi?

I would like to cash...
Vorei incassare ...

this traveler's check.
questo assegno turistico.

What is the maximum amount I can withdraw?
Qual è l'importo massimo per un assegno?

Your check card, please.
La carta assegni, per favore.

Could I please see...
Potrei vedere per favore ...

your ID card?
la Sua carta d'identità?

your passport?
il Suo passaporto?

Sign here, please.
Firmi qui, per favore.

account	conto
amount	importo
ATM	il bancomat, sportello automatico
bank	banca
bank card	carta di banca
bill (money)	banconota

cash	i contanti
cent	centesimo
change	gli spiccioli, moneta
check	assegno
to issue a check	rilasciare un assegno
code number	numero segreto
coin	moneta
credit card	carta di credito
currency	le divise/valute estere
currency	valuta
euro	euro
exchange rate	corso dei cambi
fixed costs	i diritti fissi
form	modulo
in cash	in contanti
money	denaro
money exchange	cambio
money order	il vaglia, assegno
to pay	pagare
payment	pagamento
receipt	ricevuta
signature	firma
smart card	tessera
Swiss franc	franco svizzero
transfer	rimessa, trasferimento
traveler's check	assegno turistico, il traveller's chèque
wire transfer	vaglia telegrafico
to exchange	cambiare

Film and Photography

> **also Photo Items**

Could you please take a photo of us?
Le dispiacerebbe farci una foto?

That's very kind (of you).
Molto gentile (da parte Sua).

Push this button.
Prema questo pulsante, per favore.

This is how you adjust the distance / aperture.
La distanza / Il diaframma si regola così.

May I take your photo?
Potrei farLe una foto?

Now we will have a nice reminder of our vacation.
Adesso abbiamo un bel ricordo delle nostre vacanze.

camera	mạcchina fotogrạfica
landscape format	formato orizzontale
photo	la foto(grạfia)
to photograph	fotografare
portrait format	formato verticale
snapshot	istantạnea

Lost and Found

> also Police

Can you please tell me where the lost and found is?
Scusi, saprebbe dirmi dov'è l'ufficio oggetti smarriti?

I have lost …
Ho perso …

I forgot my handbag on the train.
Ho lasciato la (mia) borsa sul treno.

Would you please notify me if someone finds it?
Mi farebbe la cortesịa di informarmi se dovesse ẹsser trovata?

Here is the address of my hotel / my home address.
Ecco l'indirizzo del mio albergo / l'indirizzo di casa.

Police

Could you please tell me where the nearest police station is?
Scusi, saprebbe indicarmi il prọssimo commissariato di polizịa?

I would like to report…
Vorrei denunciạre …

  a robbery
  un furto.

  an assault
  un assalto / un'aggressione.

Someone stole…
Mi è stata/o rubata/o …

  my handbag.
  la borsa.

  my wallet.
  il portafọglio.

  my camera.
  la mạcchina fotogrạfica.

my car / my bicycle.
la macchina / la bicicletta.

Someone has broken into my car.
La mia macchina è stata forzata.

Someone stole... from my car.
Dalla mia macchina è stato rubato ...

I have lost...
Ho perso ...

My son / my daughter has disappeared.
Mio figlio / Mia figlia è scomparso/a.

This man is bothering me.
Quest'uomo mi sta molestando.

Could you please help me?
Mi può aiutare, per favore?

Precisely when did that happen?
Quando è successo esattamente?

Your name and your address, please.
Il Suo nome e indirizzo, per favore.

Please consult with the American / Canadian consulate.
Per favore, si rivolga al consolato americano / canadese.

to arrest	arrestare
to beat up	picchiare
to bother	molestare
to break in	forzare, scassinare
car radio	l'autoradio f
check	assegno
check card	carta assegni
confiscate	sequestrare
contraband	contrabbando
court	il tribunale
credit card	carta di credito
crime	delitto
custody	la detenzione preventiva
drugs	gli stupefacenti
guilt	colpa
ID card	carta d'identità
judge	il giudice
key	la chiave
lawyer	avvocato
to lose	perdere
papers	i documenti
passport	passaporto
pickpocket	borsaiolo, lo scippatore

police	polizia
police car	auto della polizia
policeman officer	l'agente *m f; (traffic)* il vigile/ la vigilessa
prison	la prigione
purse	borsellino
rape	violenza(carnale), stupro
registration	libretto di circolazione
to report	denunciare
sexual harassment	molestia sessuale
theft	furto
thief	ladro

Post Office

In places where there are lots of tourists, the post offices are generally open until 8:00 P.M. during the week.

Excuse me, could you please tell me where ... is?
Scusi, saprebbe indicarmi...

the nearest post office
il prossimo ufficio postale?

the nearest mail box
la prossima cassetta postale?

How much does it cost for a letter / a postcard...
Quanto costa una lettera / una cartolina per ...

to America?
l'America?

to Canada
il Canada?

to Switzerland?
la Svizzera?

Postcards cost exactly the same as letters. If you want your mail to be delivered more quickly, in the post office or a tobacco shop you can get stamps marked *Posta Prioritaria*. They are a little more expensive than the regular stamps, but they will get a postcard delivered within three days inside Europe.

Three stamps for ..., please.
Tre francobolli da ..., per favore.

This letter by..., please.
Questa lettera ..., per favore.
  airmail / priority.
  con posta prioritaria.

How long does it take a letter to reach America?
Quanto tempo impiega una lettera per l'America?

Do you also have special issue stamps?
Ha anche delle emissioni speciali?

I would like to withdraw ... Euros from my savings account.
Vorrei prelevare ... Euro dal mio libretto postale di risparmio.

➢ **also Bank**

address	indirizzo
addressee	destinatario
airmail	posta aerea
charge	tariffa
customs declaration	la dichiarazione doganale
declaration of value	il valore dichiarato
dispatch form	bollettino di spedizione dei pacchi postali
fax	fax
to fill out	compilare
form	modulo
to forward	recapitare
general delivery	fermo posta
letter	lettera
mailbox	cassetta postale
main post office	posta centrale
package	pacco
packet	pacchetto
pickup	levata
post office	ufficio postale
postage	affrancatura
postal code	CAP (codice di avviamento postale)
postal money order	il vaglia postale
postcard	cartolina postale
priority letter	posta prioritaria
priority mail	con posta prioritaria
registered letter	raccomandata
savings book	libretto di risparmio postale
sender	il mittente
special issue stamp	l'emissione *f* speciale
stamp	francobollo
to stamp	affrancare

stamp machine	il distributore automatico per francobolli
telegram	il telegramma
weight	peso

Using the Telephone

You can use coins (10, 20, and 50 cents, plus a euro) and telephone cards (watch out for the expiration date!) to make a call. In calling a foreign country from Italy, you have to dial a country code, then the appropriate area code, and then the number of the person or the business. The best course is to check a phone book in Italy for a list of country codes. Calls placed inside Italy require the area code before the specific phone number, even for local calls.
There are public telephones in phone booths, bars, and restaurants.

Can you please tell me where the nearest phone booth is?
Scusi, saprebbe indicarmi la prossima cabina telefonica?

I would like a phone card, please.
Vorrei una scheda telefonica, per favore.

Pardon me, what is the prefix for…?
Scusi, qual è il prefisso di/per …?

I would like to place a long-distance call to…
Per favore, un'interurbana per …

I would like to make a collect call.
Vorrei annunciare una telefonata a carico del ricevente.

Go to booth number…
Vada nella cabina numero …

A Phone Conversation

This is…
Qui parla …

Hello; who is this, please?
Pronto, scusi, con chi parlo?

Could I please speak to Mr. / Mrs. /Miss… ?
Scusi, potrei parlare con il signor / la signora / la signorina …?

I'm sorry, but he/ she is not here.
Mi dispiace, ma non c'è.

182

Can he/she call you back?
La posso far richiamare?

Would you like to leave a message?
Vuol lasciar detto qualcosa?

Would you please tell him/her that I called?
Gli/Le potrebbe dire che ho chiamato, per favore?

"This number is not in service."
"È stata raggiunta una numerazione inesistente."

answering machine	segreteria telefonica
appointment	preavviso
area code	prefisso
busy	occupato
call	telefonata
to call	telefonare
cell phone	il cellulare/telefonino
charge	tariffa
collect call	la comunicazione telefonica a carico del ricevente
connection	la comunicazione
conversation	la conversazione
to dial	formare il numero
information	informazioni
local call	telefonata urbana
long distance	interurbana
overseas call	la comunicazione internazionale
phone book	elenco telefonico
phone booth	cabina telefonica
phone card	carta telefonica
phone number	numero telefonico
to pick up	rispondere al telefono
portable phone	telefono portatile
public telephone	telefono pubblico
receiver	il ricevitore
telephone	telefono

Toilet and Bathroom

Where is the toilet, please?
Scusi, dov'è il bagno?

May I please use your bathroom?
Scusi, ma dovrei andare in bagno. Posso?

Would you please give me the key for the bathroom?
Potrebbe darmi la chiave per il bagno, per favore?

clean	pulito
dirty	sporco
flush	lo sciacquone
hand towel	asciugamano
Men	Signori
sanitary napkins	gli assorbenti
sink	lavabo, lavandino
soap	il sapone
tampon	tamponi
toilet paper	carta igienica
urinal	gabinetto alla turca/vespasiano
Women	Signore

Articles (Gender Indicators)

Definite Article in the Singular and Plural

	Sing.	Plur.	
feminine	la	le	before consonant e.g., la bambina / le bambine
	l'	le	before vowel, e.g., l'ora/le ore
masculine	il	i	before consonant, but not before s + consonant (sb, st, sc, etc.), z, gn e.g., il treno/I treni
	lo	gli	before s + consonant (sb, st, sc, etc.), z, gn e.g., lo zaino/gli zaini
	l'	gli	before vowel, e.g., l'amico/gli amici

- The following are used with the definite article:

  —Possessive adjectives (see p.190)
  —Title and name: Dov'è **il signor Neri**? Where is Mr. Neri?
   (except in direct address: Buongiorno, signor Neri.)
  —Country names: Conosce **l'Italia?** Are you familiar with Italy?
   (except with *in* + a feminine name: in Italia / in or to Italy)
  —Clock time: è **l'una**. It is one o'clock. Sono **le due**. It is two o'clock.
  —Nouns used in a general sense:
  La benzina costa molto. Gas is expensive.

- Expressions with the article: • Expressions without the article:

chiuso il lunedì/il martedì
closed Mondays / Tuesdays

partire lunedì/martedì
to leave on Monday / Tuesday

l'anno prossimo
next year

in maggio/aprile
in May / April

fare il bagno to bathe

fare il pieno to fill up (the car)

andare in città
to go into the city

fare il biglietto
to cancel the tickey

andare in treno/macchina
to take the train / car

Indefinite Article

feminine	una	before a consonant
		e.g., una ragazza
	un'	before a vowel
		e.g., un'amica
masculine	un	before a vowel or a consonant, but not
		before s + consonant (sb, st, sc, etc.), z, gn
		e.g., un minuto, un uomo
	uno	before s + a consonant (sb, st, sc, etc.),
		z, gn e.g., uno sciopero

Nouns

Singular and Plural Nouns

In Italian there are
1. masculine nouns that end in -o (plural with -i)
   -e (plural with -i)
   -a (plural with -i)
2. feminine nouns that end in -a (plural with -e)
   -e (plural with -i)
   -o (plural with -i)

	Singular		Plural	
masculine	il	ragazzo	i	ragazzi
	il	padre	i	padri
	il	problema	i	problemi
feminine	la	ragazza	le	ragazze
	la	madre	le	madri
	la	mano	le	mani

- A number of nouns that refer to people (most of which end in -ante, -ente, -ese, or ista) are used for both males and females, e.g.
  il cliente/la cliente il turista/la turista
- Always used in the singular: la gente the people, la roba the things
- Always used in the plural: gli occhiali the glasses, i pantaloni the pants i soldi the money

Adjectives (Descriptive Words)

Agreement with Nouns

In Italian there are the following:
1. Adjectives that end in –o; they form their feminine form with the ending –o;
2. Adjectives that end in –e; they have just one form for both genders. The plural is handled in the same way as with nouns: o→ i, a→ e, e→ i.

	Singular	Plural
1. masculine feminine	il ragazzo contento la ragazza contenta	i ragazzi contenti le ragazze contente
2. masculine and feminine	il ragazzo la ragazza gentile	i ragazzi le ragazze gentili

Adjective Position

Generally the adjective follows the noun it modifies.

la valigia **nera/rossa/pesante**	the black/red/heavy suitcase
un giornale **italiano/inglese**	an Italian/English newspaper

- The following may be placed before the noun:

bello	beautiful	buono	good	grande	large
lungo	long	brutto	ugly	cattivo	lousy
piccolo	small	bravo	skillful		

  Before masculine singular nouns (except before z, gn, or s + a consonant), *buono* and *bello* are shortened to *buon* and *bel*:
  Buon viaggio! Have a good trip!
  Che **bel** bambino! What a beautiful child!

Adverbs

Some words function primarily as adjectives, such as *tardi* (late); others are formed from adjectives.
Derived adjectives are formed by adding the ending –*mente* to the feminine form of an adjective.

lento, -a:	Parla **lentamente.**	He speaks slowly.
veloce:	Corre **velocemente.**	He runs fast.

- With adjectives that end in *–le* or *–re*, the *e* is omitted before adding *–mente*.
  facile <small>easy</small> – facilmente

- The adverbs that correspond to the adjectives *buono* and *malo* are *bene* and *male*: Lavora **bene / male.** <small>He works well / poorly.</small>

The Partitive Article: Expressing Quantities with *di*

The partitive article consists of *di* + the definite article.
It designates a quantity or number that is not specified precisely.

indefinite quantity/number	Mi dia **dell'**acqua.	<small>Give me (some) water.</small>
	Vorrei **del** vino rosso.	<small>I would like (some) red wine.</small>
	Ha fatto **delle** foto?	<small>Did you take (some) photos?</small>

Di is used by itself after nouns that refer to a specific quantity or number.

specific quantity/number	un litro **di** vino	<small>a liter of wine</small>
	un piatto **di** spaghetti	<small>a plate of spaghetti</small>
	due chili **di** arance	<small>two kilos of oranges</small>
	un milione **di** euro	<small>a million euro</small>

- **un po' di** vino (pane)   <small>a little/some wine (bread)</small>
  un paio di scarpe   <small>a pair of shoes</small>

Pronouns

Personal Pronouns

Personal Subject Pronouns

	Singular					Plural				
(Who?)	io	tu	lui	lei	Lei	noi	voi	Voi	loro	Loro
	ich	du	er	sie	Sie	wir	ihr	Sie	sie	Sie

- Normally the subject pronouns are not used with verbs:
  Partiamo oggi. <small>We are leaving today.</small>
  They are included only when the speaker wishes to emphasize the subject: Ordino **io?** <small>Shall I order?</small>

- In polite conversation, the following generally are used:
  —the third person singular when addressing someone;
  —the second person plural or (in very formal circumstances) the third person plural, when addressing several people.

Direct and Indirect Object Pronouns

	Singular					Plural						
Whom? To/for whom?	mi me	ti you	lo him	la her	La you (formal)	ci us	vi you	Vi you (formal)	li they	le they	Li you (formal) (m)	Le you (formal) (f)
									(m)	(f)		
To/for whom?	mi me	ti you	gli him	le her	Le you (formal)	ci us	vi you	Vi you (formal)	gli them	Loro you (formal)		

e.g.: Vedi Maria? Sì, la vedo.
Stasera incontro Maria e le do il libro.

Do you se Maria? Yes, I see her.
Tonight I am meeting Maria and giving her the book.

Reflexive Pronouns and Verbs

Reflexive pronouns are placed in front of the verb.
The past tense of reflexive verbs is constructed using *essere* (to be).
In such cases, the past participle agrees in gender and in number with the subject:

I *bambini* si sono lavati.   The children have washed (themselves).

Present		Perfect	
mi lavo	I wash	mi sono lavato, -a	I washed
ti lavi	you wash	ti sei lavato, -a	you washed
si lava	he/she washes	si è lavato, -a	he/she washed
ci laviamo	we wash	ci siamo lavati, -e	we washed
vi lavate	you wash	vi siete lavati, -e	you washed
si lạvano	they wash	si sono lavati, -e	they washed

Possessive Adjectives

| | Object Possessed: Singular | | Object Possessed: Plural | |
	masculine	feminine	masculine	feminine
one possessor	il mio *my*	la mia	i miei	le mie
	il tuo *your*	la tua	i tuoi	le tue
	il suo *his/her*	la sua	i suoi	le sue
	il Suo *your*	la Sua	i Suoi	le Sue
several possessors	il nostro *our*	la nostra	i nostri	le nostre
	il vostro *your*	la vostra	i vostri	le vostre
	il loro *their*	la loro	i loro	le loro
	il Loro *your*	la Loro	i Loro	le Loro

- Possessive adjectives are normally used with the definite article:
  Dov'è **la mia** borsa? Where is my handbag?
  However, they are used without articles in the following instances:
  —before singular nouns designating relatives: **mio zio** my uncle
  —in certain expressions, e.g., a casa **mia** at my house
- *Suo* refers to a masculine or a feminine possessor; *loro* refers to several possessors:
  la **sua** chiave his/her key – la **loro** chiave their key

Demonstrative Adjectives

| Singular | | Plural | |
masculine	feminine	masculine	feminine
questo *this*	questa	questi	queste
quello *that*	quella	quelli	quelle

When *quello* is used instead of an article, it takes the form of the definite article:

Singular		Plural	
quel pacco	that package	quei pacchi	those packages
quello scolaro	that student	quegli scolari	those students
quell' uomo	that man	quegli uomini	those men
quella donna	that woman	quelle donne	those women

Questa borsa mi piace. I like this handbag. **Quest'** anno andremo a Roma. This year we will go to Rome.	*Questo* refers to people or to things that are in the immediate vicinity.
Conosce **quel** signore? Do you know that man? Che abito prende? – **Quello** rosso. Which dress …? That red one.	*Quello* refers to people or things that are not in the immediate vicinity.

Question Words

Who? Whom? To/for whom?	**Chi** è venuto? Who came? **Chi** conosce? Whom do you know? **A chi** scrive? To whom are you writing?
What? What kind?	**Che cosa** desidera? What do you want? **Che libro** è questo? What kind of book is this?
Which?	**Quale** strada? Which street? **Qual** è la sua macchina? Which car is yours?
How much/ many?	**Quanto** costa? How much does it cost? **Quanti** chilometri? How many kilometers?
Where?	**Dove** si trova …? Where is…? **Dove** va? Where are you going? **Di dov'è?/Da dove** viene? Where are you from?
When? At what time? How long?	**Quando** aprono i negozi? When do the stores open? **A che ora** parte? What time are you leaving? **Quanto** devo aspettare? How long do I have to wait?
How? Why?	**Come** funziona? How does it work? **Perché** non funziona? Why doesn't it work?

GRAMMAR IN BRIEF

Verbs (Action Words)

The Present Tense

- Verb forms generally are used without personal pronouns (see p.188): **Abbiamo** tempo. We have time.
- To show politeness, people use
  —the third person singular in addressing a person directly:
    Ha tempo, signor/signora Neri? Do you have time, Mr./Mrs. Neri?
  —the second person plural or (very formally) the third person plural in addressing several people:
    Avete tempo? / **Hanno** tempo, signori? Do you have time, gentlemen / ladies and gentlemen?

avere, essere

	avere	to have	essere	to be
io	ho	I have	sono	I am
tu	hai	you have	sei	you are
lui	ha	he has	è	he is
lei		she has, you (formal) have		she is, you (formal) are
noi	abbiamo	we have	siamo	we are
voi	avete	you have	siete	you are
loro	hanno	they have, you (formal) have	sono	they are, you (formal) are

- c'è there is – ci sono there are

Regular Verbs
Verbs in Italian are grouped into three categories (conjugations) depending on their infinitive endings.

	Verbs ending in -are		-ere	-ire	
	parlare		vendere	partire	capire
	to speak		to sell	to leave	to understand
io	parlo	I speak	vendo	parto	capisco
tu	parli	you speak	vendi	parti	capisci
lui		he speaks			
lei	parla	she speaks	vende	parte	capisce
lei		you (formal) speak			
noi	parliamo	we speak	vendiamo	partiamo	capiamo
voi	parlate	you speak	vendete	partite	capite
		you speak			
loro	parlano	they speak	vendono	partono	capiscono
		you (pl., formal) speak			

- Some verbs in *–ere* are stressed on the stem (e.g., vendere), and others on the ending (e.g., vedere, to see)
- The following verbs are conjugated like *capire*: finire (to finish), preferire (to prefer), construire (to construct), spedire (to send), ubbidire (to follow), and pulire (to clean)
- The following verbs are conjugated like *partire*: dormire (to sleep), sentire (to hear), and aprire (to open)
- With verbs that end in *–care* or *–gare*, a mute *h* is added before an *i* in the ending: pa**gh**i.

The Perfect Tense (Completed Action)

The Past Participle

Helping Verb		Regular Verbs Ending in		
		-are	-ere	-ire
avere	essere	parl**are**	vend**ere**	cap**ire**
avuto	**stato**	parl**ato**	vend**uto**	cap**ito**
had	been	spoken	bought	understood
Ending of participle:		-ato	-uto	-ito

• Verbs with irregular past participles:

accendere to light	acceso	offrire to offer	offerto
aprire to open	aperto	rompere to break	rotto
chiedere to ask (for)	chiesto	scendere to get out/go down	sceso
chiudere to close	chiuso	scrivere to write	scritto
correre to run	corso	spegnere to turn off	spento
fare to make/do	fatto	spendere to spend	spend
leggere to read	letto	vedere to see	visto
mettere put/place/put on	messo	vivere to live	vissuto

The Perfect with *avere* and *essere*

The Perfect is constructed using the present tense of the helping verb

—*avere* (to have) + past participle: ho avuto, I had, have had, did have

—*essere* (to be) + past participle: in this case the participle agrees in gender and in number with the subject:

Le mie amiche sono stat**e** *a Roma.* My friends have been to Rome.

The Perfect Tense with *avere*	The Perfect Tense with *essere*	
	masculine subject	feminine subject
ho capito I have understood	sono andato I have gone	sono andata
hai capito you have understood	sei andato you have gone	sei andata
ha capito he/she has understood you (formal) have understood	è andato he has gone you (formal) have gone	è andata she has gone you (formal) have gone
abbiamo capito we have understood	siamo andati we have gone	siamo andate
avete capito you have understood you (formal) have understood	siete andati you have gone you (formal) have gone	siete andate
hanno capito they have understood you (formal) have understood	sono andati you have gone you (formal) have gone	sono andate

- The perfect tense
  —of reflexive verbs is constructed with *essere* (see p.165)
  —is constructed using *avere* in the case of *viaggiare* (to travel), *passeggiare* (to take a walk), *nuotare* (to swim), and *sciare* (to ski).
  Abbiamo viaggiato molto. We have traveled a lot.
  —of modal verbs (*potere, dovere, volere*) is constructed using *essere* or *avere*.
  Non ho voluto mangiare. I didn't want to eat.
  É voluto andare a Roma. He wanted to go to Rome.

Future and Conditional

The Future

	-are		-ere	-ire
	comprare		vendere	partire
io	comprerò	I shall buy	venderò	partirò
tu	comprerai		venderai	partirai
lui lei	comprerà		venderà	partirà
noi	compreremo		venderemo	partiremo
voi	comprerete		venderete	partirete
loro	compreranno		venderanno	partiranno

The Conditional Tense

io	comprer**ei**	I would buy	vend**erei**	part**irei**
tu	comprer**esti**		vend**eresti**	part**iresti**
lui	comprer**ebbe**		vend**erebbe**	part**irebbe**
lei				
noi	comprer**emmo**		vend**eremmo**	part**iremmo**
voi	comprer**este**		vend**ereste**	part**ireste**
loro	comprer**ebbero**		vend**erebbero**	part**irebbero**

- The conditional tense is often used in polite statements:
  Vorrei una camera singola. I would like a single room.
  Avrebbe un fiammifero? Would you have a match?
  Mi **potrebbe** aiutare? Could you help me?

- Verbs that end in –*care* or –*gare* insert a mute *h* before an *e* in the ending: pag**h**eremo we shall pay

Word Order

The regular word order in a declarative sentence is as follows:

	Subject	Verb	The Rest of the Sentence	
	Carla	compra	la borsa.	C. buys the handbag.
Oggi	Carla	ha comprato	la borsa.	C. bought the handbag today.

However, the subject comes after the verb in the following cases:

Oggi è arrivata Carla. Carla arrived today.	when emphasis is placed on the subject
Dov'è la mia borsa? Where is my handbag?	in questions

- Questions without a question word generally follow the regular word order of the declarative sentence:
  Ha visto il signor Neri? Have you seen Mr. Neri?

Negation

no

È stanco? – **No**, signora. Are you tired?—No.
Pioverà? – Speriamo **di no**. Will it rain?—We hope not.

non

	non Verb	
Perché	**non** è venuto?	Why didn't he come?
Gina	**non** ha tempo.	Gina has no time.

- Non-accentuated pronouns such as *ci* (there) and *ne* (some) come between *non* and the verb:
  Non lo vedo.   I don't see him/it.
  Non ci sono panini.   There are no rolls.

non ... nessuno/nulla/niente/mai, etc.

Non c'è **nessuno**.	No one is there.
Non voglio **nulla/niente**.	I don't want anything.
Non fumo **mai**.	I never smoke.
Non fumo **più**.	I no longer smoke.
Non beve **né** vino **né** birra.	He drinks neither wine nor beer.

- If the second element of negation is placed before the verb, *non* is omitted: Nessuno è venuto. Nobody came.

A

a to (direction), toward; per; vicino a *(near)* at

a casa (at) home

a livello del suolo at ground level

a mezzogiorno at noon

a quest'ora at this time

a tinta unita of a single color

a volte sometimes

abat-jour *m* bedside lamp

abbandonare to leave

abbastanza quite, rather

abbazia abbey

abbigliamento clothing; ~ per bambini children's clothing

abbonamento giornaliero day pass

abbonamento settimanale week pass/ticket

abbracciare to hug

abbreviazione *f* abbreviation

abbronzato brown (tanned)

abitante *m/f* inhabitant, resident

abitare to live

abito suit; ~ da sera evening dress

abituale customary

abituato, essere ~ to be used to

aborto abortion

accadere to happen

accappatoio bathrobe

acceleratore *m* **a mano** manual control (car)

acceleratore *m* accelerator

accendere to light; to turn on (lights)

accensione *f* ignition

accessibilità accessibility

accessori *m pl* **per la riparazione di forature** tire repair kit

accettare to accept (invitation), to confirm

accettazione *f* acceptance

acclimatarsi to acclimatize oneself

accomiatarsi to say good-bye

accompagnare to accompany

accompagnatore(-trice) companion

acconsentire to consent

accordarsi su to agree on

aceto vinegar

acetone *m* nail polish remover

acidità di stomaco heartburn

acqua water; ~ calda hot water; ~ di raffreddamento coolant; ~ fredda cold water; ~ minerale mineral water; ~ potabile drinking water

acquaforte *f* etching

acquaio kitchen sink

acquerello watercolor

adattatore *m* adapter

adatto right (appropriate); ~ per carrozzelle wheelchair accessible

addome *m* groin
aderire to acquiesce
adirato angry
adoperare to use
Adriatico Adriatic
adulto/adulta adult
aerobica aerobics
aeroporto airport
affamato, essere ~ to be
  hungry
affermare to affirm
affettuoso affectionate
affittare to rent; lease
affitto rent
affrancare to stamp (a letter)
affrancatura postage
affrettarsi to hurry
affumicato smoked
afoso stuffy, sultry
agente *m f* policeman
agenzia agency; ~ di viaggi
  travel agency
aggiungere to add
aggressione *f* assault
aglio garlic
ago needle
agosto August
agro sour
air terminal *m* terminal
aiutare qd to help someone
aiuto help; support
al di sotto di underneath
ala wing
albero tree
albicocche apricots
album *m* coloring book
alcuni some; a few
alcuni/alcune a few
alimentazione *f* feeding;
  catering
aliscafo hydrofoil
alla griglia from the grill
alle around (time expressions)

allegro happy
allergia allergy
alloggio lodging
allora so; then; at that time
alloro laurel
allungare to lengthen
almeno at least
alpinismo mountain climbing
alt! Halt!
alta marea high tide
alta stagione *f* busy season
altare *m* altar
altezza height
alto high; tall (stature)
altoparlante *m* loudspeaker
altro other; another; ~ ieri the
  day before yesterday
altrove elsewhere
alzare to lift; (prices) to raise
alzarsi to stand up
amabile sweet (wine)
amare to love
amaro bitter
ambasciata embassy
ambiente *m* environment;
  surroundings
americano American *(adj.)*
amici/amiche, essere ~ to be
  friends
amico/amica friend
ammenda fine
ammesso authorized
amministrazione *f* administration
ammirare to admire
amore *m* love
ampio wide
analcolico alcohol-free
analgesici *m pl* pain pills
ananas *m* pineapple
anca hip
anche also
ancora still

andar via to go away

andare to go, drive; ~ a letto to go to bed; ~ a trovare qd to visit someone; ~ in bicicletta to ride a bike

anello ring

anestesia anesthesia

anfiteatro amphitheater

angina angina

angolo corner

anguilla eel

animale *m* animal

animali *m pl* **domestici** house pets

anno year; ~ prossimo next year

annuale *(adj)*; **annualmente** *(adv)* yearly

annuale annual

annunciare to announce

antibiotico antibiotic

anticipo advance; in in ~ advance

antico old (from an earlier time)

anticoncezionale *m* contraceptive

antigelo antifreeze

antipasto appetizer

ape *f* bee

aperto open

apoplessia cerebrale stroke

apparecchio device; ~ caricabatterie batterie, battery charger

appartamento apartment

appartenere to belong

appena scarcely

appendicite *f* appendicitis

appetito appetite

applauso applause

appuntamento appointment

apribottiglie *m* bottle opener

aprile April

apriporta *m* **automatico** automatic door opener

aprire to open

apriscatole *m* can opener

arance oranges

arancione orange

archeologia archeology

architetto architect

architettura architecture

arco arch

area di rigore penalty area

arena arena

argento silver

aria air; ~ condizionata air conditioning

aringa herring

armadio cupboard

arrabbiarsi (per qc/con qd) to become angry about

arrabbiato angry; mad; irritated

arrestare to arrest

arrivare to arrive

arrivo arrival

arrostito roasted; baked

arte *f* art ~ di vasaio pottery ~ grafica graphic art ~ orafa goldsmith's art

articolazione *f* joint

articoli *m pl* **sportivi** sporting goods

artigianato handicrafts

ascensore *m* elevator

ascesso abscess

asciugamano towel

asciugare to dry; ~ con il fon fon, to blow dry

asciugatrice *f* dryer (for laundry)

asciutto dry

ascoltare (qd) to listen to someone

ascoltare musica to listen to music

asino donkey

asma *m/f* asthma

asparagi *m pl* asparagus

aspettare to wait for; expect

aspettarsi to await

aspirina aspirin

assaggiare to try (foods)

assalto attack, assault

assegno check ~ turistico traveler's check

assetato, essere ~ to be thirsty

assicurazione *f* insurance ~ di totale copertura comprehensive insurance; ~ parziale per tutti i rischi fire and theft insurance

assistente *m/f* **di bordo** steward/ess

assistenza ai bambini child care

associazione *f* association, club; ~ handicappati/ svantaggiati handicap association

assolutamente absolutely; unconditionally

assomigliare to compare

assorbenti *f pl* **sottili** panty liners

assorbenti *m pl* sanitary napkins

atletica leggera track and field

attacco ski binding

attacco cardiaco heart attack

attento attentive; careful

attenzione! Attention! fare attenzione (a) pay attention to

atterraggio landing

atto act

attore/attrice actor / actress

attore /attrice di cinema movie actor / actress

attraversare to cross

attraverso across; through

attrezzatura da sub diving gear

attrezzo tool

augurio wish

aumentare to raise (price); to grow

America America

americano American (person)

autentico authentic

auto *f* car

auto della polizia police car

autoambulanza ambulance

autobus *m* bus ~ interurbano intercity; ~ urbano city bus

autogrill *m* service area

automatico automatic; *(adv)* automaticamente automatically

autoradio *f* car radio

autorità authority

autoscatto automatic shutter release

autosoccorso towing service

autostrada highway

autunno autumn

avanti Come in! Forward!

aver bisogno di to need

avere to have aver bisogno di to need aver fretta to be in a hurry avere il mal di mare to be seasick

avocado *m* avocado

avvelenamento poisoning

avvenimento event

avvertire to inform; ~ di to, warn about

avvicinarsi to approach

B

babyfon *m* baby intercom

baby-sitter *m/f* babysitter
baciare to kiss
bacio kiss
badminton *m* badminton
baffi *m pl* mustache
bagagliaio trunk
bagaglio baggage
bagnato wet
bagnino lifeguard
bagno *m* **per handicappati** handicap toilet
bagno bathroom
baita hut (mountain)
balcone *m* balcony
ballare to dance
ballerino/a dancer
balletto ballet
ballo dance; ball (celebration)
bambini children
bambino child
banane bananas
banca bank
banchina pier
bancomat *m* ATM
banconota banknote
barba beard
barca a remi rowboat
barca a vela sailboat
barocco baroque
barzelletta joke
basette sideburns
basilico basil
basket(-ball) *m* basketball
bassa marea low tide
bassa stagione *f* slow season
basso low; deep; short (stature); a bassa voce softly
bastare to suffice
bastoncini *m pl* **igienici** cotton swabs *pl*
bastone *m* stick; ~ **per ciechi** cane ~ **da sci** ski pole
batteria battery

beach-volley *m* beach volleyball
beige beige
bello beautiful
belvedere *m* lookout point
ben cotto well done
benché although
benda elastica rubber band
bene *m* good; *(adv.)* well
benestante well to do
benvenuto welcome
benzina gasoline fare ~ to fill up
bere to drink
berretto cap
bevanda drink
biancheria da letto bed linens
biancheria intima underwear
bianco white
biberon *m* baby bottle
bibita refreshment (drink)
bicchiere *m* glass; ~ **da acqua** water glass ~ **da vino** wine glass
bicicletta bicycle; ~ **da corsa** racing bike ~ **da trekking** touring bike; ~ **per disabili** hand-operated bike
bidone *m* wastebasket
bigiotteria fashion jewelry
biglietteria ticket window
biglietto ticket; ~ **a più obliterazioni** multiple trip ticket; ~ **d'ingresso** admission ticket; ~ **di andata e ritorno** round-trip ticket; ~ **giornaliero** day ticket; ~ **per ragazzi** children's ticket
bigodini *m pl* hair curler
bikini *m* bikini
binario platform (railroad station)
biondo blonde
biro *f* ballpoint pen
birra beer; ~ **analcolica** alcohol-free beer

biscotti *m pl* biscuits; cookies

bisognoso di cure in need of care

bizantino Byzantine

blazer *m* blazer

blocco, ~ di carta note pad

blu blue

blues *m* blues

bocca mouth

body *m* body

bollettino meteorologico weather report

bollito boiled

bombola di gas gas bottle

bonaccia calm

borotalco body powder

borsa bag, handbag; **~ a tracolla** shoulder bag; **~ da viaggio** travel bag; **~ frigo** insulated bag

borsaiolo pickpocket

bosco woods

bottiglia bottle

bottiglieria liquor store

boutique *f* boutique

bowling *m* bowling

braccialetto bracelet

bracciali *m pl* **salvagente** water wings *pl*

Stati Uniti United States

brasato braised

breve brief (time); **a ~ termine/ scadenza** short term

brillo drunk

brividi *m pl* shivers; shudder

bronchi *m pl* bronchi

bronchite *f* bronchitis

bronzo bronze

bruciare to burn

brutto ugly; disgusting; *(weather)* lousy

bucato laundry

buco hole

buffet *m* **della colazione** breakfast buffet

buffet *m* **delle insalate** salad bar

bugia lie

bungalow *m* bungalow

bungeejumping *m* bungee jumping

buono *(adj.)* good; *m* coupon; **~ per le cure mediche** medical insurance record card

burro butter

bussola compass

busta envelope

bustina di tè teabag

bypass *m* bypass

C

c'è there is; **c'è Luigi?** Is Luigi there?

cabaret *m* cabaret

cabina cabin **~ telefonica** phone booth

cadere to fall; fall down

caffè *m* coffee; café

calamaro cuttlefish

calcio soccer

calcolare to calculate; to reckon

calcolatore *m* **tascabile** pocket calculator

calcolo renale kidney stone

caldo warm; hot

calligrafia handwriting

calmante *m* sedative

calzamaglia pantyhose

calze stockings

calzini *m pl* socks

calzolaio cobbler

calzoni *m pl* pants ~ della tuta sweat pants

cambiamento change

cambiare to change; exchange; to change money; to change (trains, planes, etc.) ~ il biglietto to change reservations

cambiarsi to change clothes

cambio change; exchange (money); exchange rate; conversion ~ automatico automatic, transmission; ~ dell'olio oil change ~ della guardia changing of the guard

camera room; ~ da letto bedroom

camera d'aria inner tube

cameriera chambermaid; waitress

cameriere waiter

camicetta blouse

camicia shirt

camminare to walk; to hike

camomilla chamomile; chamomile tea

campanello bell

campanile *m* church tower

campeggiare to go camping

campeggio camping

camper *m* camping vehicle

camping *m* camping; campground

campo field ~ sportivo athletic field

Canada Canada

canadese Canadian

canale *m* canal

cancro cancer

candela candle

candele candles

cane *m* dog; ~ guida per ciechi seeing eye dog

canna da pesca fishing rod

cannuccia drinking straw

canoa canoe

canottiera undershirt

canotto pneumatico inflatable boat

canovaccio per asciugare i piatti dish towel

cantante *m/f* singer

cantare to sing

cantiere edile construction site

canto song

canzone *f* song

CAP (codice di avviamento postale) postal code

capanna hut

capelli *m pl* hair

capire to understand

capitale *f* capital

capitano captain

capo head; object; leader

capogiro dizziness; dizzy spell

Capodanno New Year

capolinea *m* terminal

cappella chapel

cappello hat ~ da sole sun hat

cappotto coat

caraffa carafe

caratteristico (per) typical of

carbonella charcoal briquettes

carciofi *m pl* artichokes

cardiostimolatore *m* pacemaker

carino pretty

carne *f* meat; ~ d'agnello lamb; ~ di maiale pork; ~ di manzo beef; ~ di montone/castrato mutton; ~ di vitello veal ~ macinata hamburger

caro dear; lovable; expensive; non ~ cheap

carote carrots

carro attrezzi tow truck

carrozzella wheelchair;
~ **elettrica** electric wheelchair;
~ **pieghevole** folding wheelchair
carta paper ~ **automobilistica**
road map; ~ **d'identità**
d'identità, ID; ~ **d'imbarco**
boarding pass; ~ **da lettere**
stationery ~ **da scrivere**
stationery; ~ **di credito** credit
card; ~ **geografica** map
~ **igienica** toilet paper;
~ **telefonica** phone card
~ **verde** green insurance card
cartoleria stationery store
cartolina illustrata picture
postcard
cartolina postale postcard
cartone *m* **animato** animated
film
cartuccia del gas gas cartridge
casa house; ~ **per le vacanze**
vacation home; **a casa** at home
cascata waterfall
casco helmet; ~ **di protezione**
cycling helmet
casinò casino
caso case, instance; **per ~**
perhaps; ~ **di emergenza**
emergency
casomai in case
cassa bank; case; ~ **automatica**
prelievi ATM; ~ **malattia**
health insurance
cassaforte *f* safe
cassetta cassette; ~ **postale**
mail box
castello castle; fortress; ~ **di**
sabbia sand castle
catena chain
cattedrale *f* cathedral
cattivo lousy; bad; mean
causa cause; reason; **a ~ di**
because of

causare to cause
cauzione *f* deposit; bottle
deposit
cavalcare to ride
cavalcata ride
cavallo horse
cavatappi *m* corkscrew
caverna cave
cavo ausiliario per la messa
in moto jumper cable
cavo da rimorchio towrope
cavo di prolungamento
extension cord
cavolfiore *m* cauliflower
cavolo cabbage
CD *m* **(compact disc)** CD
(compact disk)
ceci *m pl* chick peas
celibe bachelor
cellulare *m* cell phone
cena dinner
centimetro centimeter
centrale *(adj.)* central; *(f)*
headquarters
centro center, downtown;
~ **città** downtown; ~ **di fitness**
fitness center; ~ **storico** the old
town; ~ **vacanze** vacation resort
ceramica ceramics
cercare to look for
cerotto band aid
certamente surely *(adv.)*
certificare to certify
certificato certificate
certo *(adj.)* certain, sure;
certamente *(adv.)* certainly
cervello brain
cespuglio bush
cesto basket
cetriolo cucumber
champagne *m* champagne

che that; *(rel. pron.)* which, who; Che peccato! What a shame! Che ...?/Che cosa? What?

chiamare to call; to name

chiamarsi to be called/named

chiaro clear

chiasso noise

chiave *f* key; ~ di accensione ignition key

chiedere to ask, request; ~ qc a qd to ask someone for something; ~ un consiglio a qd to ask someone for advice

chiesa church

chilogrammo kilo

chilometro kilometer

chiodi *m pl* di garofano cloves

chiostro monastery

chirurgo surgeon

chiudere (a chiave) to lock

chiudere to close; lock in; ~ a chiave to lock

chiuso closed

ci us; *(adv.)* there, here; ci sono there are; Ci sono i nonni? Are the grandparents here?

cibo dietetico health food

cicatrice *f* scar

cicerone *m* guide

ciclismo cycling

ciclopista bicycle path

cielo sky

ciliegie cherries

cima summit

cimitero cemetery

cinema *m* movie

cinema *m* all'aperto outdoor movie

cintura belt; ~ di sicurezza seat belt

ciò nonostante nevertheless

cioccolata chocolate

ciondolo pendant

cipolle onions

cipria face-powder

circa approximately

circolo clubhouse ~ golfistico clubhouse (on golf course)

circonvallazione beltway

cistifellea *f* gallbladder

città city

cittadino unitario EU citizen

ciuccio pacifier

clacson *m* horn (of car)

classe *f* class

classicismo classicism

classico classical

clavicola collarbone

cliente *m/f* client

clima *m* climate

club *m* club, clubhouse

codice *m* per la porta della camera door code

cofano hood (of car)

cogliere to pick, pluck

cognata sister-in-law

cognato brother-in-law

cognome *m* family name; ~ di nascita, ~ da nubile birth/maiden name

coincidenza coincidence

colazione *f* breakfast; fare ~ to have breakfast

colera *m* cholera

colica colic

collana chain

collant *m* pantyhose

collega *m/f* colleague

collegamento binding

collina hill

collirio eye drops

collisione *f* collision

collo throat

colonna column; ~ vertebrale spinal column

color oro gold color
colore *m* color; **a colori** colored
colpa guilt
colpi *m pl* **di sole** strands *(hair style)* *pl*
colpire to hit
colpo apoplettico stroke
colpo della strega lumbago
colpo di sole sunstroke
coltello knife; ~ **tascabile** pocket knife
combustibile *m* fuel
come as *(comparison, question)*; how
cominciare to begin
comitiva group, circle of friends
commedia comedy; theater; ~ **musicale** musical ~ **popolare** folk play
commerciante *m/f* **in oggetti d'arte** art dealer
commestibile edible
commozione *f* **cerebrale** concussion
comodino night table
comodo comfortable
compagnia aerea airline company
compagnia teatrale theater group
compagno di giochi playmate
compassione *f* compassion
competente competent
compilare to fill out
compleanno birthday
complesso complex; musical group
completo *(adj)* complete; **al** ~ full
compositore/compositrice composer
comprare to buy
compreso included

compressa tablet
compresse contro il dolore pain pills
compresse contro il mal di testa headache pills
comune *m* municipality; *(adj.)* common; customary
comunicazione *f* communication; (tele) connection; ~ **internazionale** international call; ~ **telefonica a carico del ricevente** collect call
con with; by means of
concerto concert; ~ **sinfonico** symphony concert
conchiglia mussel
condire to season
condimento per l'insalata salad dressing
condizione *f* condition; state
conducente *m/f* driver
confermare to confirm
confine *m* border, border crossing
confortevole comfortable
confrontare to compare
congedarsi to take one's leave
congratularsi to congratulate
coniglio rabbit
connazionale *m/f* fellow citizen
conoscente *m/f* acquaintance
conoscenza knowledge; acquaintance; **fare la** ~ **di qd** to get to know someone
conoscere to know
consegna del bagaglio baggage consignment
consegna delle chiavi key return
consegnare to drop off; (baggage) hand over
conservare to preserve, conserve
consigliare to advise
consiglio advice, tip

consolato consulate
consumo consumption; ~ d'acqua water consumption
contagioso contagious
contanti *m pl* cash
contare to count
contatto contact; touching; binding
contemporaneo contemporary
contenere to contain
contento happy, content
contenuto contents
conto bill
contrabbando contraband
contrario opposite; al ~ on the contrary; essere ~ to be against
contrattempo incident
contratto contract
contro against
controllare to control, test
controllo dei passaporti passport check
controllo di sicurezza security check
controllo radar radar control
controllore *m* conductor
contusione *f* bruise
convalidare to validate
convento convent
conversare to converse
conversazione *f* conversation
conversione *f* conversion
convincere to convince
coperta blanket; ~ di lana wool blanket
coperto place setting
copia copy
coppia couple
corda rope; ~ per stendere il bucato clothesline
cordiale *(adj)* hearty
cordialmente *(adv)* heartily
coro choir; chorus

corona crown
corpo body
corrente *f* current; *(adj.)* common; current, fluent; ~ d'aria draft ~ elettrica electrical current
correre to run
corridoio corridor; hallway
corrimano handrail
corrotto corrupt (morally)
corso course; ~ da nuoto swimming lessons; ~ dei cambi exchange rate; ~ di sci ski instruction
cortese polite
cortile *m* courtyard; ~ interno inner courtyard
corto short
corto circuito short circuit
cortometraggio short feature (film)
cosa thing; what?
cose *f pl* da vedersi sights, tourist attractions
così thus
costa coast
costare to cost
costipazione *f* cold; constipation
costituito, essere ~ da to consist of
costoletta cutlet
costringere to force
costruzione *f* construction
costume *m* custom, practice; dress; ~ da bagno bathing trunks, bathing suit; ~ regionale regional dress
cotone *m* cotton ~ idrofilo absorbent cotton
cotto cooked; ~ a vapore steamed
cozze *f pl* mussels

207

crampo cramp
cravatta necktie
creativo creative
credere to believe, opine
crema cream; ~ per le mani hand lotion; ~ solare sun cream
cremagliera cog railway
crescere to grow
cric *m* jack (auto)
cristallo crystal
cristianesimo Christianity
criticare to criticize
croce *f* cross
crociera cruise
crudo raw
cucchiaino teaspoon
cucchiaio spoon
cucina kitchen
cucina a gas gas stove
cucina elettrica electric stove
cucinare to cook
cucinino kitchenette
cucinotto kitchenette
cucire to sew
cuffia bathing cap; headphone
cugino/cugina cousin
cultura culture
culturismo bodybuilding
cumino cumin
cuoco cook
cuore *m* heart
cupola cupola
curare to treat
curioso curious
curling *m* curling
curva curve
cuscino pillow
custodire to preserve, watch over

D

da from (direction); since (time)
danneggiare to damage; to harm
danno damage; harm
dannoso harmful; unhealthy
danza dance
dappertutto everywhere
dare to give
data date; ~ di nascita date of birth
dato che since (at start of sentence)
datteri dates
davanti before; ~ a (spatial) in front of
debito debt (money)
debole weak
decidere to decide; to conclude
decidersi to decide, make up one's mind
decollo takeoff
definitivamente *(adv.)* finally
definitivo *(adj.)* final
del posto domestic, local
delega proxy; power of attorney
delitto crime
deluso disappointed
denaro money
dente *m* tooth
dente *m* **del giudjzio** wisdom tooth
dentifricio toothpaste
dentro inside, within
denunciare to report
deodorante *m* deodorant
depositare to deposit
deposito a cassette mailbox
deposito bagagli baggage check
derivare to derive from
descrivere to describe

desiderare to desire, wish

desinare *m* lunch

dessert *m* dessert

destinatario addressee

destro right; **a destra** right, to the right

detenzione *f* **preventiva** custody

detersivo detergent; ~ **per le stoviglie** dishwashing detergent

deviazione detour

di from (origin); of (material); than (comparisons)

di mala voglia unwillingly

diabete *m* diabetes

diabetico diabetic

diagnosi *f* diagnosis

diarrea diarrhea

dicembre *m* December

dichiarare to explain

dichiarazione *f* **doganale** customs declaration

dieci minuti fa ten minutes ago

dieta *f* diet

dietro behind; backward

difetto defect; lack

differenza difference

difficile hard, difficult

difficoltà di respirazione difficulty breathing

difterite *f* diphtheria

digestione *f* digestion

digitare to type in, (comput.) to input

digiuno to fast (on empty stomach)

dimenticare to forget

dinamo *f* generator

dinastia dynasty

dintorni *m pl* surroundings

Dio God

dipingere to paint

dipinto painting

dire to say

diretto *(adj.)* direct

direttore/direttrice director

direttore/direttrice d'orchestra orchestra conductor

direzione *f* direction

diritto straight; right

diritti *m pl* **aeroportuali** airport taxes

diritti *m pl* **fissi** handling charges

disabile *m/f* **in sedia a rotelle** person in a wheelchair

disabitato uninhabited; lonely

disdire to cancel

disegnare to draw

disegno drawing; ~ **di nudi** drawing from a model

disgrazia bad luck

disinfettante *m* disinfectant

disinfettare to disinfect

disoccupato unemployed

disperato desperate

dispiacere *m* to displease; to be sorry, regret

distinto distinguished

distributore *m* distributor; ~ **automatico** gas station; ~ **automatico di biglietti** automatic ticket machine; ~ **automatico per francobolli** stamp machine

distruggere to destroy

disturbare to disturb

disturbi *m pl* **circolatori** circulatory disorder; ~ **cardiaci** heart trouble

dito finger; ~ **del piede** toe

ditta company

divano letto fold-out couch

diventare to become

diverso *(adj.)* different;
  diversamente *(adv.)* differently
divertimento entertainment,
  enjoyment
divertirsi to entertain oneself, to
  have fun
dividere to divide; ~ **con qd** to
  share with someone
divieto prohibition
divise *f pl* **estere** foreign
  currency
doccia shower
documentario documentary film
documenti *m pl* documents
dogana customs
dolce *m* cake, dessert; *(adj.)*
  sweet, mild
dolcetto di cioccolata
  chocolate bar
dolciumi *m pl* sweets
dolore *m* **alla schiena**
  backache
domanda question; request
domandare to ask
domenica (on) Sunday
domicilio residence
donna lady
dopo after; *(prep.)* after; ~
  domani the day after tomorrow
doppio *(adj.)* double
dormire to sleep
dovere *m* duty; *(verb)* to have to;
  must; to owe
dramma *m* drama
drogare to spice
due two; **tutte/tutti** *f/m/l*
  e due both *f/m*
dunque thus
duomo cathedral
durante *(prep.)* during
durare to last; to hold out
durata duration; resistance
durevole durable

duro hard; solid

e and
eccellente excellent
eccetto except
ecco here is, there is, look
economico inexpensive
edificio building
educazione *f* education, good
  breeding
edulcorante *m* sweetener
eisschiessen curling
elastico per capelli hair band
elenco directory; ~ **telefonico**
  telephone book
elettricista *m* electrician
elettrico electric
elettrodomestici electric
  appliances; **negozio di~** electric
  appliance store
elevatore *m* elevator
emblema *m* emblem
emicrania migraine
emissione *f* **speciale** special
  issue stamp
emorragia hemorrhage;
  ~ **nasale** nosebleed
ente *m* corporation; institution;
  ~ **per il turismo** tourist office
entrare to enter, go in, come in
  ~ **in**
entrata entrance; **entrata in**
  territorio straniero entry into
  foreign territory
entusiasta (di) enthusiastic
  (about)
epigrafe *f* inscription
epilessia epilepsy

epoca epoch
equipaggio crew *(ship)*
erbette herbs
ernia rupture; ~ inguinale hernia
errore *m* error
eruzione *f* cutanea rash
esagerato exaggerated
esame *m* examination
esaminare to examine
esantema *m* eruption
esaurito exhausted
escursione *f* a terra land tour
escursione *f* excursion; fare un'~ to take a hike
esempio example; per ~ for example
esente da dazio doganale toll-free
esercitare to practice; (profession) to ply, practice
esercizio practice, exercise
esigere to require
esitare to hesitate
esofago esophagus
esposimetro light meter
esposizione *f* exposition
espressamente expressly
espressione *f* expression
espressionismo expressionism
essere to be
est *m* east; a ~ di east of
estate *f* summer
estero overseas; foreign
estintore *m* fire extinguisher
estraneo/a stranger
età age
euro euro
Europa Europe
europeo European *(adj)*
europeo/europea European *(person)*
evacuazione *f* evacuation; bowel movement

evitare to avoid

F

fabbrica factory
faccia face
facciata façade
facile simple, easy
fagioli *m pl* beans
fagiolini *m pl* green beans
famiglia family
famoso famous
fanalino posteriore taillight
fango mud; dirt
far benzina to fill up (auto)
far scalo a to have a stopover in
far segno to save
fare to make; to do
fare contrabbando to smuggle
fare della musica to play music
fare escursioni to hike
fare il check-in to check in
fare jogging to jog
fare lo snorkeling to go snorkeling
farina flour
fari *m pl* abbaglianti high beams (headlights)
farmacia drugstore
farmaco medicine
faro lighthouse; headlight
fascia coprireni kidney belt
fascia di garza gauze bandage
fasciare to wrap
fasciatoio changing table
faticoso strenuous, tiring
fatto fact; incident
fatto a mano handmade
fatto in casa homemade

fattore *m* **protettivo** protection factor (sunscreen)

fattoria farmhouse

favore *m* favor

favorevole, essere ~ to be favorably disposed

fazzoletto handkerchief ~ **di carta** paper tissue

febbraio February

febbre *f* fever

fede *f* faith; wedding ring

fedele faithful

fegato liver

felice happy

felicità happiness

femminile feminine

ferie *pl* vacation

ferire to hurt

ferita wound, injury; ~ **da taglio** cut

ferito/ferita injured person

fermare to shut off (mech)

fermarsi to stop, stay

fermata stop

fermo posta general delivery

festa celebration, party

festival *m* festival

fetta slice

fiammifero match

fiaschetteria wine shop

fichi figs

fidanzato/fidanzata fiancé(e)

fidarsi di to trust; **non fidarsi di qc/qd** to distrust something/someone

fidato reliable

fiducia trust

fiera fair

figlia daughter

figlio son

fila row; **fare la ~** to stand in line

film *m* film; **~ in bianco e nero** black and white film

filo wire

finalmente finally

fine *f* end; refined; **alla fine** at the end, lastly

finestra window

finire to finish

fino a until

finocchio fennel

finora so far

fiocchi *m pl* **d'avena** oatmeal

fioraio flower shop

fiore *m* flower

fiorire to bloom

firma signature

firmare to sign

fissare to establish; to agree

fiume *m* river; stream

flash *m* flash attachment

flatulenza flatulence

fleboclisi *f* infusion

foglia leaf (foliage)

foglio sheet (paper)

föhn *m* hair dryer

folclore *m* folklore

folle *m/f* fool; *(adj.)* crazy; **in folle** in neutral (gear)

fontana spring

fonte *f* spring; fountain

forbici *f pl* scissors; **~ per le unghie** nail clippers

forchetta fork

foresta forest

forfait *m* flat rate **forfait per il fine settimana** weekend rate

forfora dandruff

forma shape; **in ~** fit

formaggio cheese; **~ di capra** goat cheese

formare to shape; **~ il numero** to dial (tele)

formato orizzontale landscape format

formato verticale portrait format

formazione *f* formation; training

fornello kitchen range; ~ a gas gas range

forse perhaps

forte strong, powerful; spicy (smell, taste)

fortezza castle, fortress

forza strength; power

forzare to force, break open

foto *f* photograph, snapshot

fotografare to photograph

fotografia photograph

foulard *m* scarf

fra between, among; ~ una settimana in a week

fragole strawberries

francese French; French person *(m* and *f)*

franco svizzero Swiss franc

francobollo stamp

frangetta bangs (hair)

frase *f* sentence

fratello brother

frattura ossea bone break

freddo cold; aver ~ to be cold

freno brake; ~ a mano handbrake

fresco fresh; cool

fretta speed; in ~ *(adv.)* quickly

frettoloso hurried

frigorifero refrigerator

fritto cooked

frizione *f* hair-setting lotion; clutch

fronte *f* forehead; di fronte a across from

frontiera border; border crossing

frutta *f* fruit

fruttivendolo fruit and vegetables merchant

fulmine *m* lightning

fumare to smoke

fumatore smoker

funicolare *f* cable car

funivia cable car

funzionare to function

fuoco fire

fuori outside, outdoors; fuori di except for

fuorigioco offside

furbo sly

furto theft

fuseaux *m pl* stretch pants

futuro future; future

G

gabbiano seagull

gabinetto closet; cabinet; ~ alla turca/vespasiano urinal

galleria passage; tunnel; gallery galleria d'arte art gallery

gamba leg

gamberetti shrimp

gancio hook

gara competition

garage *m* garage

garanzia guaranty; security

garbare to please; appeal to

gatta/gatto cat *(f. and m.)*

gel *m* per capelli hair gel

gel *m* per la doccia shower gel

gelo frost

gengiva gum (of mouth)

genitori *pl* parents

gennaio January

gente *f* people

gentile likeable; nice

213

gettare to throw

ghiaccio ice

già already

giacca jacket

giacca a vento windbreaker

giacca di lana wool jacket

giacca di pelle leather jacket

giacere to lie

giallo yellow

giardino garden; ~ pubblico
park; ~ botanico botanical
garden

gilè m vest

ginnastica gymnastics; ~ jazz
jazzercize

ginocchio knee

giocare to play

giocattoli m pl toys

gioco dei birilli nine-pins

gioco del volano badminton

gioia joy

gioielleria jeweler

gioielli m pl jewelry, jewels

giornalaio newspaper seller

giornale m newspaper

giorno day; il ~ all day;
~ d'arrivo arrival day; nei
giorni feriali on workdays

giovane young

giovedì Thursday

giro walk, tour, excursion;
~ dell'isola an island tour;
~ turistico della città city tour

gita excursion, trip; ~ di un
giorno day trip; ~ in barca a
vela a sailing cruise

giù under; in ~ downward,
downhill

giubbetto di salvataggio life
jacket

giugno June

giusto right; appropriate; essere
~ to be correct

gocce f pl drops; ~ per gli
occhi eye drops; ~ per gli
orecchi ear drops

godere to enjoy

gola ravine; throat; gorge

golf m golf; wool jacket

golfo gulf, bay

gomma a terra flat tire

gomma da masticare
chewing gum

gonfio swollen

gonfiore m swelling

gonna skirt

gotico gothic

governo government

gradino step

grammo gram

granchi crabs

grande big

grande magazzino m
department store

grandezza largeness (spiritual,
spatial)

granturco corn

grasso thick; fat; fatty

gratinare to put into the oven

gratis free, cost-free

gravidanza pregnancy

Grecia Greece

greco Greek

gridare to yell

grigio gray

griglia grill

grosso big; thick

grotta grotto; cave

gruccia crutch

gruccia per i panni coat
hanger

gruppo group; ~ sanguigno
blood type

guadagno profit; income

guanti gloves

guanto di spugna washcloth

guardare to look at, watch
guardaroba m wardrobe
guasto trouble; defect; *(adj.)* faulty, ruined; defective
guida direction, leadership; travel guide
guida dei campeggi camping guide
guida turistica tourist guide
guidare to guide; to drive
gusto taste

H

hall f reception hall
handicap m fisico physical handicap
hockey m su hiaccio ice hockey
hostess f hostess
house boat f houseboat
hovercraft m hovercraft

I

idea idea; conception
idoneo per carrozzelle wheelchair-accessible
idoneo per/a misura degli handicappati handicap-accessible
ieri yesterday
il the
imballaggio packaging
imboccatura mouth (of river)
imbroglione *(m)* cheat
immondizia trash

imparare to learn
impedire to impede, hinder
imperatore/imperatrice emperor, empress
impermeabile m raincoat
impianto establishment; ~ di risalita per bambini kiddy-tow
impiego employment; job
importante important, significant, large; poco ~ unimportant
importo amount, sum
impossibile impossible
impressionante impressive
impressione f impression
impressionismo impressionism
improbabile improbable
improvviso *(adj)* sudden; all'~ suddenly)
in in; to (direction); in italiano in Italian; in contanti in cash; in fretta quickly; in nessun luogo nowhere; in più in addition; in secondo luogo secondly
inadatto inappropriate
incantevole charming, captivating
incartare to wrap in paper
incendio fire
incidente m accident; occurrence; avere un incidente to have an accident
incontrare to meet
incredibile incredible
incrocio intersection
indecente improper, indecent
indeciso undecided
indicazione f designation; information
indietro back; all'~ backwards
indigestione f indigestion
indirizzo address
indivia del Belgio chicory

infarto heart attack
infastidire to annoy
infermiera nurse
infezione f infection
infiammabile flammable
infiammazione f inflammation
influenza flu
informare to inform, instruct; ~ qd to notify someone
informarsi to inquire
informazione f information
infortunio accident; avere un ~ to have an accident
inganno deceit (cheating)
inglese English; English person (m and f)
ingorgo obstruction
ingresso entrance
iniezione f injection (shot)
iniziare to start, begin
inizio start, beginning
innocente innocent
inoltre in addition, besides
insalata salad; ~ verde green salad
insalatiera salad bowl
insegna sign
insegnare to teach, instruct
insetto insect
insieme (adv) together
insistere su to insist on
insolito unusual
insonnia insomnia
insopportabile unbearable
insulina insulin
intaglio wood carving
intelligente intelligent
intendere to intend
intendersi to agree; to understand one another
intensità del vento wind speed

intenzione f intention; avere l'intenzione di to intend to
interessante interesting
interessarsi (a, di) to be interested in
internazionale international
intero (adj.) entire; interamente, interamente (adv.) entirely
interrail m Interrail
interrompere to interrupt; to break off
interruttore m light switch
interurbana long-distance call
intervallo half-time
intestino intestine
intorno a around
intossicazione f da alimenti food poisoning
invalido/a severely handicapped person (m and f)
invano in vain
invece di instead of
inverno winter
inverso reversed
invitare to invite
io I
iogurt m yogurt
ipodermoclisi f infusion
iscrizione f inscription
isola island
istantanea snapshot
istante m moment, instant
istruire to instruct
istruzione (f) instruction, training
istruzione scolastica academic training
Italia Italia
italiano Italian; in ~ in Italian
itinerario itinerary, travel route; ~ in bici(cletta) bicycle tour

J

jazz *m* jazz
jeans *m pl* jeans

K

ketchup *m* ketchup

L

la the *(definite article, f)*; *(dir. obj. pron., f)* it, her
là there
labbro lip
laccio da tenda tent rope
laccio per scarpe shoelace
ladro thief
lago lake
lamentarsi (di) to complain (about)
lampada lamp
lampadina (ad incandescenza) light bulb
lampeggiatori *m pl* d'emergenza emergency flashers
lana wool
larghezza width
largo wide; broad
lasciare to leave; to leave behind
lassativo laxative
lato side
latta water can
latte *m* milk; latte magro low-fat milk
lattina drink can

lattuga lettuce
lavabo sink
lavanderia laundry ~ a gettone laundromat
lavandino wash basin, sink
lavare to wash
lavare/pulire a secco dry cleaning
lavastoviglie *f* automatic dishwasher
lavatrice *f* washing machine
lavorare to work
lavoro work
le *(def. art., f pl.)* the; *(ind. obj. pron,. f s.)* her
Le *(ind. obj. f sing; polite form)* you
leale fair
leggere to read
leggero light (weight)
legno wood
Lei you (formal); lei *(subj. pron., f s.)* she; a lei *(accentuated form)* her
lente *f* lens
lenticchie *f pl* lentils
lento *(adj)*, **lentamente** *(adv.)* slow(ly)
lettera letter
lettino (per bambini) child's bed
letto bed; ~ a castello bunk bed
lettore *m* CD CD player; ~ portatile portable CD player
levata emptying
lezione *f* lesson
li *(dir. obj. pron., m pl.)* them
lì there
libero free
libreria bookstore
libretto di circolazione driver's license

libretto di risparmio postale post office savings book

libretto di vaccinazione vaccination record

libro book; ~ **da colorare** coloring book; ~ **di cucina** cookbook; ~ **tascabile** pocket book

licenza di pesca fishing license

lieto (di) glad

lilla lilac

limite *m* limit; ~ **massimo consentito di alcol nel sangue** maximum allowable blood alcohol level

limonata lemonade

limoni *m pl* lemons

linea line; cable (tel., elec.); (train) line

lingua language

linguaggio mimico/a segni sign language

lino linen

liquido liquid

lisca fishbone

lista delle vivande menu

lite *f* dispute

litro liter

livello, a ~ del suolo at ground level

lo him; it; *(def. art., m s.)* the

locale *(m)* place (premises); bar

località locality; ~ **marittima** bathing resort

lodare to praise

lontananza distance

lontano distant, far

Loro *pl* you; **loro** *(subj. pron. pl.)* they; them; *(pl. poss. pron.)* their

lozione *f* after-shave lotion

luce *f* light **luci anabbaglianti** low beams; **luci di arresto** break lights **luci di posizione** parking lights

lucido per scarpe shoe polish

luglio July

lui he; *(accentuated form)* him; **a ~** *(accentuated form)* to/for him

luna moon

lunedì Monday

Lunedì dell'Angelo Easter Monday

lunedì scorso last Monday

lunghezza length

lungo long; far

luogo place; **aver ~** to take place; ~ **di nascita** place of birth ~ **di pellegrinaggio** pilgrimage site

lussuoso luxurious

M

ma but; however; but rather

macchia spot

macchina machine; car; automobile; ~ **del caffè** coffee machine; ~ **fotografica** camera; ~ **fotografica a sviluppo immediato** instant Polaroid camera; ~ **fotografica digitale** digital camera; ~ **fotografica subacquea** underwater camera

macelleria butcher shop

madre *f* mother

maestro/a teacher; ~ **di sci** ski instructor

maggio May

maglietta T-shirt

maglione *m* sweater

magnifico magnificent

magro lean; thin

mai never

mais *m* corn

mal *m* pain

  mal di denti toothache

  mal di stomaco stomachache

  mal di testa headache

  mal di gola sore throat

malato sick

malattia illness; ~ infantile childhood sickness

male *(adv.)* badly; fare ~ to hurt

malinteso misunderstanding

malleolo ankle

mancare to be lacking, to miss

mancia tip

mancorrente *m* handrail

mandare to send

mandarini *m pl* mandarin oranges

mandorle *f pl* almonds

mangiare *m* to eat; food

maniche sleeve

manifestazione *f* exhibition

manifesto poster

maniglia handle

mano *f* hand

manopola washcloth

manopola sul volante steering knob (auto)

mappa dei sentieri hiking map

marcia gear (car); speed

marcia di un giorno day tour

marcia indietro reverse

marcio rotten, ramshackle

mare *m* sea

margarina margarine

marito husband

marmellata marmalade

marrone brown

martedì Tuesday

marzo March

mascara *m* mascara

mascella jaw

maschera *f* diving mask

maschile masculine

massaggio massage

massimo maximum, highest; al massimo at most

materassino air mattress

materasso mattress

materiale *m* material; ~ di pronto soccorso bandage

matita colorata colored pencil

mattina morning

mattino morning

maturo mature, ripe

mazza da golf golf club

mazzo bouquet

me *(accentuated form)* me; a me *(accentuated form)* to/for me

méches *f pl* strands

mediatore *m* broker, agent

medicamento per disturbi circolatori circulatory medicine

medicina medicine; medication

medio *(adj.)* average; in media *(adv.)* on the average

Medioevo Middle Ages

Mediterraneo Mediterranean

meglio (di) better (than)

melanzane eggplants

mele apples

melone *m* melons

membrana del timpano eardrum

meno minus; per lo ~ at least

menomato nella vista visually impaired

menomazione *f* fisica physical handicap

mensile *(adj.)* **mensilmente** *(adv.)* monthly

mentre *(conj.)* while

menu *m* menu

meravigliarsi (di) to wonder (about)

meraviglioso wonderful

mercanteggiare to haggle

mercato market; **a buon ~** cheap; **~ delle pulci** flea market

mercoledì Wednesday

mese *m* Month

messa mass (church)

messa in scena production (theater)

mesticheria hardware store

mestruazione *f* menstruation

metà half

meta goal

metro meter; **~ quadrato** square meter

metropolitana subway

mettere put, place; lay; **~ in valigia** to pack (in a suitcase)

mettersi to put on (clothing)

mettersi d'accordo to agree

mezza porzione *f* child's portion

mezzapensione *f* half pension

mezzo half; middle; **in ~ a** in the middle of; **~ chilo** pound

mezzogiorno noon; **a mezzogiorno** at noon

mi me; to/for me

micosi *f* fungus, mold

microonda microwave

miele *m* honey

migliorare to improve

migliore *m/f* better; *(with def. art.)* best

millimetro millimeter

minestra soup

minibar *m* mini-bar

minigolf *m* miniature golf

minorenne *m/f* youngster, minor

minuto minute

mio my

mio, il mio my, mine

mirino viewfinder

misto mixed

misura measurement; size (clothing, shoes)

mite mild

mitili *m pl* mussels

mittente *m* sender

mobile *m* furniture; mobile

moda fashion

modello model

moderno modern

modo manner, way

modulo form

moglie *f* wife

molestia sessuale sexual harassment

molletta (per stendere la biancheria) clothespins

mollette *f pl* **(per capelli)** barrettes (hair)

molo breakwater, pier

molto very; lots

monastero monastery

mondo world

moneta coin

monopattino in-line skate

montagna mountains

monte *m* mountain

monumenti *m pl* monuments, sights

monumento monument; **~ commemorativo** memorial; **~ sepolcrale** tomb

morbido soft

morbillo measles

mordere to bite

more mulberry; blackberry

morire to die

morte *f* death

morto dead

mosaico mosaic

mosca fly
mostarda *f* mustard
mostra exhibition
mostrare to show
motel *m* motel
motivo motive; cause
moto ondoso sea conditions
motore *m* motor
motorino d'avviamento starter
motoscafo motorboat
mountain bike *f* mountain bike
mucchio, un ~ di quantity
müesli *m* granola
multa fine
multicolore multicolored
municipio town hall
muro wall
muscolo muscle
museo museum
musica music; ~ classica classical music; ~ dal vivo live music; ~ popolare popular music
musical *m* musical
muta *f* neoprene suit
mutande underpants
muto mute

N

nascondere to hide, conceal; di nascosto *(adv.)* secretly
naso nose
nato born
natura nature; ~ morta still life
naturale *(adj.)*; **naturalmente** *(adv.)* natural, naturally
nausea nausea

nave *f* steamer
nazionalità nationality
nebbia fog
necessario necessary
nefrite *f* nephritis
negativo negative
negozio di antichità antique shop
negozio di calzature shoe store
negozio di ferramenta hardware store
negozio di generi alimentari food store
negozio di giocattoli toy store
negozio di prodotti biodinamici health food store
negozio di souvenir souvenir shop
nei dintorni di in the vicinity of
neonato baby, newborn
neppure not even
nero black
nervo nerve
nervoso nervous
nessuno nobody, no one
neve *f* snow; **neve farinosa** powder snow
niente nothing; ~ affatto absolutely not
night *m* bar
night-club *m* nightclub
nipote *m/f* grandson; granddaughter; nephew, niece
noci *f pl* nuts **noce di cocco** coconut; **noce moscata** nutmeg
noi *(dir. obj. pronoun, accentuated form)* us; we; a ~ *(ind. obj. pronoun, accentuated form)* to us
noioso boring; tiresome
noleggio rent
nome *m* name

non not; **non ancora** not yet; **non ubriaco** sober; **non udente** deaf

nonna grandmother

nonno grandfather

nord *m* north; **a ~ di** north of

normale normal

normalmente normally

nostro, il nostro our

notare to note, notice; to jot down

notebook *m* notebook

notizia news, notice

noto well-known

notte *f* night; **la notte** at night

novembre November

novità novelty; newness

nozze *f pl* marriage

nubile single (woman)

nudo nude

numero number; **~ civico** house number; **~ del vagone** vehicle number; **~ segreto** personal identification number; **~ telefonico** phone number

nuotare to swim; **~ sott'acqua** to skin dive

nuovo new; **di ~** again

nuvola cloud

nuvoloso cloudy

O

o ... o ... either...or

obbligato, essere ~ to be obliged

obiettivo rational

obliteratore *m* automatic ticket-stamping machine

occasionalmente *(adv)* occasionally

occasione *f* occasion, opportunity

occhi *m pl* eyes

occhiali *m pl* ski goggles

occuparsi di to take care of

occupato busy; occupied *(seat)*

odorare to smell

odore *m* smell

offesa offense

offrire to offer

oggetto object; **oggetti di valore** valuables

oggi today

ogni *(adj.)* every, each; **~ giorno** every day; **~ ora** hourly; **~ settimana** *(adv.)* weekly

ognuno *(pron.)* everyone

olio oil; **~ d'oliva** olive oil; **~ per freni** brake fluid; **~ solare** suntan oil

olive olives

ombra shade

ombrello umbrella

ondata di caldo heat wave

opera work; opera; **~ teatrale** play

operazione *f* operation

operetta operetta

opinione *f* opinion, view

opposto opposite

oppure or

opuscolo del programma program (booklet)

ora now; hour; **un quarto d'ora** a quarter-hour; **una mezz'ora** a half-hour; **a quest'ora** at this time

orario itinerary; **~ d'apertura (al pubblico)** business hours; **~ d'arrivo** arrival time; **~ di visita** office hours, visiting hours

orchestra orchestra, dance band
ordinazione *f* order
orecchini *m pl* earrings
orecchio ear
orecchioni *m pl* mumps
originale *m* original
oro gold
orologiaio watchmaker
orologio da polso wristwatch
osare to dare
ospedale *m* hospital
ospitalità hospitality
ospite *m/f* host; guest
osservare to observe; watch; notice
osservatorio astronomico astronomical observatory
ossigenatore *m* respirator
osso bone
oste *m* innkeeper
osteria bar
ostriche oysters
otite *f* inner ear infection
ottico optician
ottobre October
ovest *m* west; a ~ di west of

P

pacchetto packet
pacco package
pacemaker *m* pacemaker
padre *m* father
padrone/padrona *m/f* owner; innkeeper; ~ di casa homeowner, host(ess)
paesaggio landscape
paese *m* country; region; town
pagamento payment

pagare to pay; ~ in contanti to pay cash
paio pair
palazzo palace
palco box, stall
palestra fitness center
palla ball; ~ a mano handball
pallacanestro basketball
pallavolo *f* volleyball
pallido pale
pallone *m* ball
palo da tenda tent pole
palude *f* swamp
panchina bench
pane *m* bread pane bianco white bread; pane nero dark bread
panificio bakery
panino roll
panna cream
panne *f* breakdown
panno cloth
pannolini *m pl* diapers
panorama *m* panorama
pantaloncini *m pl* shorts
pantaloni *m pl* pants; ~ da sci ski pants
paprica paprika (spice)
parabrezza *m* windshield
paracadutismo sky diving
paralisi *f* paralysis
parapendio hang-glider
paraplegico paraplegic
paraurti *m* bumper
parcheggiare to park
parcheggio parking space
parco park; ~ divertimenti amusement park; ~ nazionale national park; nature preserve
parente di related to
parete *f* wall
pari undecided
parlare to speak, converse

parola word

parrucca wig

parrucchiere *m* hairdresser, barber

parte *f* part

partecipare (a) to take part in

partenza departure

particolare particular

partire to leave, depart; to start *(da,* from); to leave *(per,* for)

partita game; ~ di calcio soccer game

Pasqua Easter

passaggio passage; crossing; voyage; di ~ on the trip; ~ di confine foreign travel

passaggio pass

passaporto passport

passare to pass, go through; to spend (time); to pass (time); ~ al forno to bake

passato past; the past

passeggero passenger; *(adj.)* temporary

passeggiare to take a walk

passeggiata walk, stroll

passerella gangway

passo pass

pasta *f* pasta

pasticca tablet

pasticceria pastry shop

pasticcio di fegato pâté

pastiglie *f pl* **per la gola** throat tablets

pasto meal

patate potatoes

patente *f* driver's license; ~ nautica boat operator's license

patino a pedali pedal boat

patria country, fatherland

pattinaggio su ghiaccio ice-skating

pattini *m pl* **per ghiaccio** ice skates

paura anxiety; fear; aver paura di to be afraid of

pavimento floor

pazienza patience

pazzo crazy

pecorino sheep's milk cheese

pedaggio autostradale highway tolls

pedalò pedal boat

pedone *m* pedestrian

pegno pledge

pelle *f* skin

pelletteria leather shop

pellicola (per la conserva- zione dei cibi) plastic wrap

pelo fur

pena penalty

pennello da barba shaving brush

pensare to think; ~ a to think about; to take care of

pensione *f* pension; ~ completa full pension

penultimo/a next-to-last

pepe *m* pepper

peperone *m* pepper (vegetable)

per for; per; by (means); by means of; on account of; per iscritto in writing; per me in my opinion

per il fine settimana on the weekend

percento percent

perché why? *(conj.)* since, because (reason)

perciò therefore

perdere to lose; to miss; to neglect; ~ l'autobus to miss the bus

perdita loss

pere pears

pericolo danger
pericoloso dangerous
periodico newspaper
periodo di divieto di caccia closed hunting season
perla pearl
permanente *f* permanent
permesso permission
permettere to permit, allow
pernottamento overnight
pernottare to spend the night
persona person
personale *m* personnel; *(adj.)* individual, personal
persuadere to persuade, convince
pertosse *f* whooping cough
pesante heavy
pesare to weigh
pescare con l'amo to fish
pesce *m* fish; ~ persico perch; ~ spada swordfish
pesche peach
pescheria fish shop
pescivendolo fishmonger
peso weight
petrolio petroleum
pettinare to comb
pettinatura hairstyle
pettine *m* comb
petto breast
pezzo piece; un ~ di pane a piece of bread; ~ d'esposizione exhibit
piacere *m* pleasure, joy
piacere to please, like; *(with introductions)*, pleased to meet you!
piacevole pleasant
piangere to cry
piano *(adj.)* even, flat; *(adv.)* slowly; softly; *m* plan; story, floor

pianta plant; ~ della città city map
pianterreno ground floor
pianura plains
piastra refrigerante cooling element
piatti *m pl* dishes
piattino saucer
piatto flat, even
piatto *m* plate; a dish; course (of a meal); ~ al tegame stir-fry ~ del giorno daily special; ~ fondo soup bowl
piazza square
piazzola di sosta rest area
piccante spicy
picchetto tent stake (camping)
picchiare to hit, strike, beat up
piccolo small
piede *m* foot
pieno full; fare il pieno to fill up the tank
pietanza dish
pietra stone
pigro lazy
pillola tablet; pillole anticoncezionali contraceptive pills
ping-pong *m* ping-pong
pinne swim fins
pinzette tweezers
pioggia rain
piombatura filling
piovoso rainy
piroscafo steamship
piscina swimming pool; ~ per bambini wading pool
piselli *m pl* peas
pista di fondo cross-country skiing
pista per pattinaggio su ghiaccio skating rink
pittore/pittrice painter

pittura painting;
~ a olio oil painting;
~ di acquerello watercolor;
~ in seta silk painting;
~ su vetro glass painting

più more; plus; ~ che/di more than; ~ tardi later

piuttosto *(adv.)* rather

pizzo lace (fabric)

platea orchestra (theater)

pneumatico tire; pneumatici da neve snow tires

poco little; un po' some, a little

poi then; afterward

poiché since

polio(mielite) *f* polio

polizia police

pollo chicken

polmone *m* lung

polmonite *f* pulmonitis

polso pulse

polvere *f* dust; powder

pomata salve; ~ per le bruciature burn cream

pomeriggio afternoon

pomodori *m pl* tomatoes

pompa d'aria air pump

pompa della benzina gas pump

pompieri *m pl* firemen

ponte *m* bridge

pontile *m* footbridge

popolo people

popone *m* melon

porcellana porcelain

porgere to offer; to give

porro leek

porta door

portacenere *m* ashtray

portale *m* portal

portamonete *m* wallet

portar via to take away

portare to bring, carry; ~ gli occhiali to wear glasses; ~ con sé to bring along

portarsi dietro to take

portata course (foods), food

portiere *m* porter; doorman

porto port

portone *m* gate

porzione *f* portion

posacenere *m* ashtray

posate place setting

positivo positive

possibile possible

possibilità possibility

posta centrale central post office

posteggio di taxi taxi stand

posteggio per handicappati handicap parking

posto place, location; area; seat; ~ al finestrino window seat

potere to be able; may

povero poor

pranzo lunch

praticare il surfing to surf

pratico practical

prato lawn, meadow; ~ per sdraiarsi sunbathing lawn

preavviso appointment

precedenza priority, right of way

preciso precise

preferire to prefer

prefisso prefix, area code

pregare to pray, beg

premio prize, reward

prendere to take; get; to use; (transportation) andare a prendere to pick up

prenotare to book, reserve

prenotazione *f* reservation, booking

preoccuparsi to worry; ~ **di** to worry about

preparare to prepare, ready

presa electrical socket; ~ **di corrente** switch

prescrivere to prescribe

presente, essere ~ to be present

presidi *m pl* **ortopedici** orthopedic aids

presentare to present; ~ **(qd a qd)** to introduce (people)

presentazione *f* presentation

preservativo preservative; condom

prestare to loan; ~ **qc da qd** to borrow something from someone

presto *(adv)* quickly; soon; early; **al più ~ possibile** as soon as possible

prete *m* priest

prevendita advance booking

previsioni *f pl* **metereologiche** weather forecast

prezzemolo parsley

prezzo price (money); ~ **del biglietto d'ingresso** admission price; ~ **del biglietto** ticket price; ~ **forfettario** flat rate; ~ **forfettario per la corrente** cost of electricity; ~ **per chilometro** price per kilometer

prigione *f* prison

prima earlier, previously; at first; ~ **di** before; ~ **colazione** *f* breakfast

prima/primo first

primavera *f* spring (season)

principale *(adj.)* principal; *(adv.)* **principalmente** mainly

principale *m* boss

privato private

privo di sensi unconscious

probabile *(adj)* probable

probabilmente *(adv)* probably

problema *m* problem; question

processione *f* procession

procura power of attorney

procurare to obtain, provide

prodotto product, result

professione *f* profession

profilattico condom

profondo deep

profumeria perfumery

profumo perfume

progetto project, plan

programma *m* program

proibire to forbid

prolunga extension cord

promettere to promise

pronto ready, prepared; hello (telephone); ~ **soccorso** first aid

pronunciare to pronounce

proposta proposal

proprietario owner

proprio own; ~ **ora** for a second (time)

prosciutto ham; ~ **cotto** boiled ham; ~ **crudo** uncooked ham

prospetto prospect

prossimo next

proteggi-slip *m pl* panty liners

protesi *f* prosthesis

protestare to protest

protezione *f* **solare** sunscreen

prova test; evidence

provenire (da) to come from

provvisorio temporary

provvista provision, supply

prugne plums

pub *m* bar, pub

pubblico public

pulire to clean, polish

pulito clean

pulizia finale final cleaning

pullover *m* pullover
pungere to prick
punta point
punto point; ~ culminante high point
puntuale *(adj.)* punctual; **puntualmente** *(adv.)* punctually
puntura shot (injection)
pure also; even
purtroppo unfortunately
pus *m* pus
puzzare to stink

Q

quadro painting
qualcosa something
qualcuno someone
quale which
qualità quality; characteristic
quando when; *(conj.)* then; when; as
quantità quantity
quartiere *m* precinct
quasi around, about
quella that *(f)*
quello that *(m)*
questa this *(f)*
questo this *(m)*
qui here

R

rabbia anger
racchetta tennis racket
raccogliere to collect, gather

raccolta collection
raccomandare to recommend
raccomandata registered letter
raccontare to tell
radiatore *m* radiator
radio *f* radio
radiografare to X-ray
radiografia radiology
raffica di vento gust of wind
raffreddore da fieno *m* hay fever
raffreddore *m* cold
ragazza girl
ragazzo boy
raggiungere to achieve
ragione *f* reason, judgment; aver ~ to be right
rallegrarsi di to be happy about
rammendare to mend
rampa entrance/exit ramp
rapidamente *(adv.)* quickly, fast
rapido *(adj.)* quick, fast
rapporto report, reference
rappresentazione *f* representation; presentation (theater)
raro *(adj.)* rare, uncommon
raramente *(adv.)* rarely
rasoio razor *(electric ~)*
re/regina king/queen
reale real
recapitare to forward
recentemente recently
reception *f* reception
recipiente *m* container
reclamare to complain; ~ per to complain about
reclamo complaint
regalare to give (as a gift)
regalino small present; souvenir
regalo gift
reggiseno bra
regia direction

regime *m* diet
regione *f* region, area
regolamento regulation
regolare to regulate
regolare *(adj.)* regular;
  regolarmente *(adv.)* regularly
relazione *f* connection
religione *f* religion
remare to row
remo oar
render possibile to make
  possible
rendere to return, give back
rene *m* kidney
reparto department
reperto archeologico
  archeological find
respirare to breathe
respiratore *m* snorkel
responsabile responsible
restare to be left
resti *m pl* remains
restituire to give back; to bring
  back
rete *f* net
retroterra *m* back country
reumatismi *m pl* rheumatism
ricci *m pl* curls
ricco rich; abundant
ricetta recipe; prescription
ricevere to receive
ricevitore *m* receiver
ricevuta receipt
ricompensa recompense, reward
ricordare a qd qc to remind
  someone of something;
  ricordarsi to remember
ridare to give back
ridere to laugh
ridicolo ridiculous
riduzione *f* reduction; ~ per
  bambini children's discount
riempire to fill

rientro return
riferire relate; refer; report
rifiutare to refuse; deny
rifiutarsi to refuse
rifornire di to supply with
rifugio shelter
riga part (in hair)
rigattiere *m* second-hand dealer
riguardo care; senza ~
  carelessly
rimandare to postpone (time); to
  send back
rimanere to stay; to be left over
rimessa remittance; garage
rimettersi to recuperate
rimorchiare to tow
rinascimento Renaissance
rinfreschi refreshments
rinfresco refreshment
ringraziare to thank
riparare to repair
ripetere to repeat
ripido steep
ripieno full
riportare to bring back
riposarsi to rest,
riposo rest
risarcimento compensation
risarcire to compensate
  (damages)
riscaldamento heat; ~
  centrale central heating
riscaldare to warm up, heat
rischio risk
riserva di caccia hunting
  preserve
riservare to reserve
riso rise
risolvere to resolve
rispondere to answer;
  respond; ~ al telefono to answer
  the phone
risultato result

ritardare to become late
ritardo delay
ritornare to return
ritorno return
ritratto portrait
rivendita di prodotti alcolici liquor store
rivista magazine
roccia cliff, rock
rock m skirt
rollerblades m pl roller blades
romanzo novel
rosa rose
rosmarino rosemary
rosolia measles
rossetto lipstick
rosso red
rotocalco magazine
rotondo round
rotto broken
roulotte f trailer
rovina ruin
rubare to steal
rubinetto faucet
rumore m noise; sound
rumoroso noisy, loud
ruolo principale leading role
ruota wheel; ~ di scorta spare tire
russare to snore

sala hall; room; ~ d'aspetto waiting room; ~ d'attesa passeggeri gate; ~ da pranzo dining room; ~ per la colazione breakfast room
salame m salami
saldo steady
sale m salt
saliera saltshaker
salire to get on
salita ascent, slope
salsa sauce
salsicce sausage
saltare to jump
salutare to greet
salvagente m life preserver
salvare to save
salvia sage
sandali m pl sandals
sandalo da mare bathing shoes
sandalo da spiaggia beach shoes
sangue m blood
sanguinare to bleed
sano healthy
santo saint
sapere m knowledge; to know; to know how; ~ di to smell like; to taste like
sapone m soap
sarto/sarta tailor
sassoso stony
sauna sauna
sazio full
sbagliarsi to be mistaken
sbagliato mistaken
sbaglio mistake, error
sbocco outlet (of river)
sbrigare to expedite
scala ladder; stair
scaldabiberon m bottle warmer
scalo stopover
scambiare to exchange

S

sabato Saturday
sacchetto bag; ~ di plastica plastic bag
sacco delle immondizie trash bag
sagra festival

scambio exchange
scapolo bachelor
scappamento exhaust
scarpa shoe
scarpe *f pl* **da ginnastica** athletic shoes
scarponi *m pl* **da sci** ski boots
scassinare to break open
scatola box; can
scatto shutter release
scavi *m pl* excavations
scegliere to choose, select
scelta choice, selection
scemo stupid
scendere to get off
scherzo joke; fun
schiena back
schiuma da barba shaving cream
sci *m* ski
sci *m pl* **nautica** water ski(ing)
sciacquone *m* flush
scialle *m* shawl
scialuppa di salvataggio lifeboat
sciare to ski
sciarpa shawl
sciatica sciatica
sciovia ski tow
scippatore *m* pickpocket
sciroppo (contro la tosse) cough syrup
scodella soup bowl
scompartimento compartment; ~ **per fumatori** smoking section; ~ **per non fumatori** non-smoking section
sconosciuto unknown; unfamiliar
sconsiderato inconsiderate; thoughtless
sconto discount
scontro collision

scopo goal; purpose
scoprire to discover
scorciatoia shortcut (route)
scorrere to flow
scottatura (solare) sunburn
scrivere to write
scrosci *m pl* **di pioggia** rain shower
scultore *m* sculptor
scultura sculpture
scuola school; ~ **di equitazione** riding school
scuro dark
scusa pardon, apology
scusare to excuse; **scusarsi** to excuse oneself
sdraiarsi to lie down
sé oneself
se if; whether
seccante boring
secco dry
secolo century
secondo second *(adj. and noun)*
secondo/a second
sedano celery
sede *f* headquarters
sedere to sit
sedersi to sit down
sedia chair; ~ **a rotelle** wheelchair
sedile *m* **auto per bambini** children's car cushion
seggiolino auto children's car seat; ~ **per bebè** infant seat (for car); ~ **per la bicicletta** child's seat (for bicycle)
seggiovia chair lift
segnalatore d'incendio *m* fire alarm
segnale *m* signal; sign
segnavia *m* signpost
segno sign

segreteria telefonica telephone answering machine

segreto secret; secretive

seguire to follow; pursue

self-service *m* self-service

selvaggio wild

selvatico wild (vegetables)

semaforo traffic light

semplice simple

sempre always

senape *f* mustard

sensibilità del film film speed

senso sense

sentiero (per escursioni) hiking path, trail

sentiero footpath

sentimento feeling

sentire to feel; to hear; to smell

senza without; ~ barriere architettoniche barrier-free; ~ impegno without obligation; ~ riguardo thoughtless

separare to separate

seppia cuttlefish

sequestrare to detain, confiscate

sera evening; la sera in the evening

serata folcloristica evening of folk entertainment

serbatoio tank

serio serious

serpente *m* snake

serratura lock

servire to serve; wait on

servirsi to help oneself

servizi *m pl* igienici bathrooms, toilets

servizio service; ~ assistenza care; ~ assistenza sociale social services center; ~ di trasporto transportation service; ~ pulman shuttle bus

sesso sex; gender

seta silk

settembre September

setticemia blood poisoning

settimana week; durante la ~ during the week; ~ supplementare week's extension

settimanale *(adj.)* weekly

sfacciato impudent

sfortuna misfortune

sforzarsi to strive, endeavor

sforzo exertion; effort

sgombro mackerel

sgridare to scold

sguardo glance

shampoo *m* shampoo

shorts *m pl* shorts

show *m* show

si *(indef. pron.)* one; *(refl. pron.)* oneself

sì yes, indeed

sicurezza security

sicuro *(adj.)* secure

sigaretta cigarette

sigaretto cigarillo

sigaro cigar

significato meaning, sense

signora lady; Mrs.

signore *m* gentleman; Mr.

signore *f pl* ladies

signori gentlemen

signorina young lady

silenzio silence; quiet

silenzioso silent; quiet

sillabare to spell

silografia woodcut

simile similar

simpatico nice

singolo single

sinistro/sinistra left; a sinistra left, to the left

sinusite *f* sinusitis

siringa syringe

sistema *m* **d'allarme** alarm system

situazione *f* situation; position

skate-board *m* skateboard

slip *m* briefs; panties

slitta sled

slogato dislocated, sprained

smalto nail polish

smarrirsi to get lost

smettere to stop

snello thin; slender

snorkel *m* snorkel

sobborgo suburb

sobrio sober; moderate

soccorso stradale roadside assistance

soddisfatto satisfied; pleased

soffitto ceiling

soggetto a dazio doganale subject to customs duties

soggiorno stay; living room

sogliola sole (fish)

sogno dream

solario solarium

sole *m* sun

soleggiato sunny

solista *m/f* soloist

solitario solitary

solito customary; usual; di solito usually

solo alone; only; just

soltanto only

soluzione *f* **elettrolitica** electrolyte solution

solvente *m* **per smalto** nail polish remover

somma amount, total

sonniferi *m pl* sleeping pills

sopportare to bear; support; endure

sopra on; over; above

sordastro hearing impaired

sordo deaf

sordomuto deaf mute

sorella sister

sorgente *f* source

sorpassare to pass

sorpreso surprised

sorvegliare to watch over

sostanza dolcificante sweetener

sostegno handle

sostituire to replace

sottile thin; slender

sotto under; underneath; beneath

sottopassaggio subway

sottotitolo subtitle

spago string

spalla shoulder

spargisale *m* saltshaker

sparire to disappear

spaventare to frighten

spaventoso frightful

spazio room, space

spazzatura trash, dirt

spazzola brush; ~ da scarpe shoe brush; ~ per le stoviglie dishwashing brush

spazzolino da denti toothbrush

specchietto retrovisore rearview mirror

specchio mirror

speciale special; particular

specialità specialty

specie *f* type

spedizione *f* **bagagli** baggage check-in

spegnere to turn off; extinguish

spendere to spend

sperare to hope

spesa purchase; fare la ~ to go shopping

spese *f pl* expenses, costs; ~ accessorie added expenses

spesso *(adj.)* thick; strong; *(adv.)* often, frequently

spettacolo performance, show

spettatore *m* spectator

spezie *f pl* spice

spiacente, essere ~ di to be sorry

spiacevole unpleasant, disagreeable

spiaggia beach; ~ **per nudisti** nudist beach

spiccioli *m pl* change

spilla brooch

spillo di sicurezza safety pin

spina fish bone; plug; ~ **di adattamento** adaptor plug; ~ **dorsale** spinal column

spinaci *m pl* spinach

spinta shove, push

spirito industriale methylated spirits

sponda bank (of river, etc.)

sporcizia dirt

sporco dirty

sport *m* sport

sport del deltaplano hang gliding

sportello accettazione bagagli baggage window

sportello automatico ATM

sportello biglietti ticket window

sportivo/sportiva athlete

sposare to marry; sposato (con), sposato (con) married (to)

sposato *(man)*/**sposata** *(woman)* married

spuntino snack

squadra sports team

squisito delicious

stadio stadium

stagione *(f)* season

stampella crutch

stanco tired

stanza room; ~ **della televisione** TV room

stanzino da bagno washroom

stare (in piedi) to stand; stare attento (a) to pay attention (to)

stato state; condition

statua statue

statura stature

stazione *f* railroad station; ~ **a monte** summit station; ~ **a valle** bottom station; ~ **centrale** main railroad station; ~ **degli autobus** bus station; ~ **di servizio** rest area

stecca rail

stella star

stendibiancheria *m* clothes rack

stesso self; lo ~ the same; fa lo ~ it doesn't matter

steward *m* steward

stile *m* style; ~ **liberty** Art Nouveau

stimare to value

stiramento pull (muscle)

stirare to iron

stitichezza constipation

stivali *m pl* boots; ~ **di gomma** rubber boots

stoffa stuff; fabric

stomaco stomach

storia story

stoviglie *f pl* dishes

straccio per lavare i piatti dishrag

strada street; road; route; per la ~ on the way; ~ **principale** main road; ~ **provinciale** country road; ~ **secondaria** secondary road

straniera foreigner; stranger *(f)*

straniero stranger; foreigner *(m)*

straordinario extraordinary
strappare to tear
strappo dei legamenti torn ligament
stretto narrow, tight
stringa per scarpe shoelace
studiare to study
studio studio
stufato stewed
stupido stupid
stupro rape
stuzzicadenti *m* toothpick
su on; over; above; in su upward; **sul Tevere** on the Tiber
sù upstairs
sua *(poss adj.)* his, her
subito immediately; right away
succedere to happen, take place
succhietto pacifier
succo d'arancia orange juice
succoso juicy
sud *m* south a ~ di south of
sudare to sweat
sufficiente sufficient
suggerimento suggestion
suo *(poss adj.)* his, her
suola sole
suolo floor, ground
suonare to sound; to ring
suora sister; nun
superiore *m/f* boss; *(adj.)* higher, better
supermercato supermarket
superstrada high-speed road
supplementare additional
supplemento supplement
supposta suppository
sveglia alarm clock
svegliare to awaken
svegliarsi to wake up
sveglio awake
svendita liquidation sale
svenimento fainting fit

sviluppare to develop

T

tabaccaio tobacco store
tabacco tobacco
tacco heel
tacere to be silent
tachimetro tachometer
tagliare to cut
taglio scalato layer cut
tailleur *m* suit
tamponi *m pl* tampons
tanica can
tanto so much; so; ~ ... quanto just as ... as
tardare to delay; to hesitate
tardi late
targa number plate; ~ di nazionalità national ID sticker
tariffe *f pl* doganali customs duties
tasca pocket (in clothing)
tassa per controlli di sicurezza security tax
tasse *pl* tax, duty
tassista *m/f* taxi driver
tavola del wind-surf wind-surfing board
tavolo table
tazza cup
te *(accentuated form)* you; a te to/for you
tè *m* tea
teatro theater
teatro-danza dance theater
Inghilterra England inglese English
telefonare to telephone, call

telefonata phone call; ~ urbana local call
telefonino cell phone
telefono telephone; ~ cordless portable phone; ~ d'emergenza emergency phone; ~ in camera phone in room
telegramma *m* telegram
teleobiettivo telephoto lens
televisore *m* television
temere to fear; be afraid of
temperatura temperature
temperino pocket knife
tempesta storm
tempio temple
tempo time; weather; in ~ *(adv.)* on time
tenda tent
tenere to hold; ~ a mente qc to keep something in mind
tenero tender; soft
tennis *m* tennis
tentare to attempt
tenuta estate; property
tergicristallo windshield wiper
termine *(m)* terminal; end
termometro thermometer
terra earth; land
terracotta terra-cotta
terraferma solid ground
terrazza terrace
terreno land; ground; field; ~ di gioco playing field
terribile terrible
terrina tureen
terzo third, thirdly
tesoro treasure
tessera smart card; ~ di campeggio camping pass
tesserino di riconoscimento per portatori di handicap handicap ID
testa head

testimone *m* witness
tetano tetanus
tettarella nipple
tetto roof; ~ apribile sunroof
thrilling thriller
ti to/for you; you
tibia shin
tifo typhus
timbro stamp
timido timid
timo thyme
timpano eardrum; tympanum
tingere to dye, tint
tinta, a ~ unita all one color
tintura di iodio tincture of iodine
tipico (per) typical (of)
tirare to pull, draw
toast *m* toast
toccare to touch
toilette *f* toilets; ~ per handicappati handicap toilets
tollerare to tolerate, endure
tomba grave
tonalità tonality; shade
tonno tuna fish
tono tone
tonsille *f pl* tonsils
tonsillite *f* tonsillitis
torbido turbid (liquid)
tornare indietro to turn around, go back
torre *f* tower
torta cake
tosse *f* cough
tostapane *m* toaster
tostato roasted
tovaglia tablecloth
tovagliolo napkin
tovagliolino di carta paper napkin
tra between, among
tradurre to translate

traffico traffic
tragedia play, tragedy
traghetto ferry
trainare to drag
tram *m* streetcar
tranne except
tranquillizzarsi to quiet down
tranquillo calm
trasferimento transfer
trasmissione *f* transmission, (radio, television), broadcast
trattare to treat
trattenersi to stay, remain
tratto period, distance
traveller's chèque *m* traveler's check
treno train; ~ locale local train; ~ traghetto auto-express
treppiedi *m* tripod
triangolo warning triangle
tribunale *m* court (justice)
triste sad
troppo too; too much; *(with adj.)* too
trovare to find; trovarsi to feel
tu you
tubo di scarico exhaust pipe
tumefazione *f* swelling
tumore *m* tumor
tunnel *m* tunnel
tuo, il tuo Yours truly
turchese turquoise
turista *m/f* tourist
tutela dei monumenti monument protection
tuttavia however
tutti i giorni every day
tutto *(adj.)* completely; all; everything; tutte/tutti everyone

ubriacarsi to get drunk
ubriaco drunk
uccello bird
udito hearing
ufficiale official
ufficio office; ~ oggetti smarriti lost and found ~ postale post office
uguale same
ulcera ulcer
ultimo last
umido humid
un/uno/una one, a
uncino hook
unico only
università university
uomo person, man
uova egg
urgente urgent
urina urine
usare to use; employ; make use of
uscire to go out, exit
uscita exit; ~ d'emergenza emergency exit
ustione *f* burning
usuale usual
utensile *m* tool
uva *f* grape

vacanze *f pl* vacation
vaccinazione *f* vaccination
vaglia *m* postale postal money order
vagone *m* bagagli baggage car

vagone *m* **ristorante** dining car

valido valid; essere ~ to be valid, in force

valigia suitcase

valle *f* valley

valore *m* value; senza valore worthless; valore dichiarato declared value

valuta currency; value

valute *f pl* estere currency

valvola (di sicurezza) fuse (elec.)

vantaggio advantage; benefit

variabile variable

varicella chicken pox

varietà *m* variety show

vasca da bagno bathtub

vasca per bambini kiddy pool, wading pool

vasellame *m* china

vaso vase

vecchio old

vedere to see

vedovo widower; vedova widow

vegetariano vegetarian

veleggiata sailing

veleno poison

velenoso poisonous

veloce *(adj.)* quick, fast

velocemente *(adv.)* quickly

velocità speed; quickness

vendere to sell

vendita sale

venerdì Friday

venire to come; ~ a sapere to learn, find out

ventilatore *m* ventilator

vento wind

ventre *m* belly

veramente *(adv.)* really

verde green

verdura vegetables

verme *(m)* worm

vero true, real, authentic

versione *f* **originale** original version

verso toward; around; ~ mezzogiorno around noon

vertigini *f pl* dizziness

vescica blister

vespa wasp

vestito dress

vetrina display window

vetrocromia glass painting

vi you

via street; way; gone, away

viaggiare to travel; ~ in autostop to hitchhike

viaggiatore/viaggiatrice traveler

viaggio journey; trip; ~ di ritorno return trip

vicino(a) near; close; beside; vicino/vicina neighbor

vicolo alley

videocamera camcorder, video camera

videocassetta videocassette

videofilm *m* video film

videoregistratore *m* video recorder

vietato prohibited

vigile/vigilessa traffic policeman

vigili *m pl* del fuoco firemen

vigna, vigneto vineyard

villa villa

villaggio village; ~ di montagna mountain town; ~ di pescatori fishing village

vincere to conquer, win

vincita victory

vino wine; ~ bianco white wine; ~ rosso red wine

viola violet

violenza(carnale) rape
virus *m* virus
visita visit; ~ guidata tour
visitare to visit; to look around; *(med.)* to examine
vista sight; view
visto visa
vita life
vite *f* screw
vitto catering
vivace lively
vivere to live
voce *f* voice
voglia desire; avere voglia di to feel like
voi you *(2nd pers. pl .subj. pron.; dir. obj. pron., stressed form);* a voi *(indir. obj. pron. stressed form)*
volano badminton
volare to fly
volentieri gladly, willingly
volere to wish
volo flight; ~ a vela gliding; ~ internazionale international flight; ~ nazionale domestic flight
volt *m* volt
volta time; una ~ once, one time
voltaggio voltage
volte, a ~ sometimes
vostro your
vulcano volcano
vuoto empty

W

watt *m* watt
western western
wurstel *m pl* sausage

Y

yoga *m* yoga

Z

zafferano saffron
zaino backpack
zanzara mosquito
zona zone, region; ~ di protezione degli uccelli bird sanctuary; zona pedonale pedestrian zone
zoo *m* zoo
zucca pumpkin
zucchero sugar

English–Italian Glossary

A

A, an, one un/uno (una)
A few alcuni
A little un po' (di)
Abbey abbazia
Abbreviation abbreviazione *f*
Abortion aborto
About circa
Above sopra, su
Abscess ascesso
Absolutely *(adv)* assolutamente
Absorbent cotton cotone *m* idrofilo
To accept *(invitation)* accettare
Acceptance accettazione *f*
Access ramp rampa
Accessibility accessibilità
Accident incidente *m*
To acclimatize acclimatarsi
To accompany accompagnare
Account conto
Acquaintance *(person)* conoscente *fm*
Acquaintanceship conoscenza
Across from di fronte
Act atto
Action film film d'azione
Actor, actress attore/attrice
Adaptor adattatore *m*
Adaptor plug spina di adattamento
To add aggiungere
Address indirizzo
Administration autorità

Administration amministrazione *f*
Administrative service ufficio, ente *m*
To admire ammirare
Admission entrata, ingresso; Admission ticket biglietto d'ingresso; Entry price prezzo del biglietto d'ingresso
Adriatic Adriatico
Adult adulto/adulta
Advance reservation preavviso
Advance sale prevendita
Advantage vantaggio
Advice consiglio
To advise consigliare
Aerobics aerobica
Affectionate tenero, affettuoso
After poi, dopo
After-shave lozione *f* dopobarba
Afternoon pomeriggio
Again di nuovo
Against contro
Age età
Agency agenzia
Ago fa; ten minutes ago dieci minuti fa
Agree mettersi d'accordo
To agree accordarsi su; intendersi
Air aria
Air conditioning aria condizionata
Air mattress materasso pneumatico

Air pump pompa d'aria
Airline compagnia aerea
Airport aeroporto
Airport bus collegamento pullman con l'aeroporto
Airport taxes i diritti aeroportuali
Alarm clock sveglia
Alarm system sistema *m* d'allarme
Alcohol free analcolico; alcohol-free beer birra analcolica
All tutti, tutte
Allergy allergia
Alley vicolo
To allow permettere
Allowed ammesso
Almonds mandorle *f pl*
Almost quasi
Alone solo
Alone unico
Already già
Also pure
Altar altare *m*
Although benché
Aluminum foil carta argentata
Always sempre
Ambulance auto-ambulanza
American *(adj.)* americano
American person americano
Among tra, fra
Amount importo, somma
Amphitheater anfiteatro
To amuse oneself divertirsi
Amusement park parco divertimenti
Amusement park parco dei divertimenti
And e
Anesthesia anestesia
Anger rabbia
Angina angina

Angry adirato, arrabbiato
Animal animale *m*
Animal preserve riserva per animali selvaggi
Animated film cartoni *m pl* animati
Ankle malleolo
To announce *(information)* annunciare
Annual *(adj)* annuale; Annually *(adv)* annualmente
To answer rispondere
Answering machine segreteria telefonica
Antibiotic antibiotico
Antifreeze antigelo
Antique antico
Antique shop negozio di antichità
Apartment appartamento
Appendicitis appendicite *f*
Appetite appetito
Appetizer antipasto
Applause applauso
Apples mele
Appointment termine *m*, data; *(doctor's, business)* appuntamento
To approach avvicinarsi
Apricots albicocche
April aprile
Arch arco
Archeology archeologia
Architect architetto
Architecture architettura
Arena arena
Armchair sedia
Around intorno a; verso; At *(time)* alle; at this time a quest'ora
Around circa, quasi
Around noon verso mezzogiorno
To arrange sbrigare
To arrange fare

241

To arrange fissare
To arrest arrestare
Arrival arrivo
Arrival day giorno d'arrivo
Arrival time orario d'arrivo
To arrive arrivare
Art arte, *f*
Art dealer commerciante *m* in oggetti d'arte
Art nouveau lo stile liberty
Artichokes carciofi *m pl*
As *(comparison)* come, quanto
As well neppure
Ashtray portacenere *m*, posacenere *m*
To ask domandare
To ask someone for advice chiedere un consiglio a qd
To ask someone for something chiedere qc a qd
Asparagus asparagi *m pl*
Aspirin aspirina
Assault assalto
Assistance servizio assistenza
Association associazione *f*
Asthma asma *m/f*
At first prima
At home a casa
At least per lo meno
At least almeno
At most al massimo
At noon a mezzogiorno
At that time allora
Athlete sportivo/sportiva
Athletic field campo sportivo
Athletic shoes scarpe *f pl* da ginnastica
ATM cassa automatica prelievi, bancomat *m*, sportello automatico
Attempt prova
Attention attenzione *f*
August agosto
Authentic vero, autentico

Auto registration libretto di circolazione
Automatic automatico; *(adv)* automaticamente
Automatic door opener apriporta automatico
Automatic ticket puncher obliteratore *m*
Automatic transmission cambio automatico
Automobile auto *f*, macchina
Autumn autunno
Average *(adj.)* medio; *(on the average)* in media
Avocado avocado *m*
To avoid evitare
Awake sveglio
To awaken svegliare
Away via

Baby neonato
Baby intercom babyfon *m*
Baby seat *(for car)* seggiolino auto per bebè
Baby's bottle biberon *m*
Babysitter baby-sitter *m/f*
Bachelor scapolo
Back schiena
Back indietro
Back country retroterra *m*
Back pain dolore *m* alla schiena
Backpack zaino
Backwards all'indietro
Bad *(adj)* cattivo; *(weather)* brutto
Badly male
Badminton badminton *m*, gioco del volano

Bag sacchetto
Bag borsa
Baggage bagaglio
Baggage cart vagone *m* bagagli
Baggage consignment consegna del bagaglio
Baggage locker deposito a cassette
Baggage registration spedizione *f* bagagli
Baggage window sportello accettazione bagagli
Baked goods biscotti *m pl*, paste *f pl*
Bakery panificio
Balcony balcone *m*
Ball palla, pallone *m*; *(party)* ballo
Ballet balletto
Ballpoint pen biro *f*
Bananas banane
Band complesso
Band-aid cerotto
Bandage benda
To bandage fasciare
Bangs frangetta
Bank banca
Bar night *m*
To bargain mercanteggiare
Baroque barocco
Barrier free senza barriere architettoniche
Basil basilico
Basket cesto
Basketball Basketball *m*, pallacanestro
Bathing cap cuffia
Bathing suit costume *m* da bagno
Bathing trunks costume *m* da bagno
Bathroom bagno
Bathtub vasca da bagno
Battery batteria

Bay golfo
To be essere
To be able potere
To be accustomed to essere abituato
To be against essere contrario
To be called chiamarsi
To be cold aver freddo
To be fine/well andare/stare bene
To be friends essere amici/amiche
To be from derivare, provenire (da)
To be happy about essere contento di
To be hungry essere affamato
To be in favor of essere favorevole
To be lacking mancare
To be left over rimanere, restare
To be located giacere
To be mistaken sbagliarsi
To be obliged essere obbligato
To be quiet tacere
To be right aver ragione
To be right essere giusto
To be seasick avere il mal di mare
To be thirsty essere assetato
To be valid essere valido
Beach spiaggia
Beach robe accappatoio
Beach sandals sandali *m pl* da mare
Beach shoes sandali *m pl* da spiaggia
Beach volleyball beach-volley *m*
Beans fagioli *m pl*
Beard barba
To beat up picchiare

243

Beautiful bello
Because perché
Because of a causa di
To become diventare
To become interested interessarsi (a qd, diqc)
Bed letto; to go to bed andare a letto
Bed linen biancheria da letto
Bedridden bisognoso di cure
Bedroom camera da letto
Bedside lamp abat-jour *m*
Bee ape *f*
Beef carne *f* di manzo
Beer birra
Before *(physically)* davanti a; *(time)* prima di
To begin cominciare, iniziare
Beginning/start inizio
Behind dietro
Beige beige
To believe pensare, credere
Bell campanello
To belong appartenere
Below al di sotto di
Belt cintura
Bench panchina
Best migliore *f, m*
Better meglio
Between tra, fra
Bicycle bicicletta
Big grande
Bike helmet casco di protezione
Bike path pista ciclabile, ciclopista
Bike seat *(for child)* seggiolino per la bicicletta
Bike tour itinerario in bici(cletta)
Bikini bikini *m*
Bill conto
Bill, banknote banconota
Bird uccello

Bird sanctuary zona di protezione degli uccelli
Birthday compleanno
Bistro locale *m*, pub *m*
To bite mordere
Bitter amaro
Black nero
Black and white film *(for camera)* pellicola in bianco e nero; *(movie)* film ~
Blackberries more
Bladder vescica
Blanket coperta
Blazer blazer *m*
To bleed sanguinare
Blind person's cane bastone *m* per ciechi
Blond biondo
Blood sangue *m*
Blood alcohol level limite *m* (massimo consentito) di alcol nel sangue
Blood poisoning setticemia
Blood type gruppo sanguigno
Bloody nose emorragia nasale
To bloom fiorire
Blouse camicetta
To blow dry asciugare con il fon
Blue blu
Blues blues *m*
Boarding gate sala d'attesa passeggeri
Boarding pass carta d'imbarco
Boating license patente *f* nautica
Body body *m*
Body corpo
Bodybuilding culturismo
Boiled bollito, cotto
Boiled ham prosciutto cotto
Bone osso
Book libro

Booklet of tickets biglietto a più obliterazioni
Bookshop libreria
Booth cabina
Boots stivali *m pl*
Border frontiera
Border crossing valico di frontiera
Boring noioso
Boring seccante
Born nato
To borrow prestare qc da qd
Boss capo *m*, superiore *m/f*, principale *m/f*
Botanical garden giardino botanico
Both tutti e due
To bother infastidire
Bottle bottiglia
Bottle opener apribottiglie *m*
Bottle warmer scaldabiberon *m*
Bouquet mazzo
Boutique boutique *f*
Bowel movement evacuazione *f*
Bowl terrina, insalatiera
Bowling bowling *m*
Box *(theater)* palco
Boy ragazzo
Bra reggiseno
Bracelet braccialetto
Brain cervello
Braised brasato
Braised stufato
Brake freno
Brake fluid olio per freni
Brake lights luci *f pl* di arresto
Bread pane *m*
Breadth larghezza
Break *(bone)* frattura
To break open forzare, scassinare
Breakdown guasto, panne *f*

Breakdown assistance soccorso stradale
Breakfast colazione *f*, prima colazione
Breakfast buffet buffet *m* della colazione
Breakfast room sala per la colazione
Breakwater molo
To breathe respirare
Bridge ponte *m*
To bring portare con sé
To bring portare
To bring back riportare, restituire
Broadcast *(radio, television)* trasmissione *f*
Broken rotto
Broken bone frattura ossea
Bronchi bronchi *m pl*
Bronchitis bronchite *f*
Bronze bronzo
Brooch spilla
Brother fratello
Brother-in-law cognato
Brown marrone; *(tanned)* abbronzato
To brown (gratinée) passare al forno, gratinare
Bruise contusione *f*
Brush spazzola
Building edificio, costruzione *f*
Bumper paraurti *m*
Bungalow bungalow *m*
Bungee jumping bungeejumping *m*
Bunk bed letto a castello
To burn bruciare
Burn ointment pomata per le bruciature
Burning ustione *f*
Bus autobus *m*

Bus station stazione *f* degli autobus
Bush cespuglio
Business hours orario d'apertura (al pubblico)
Busy season alta stagione *f*
But ma
Butcher shop macelleria
Butter burro
To buy comprare
By da
By chance per caso
By means of per, con
Bypass bypass *m*
Bypass circonvallazione *f*
Byzantine bizantino

C

Cabaret cabaret *m*
Cabbage cavolo
Cable car funivia, funicolare *f*
Café caffè *m*
Cake dolce *m*, torta
To calculate calcolare
Calculator calcolatore *m* tascabile
To call chiamare
Calling card carta telefonica
Calm bonaccia
To calm oneself tranquillizzarsi
Camcorder videocamera
Camera macchina fotografica
Campground campeggio
Camping camping *m*, campeggio
Camping guide guida dei campeggi
Camping permit tessera di campeggio

Camping vehicle camper *m*
Can scatola
Can opener apriscatole *m*
Canal canale *m*
To cancel *(room reservation, travel tickets)* disdire
Cancer cancro
Candle candela
Candles candele
Canoe canoa
Cap berretto
Capital capitale *f*
Captain capitano
Car radio autoradio *f*
Car seat *(for child)* seggiolino auto
Carafe caraffa
Cardigan golf *m*
Careful attento
Carrots carote
Case cassa
Cash contanti *m pl*
Cash register cassa
Casino casinò
Cassette cassetta
Castle fortezza
Castle castello
Cat gatta *f*, gatto *m*
To catch prendere
Cathedral duomo
Cathedral cattedrale *f*
Cauliflower cavolfiore *m*
To cause causare
Cave grotta, caverna
CD/compact disk CD *m* (compact disc)
CD player lettore *m* CD
Ceiling soffitto
Celebration festa
Celery sedano
Cell phone cellulare *m*, telefonino
Cell phone telefono cordless

Cemetery cimitero
Center centro
Centimeter centimetro
Central centrale
Central heat riscaldamento centrale
Central post office posta centrale
Century secolo
Ceramics ceramica
Certain *(adj)* certo; *(adv)* certamente
Certificate certificato
Chain collana, catena
Chair sedia
Chairlift seggiovia
Chamber maid cameriera
Chamomile tea camomilla
Champagne champagne *m*
Change spiccioli *m pl*, moneta
To change cambiare
Change cambio; cambiamento; *(money)* moneta, spiccioli *m pl*
To change a ticket cambiare il biglietto
To change clothes cambiarsi
Changing of the guard cambio della guardia
Changing table fasciatoio
Channel canale *m*
Chapel cappella
Charcoal carbonella
Charger apparecchio carica-batterie
Charges tasse *pl*
Charges spese *f pl* (accessorie)
Charming incantevole
Cheap economico, a buon mercato
To check controllare
To check in fare il check-in
Cheese formaggio
Cherries ciliegie

Chest petto
Chewing gum gomma da masticare
Chick peas ceci *m pl*
Chicken pollo
Chicken pox varicella
Child bambino
Child care assistenza ai bambini
Childhood disease malattia infantile
Children's clothing abbigliamento per bambini
Children's discount riduzione *f* per bambini
Children's ticket biglietto per ragazzi
Child's bed lettino (per bambini)
Child's portion mezza porzione *f*
Chills brividi *m pl*
Chocolate cioccolata
Chocolate bar dolcetto di cioccolata
Choice scelta
Choir coro
Cholera colera *m*
To choose scegliere
Chop costoletta
Christianity cristianesimo
Church chiesa
Church tower campanile *m*
Cigar sigaro
Cigarette sigaretta
Cigarillo sigaretto
Circulatory troubles disturbi circolatori
City città
City bus autobus *m* urbano
City map pianta della città
Class classe *f*
Classic classico
Classical music musica classica
Classicism classicismo

247

Clay argilla, creta
Clean pulito
To clean pulire
Clear chiaro
Clearance sale svendita
Client cliente *(m,f)*
Climate clima *m*
Cloister chiostro
Close to vicino a
Closed chiuso
Closed season periodo di divieto di caccia
Cloth panno
Clothesline corda per stendere il bucato
Clothespin molletta (per stendere la biancheria)
Clothing abbigliamento
Cloud nuvola
Cloudy nuvoloso
Clove i chiodi di garofani
Clubhouse circolo, club *m*
Clutch frizione *f*
Coach *(bus)* autobus *m* interurbano
Coast costa
Coat cappotto, soprabito
Coat hanger gruccia (per i panni)
Coat room guardaroba *m*
Coconut noce *f* di cocco
Coffee caffè *m*
Coffee machine macchina del caffè
Cog railway cremagliera
Coin moneta
Cold freddo
Cold *(sickness)* raffreddore *m*, costipazione *f*
Cold water acqua fredda
Colic colica
Collarbone clavicola
Colleague collega *(f, m)*

To collect raccogliere
Collect call comunicazione *f* telefonica a carico del ricevente
Collision scontro, collisione *f*
Color tingere
Colored a colori
Colored pencil matita colorata
Coloring book album *m* da colorare, libro da colorare
Column colonna
Comb pettine *m*
To comb pettinare
To come venire
Come in! avanti!
Comedy commedia
Comfortable comodo, confortevole
Common *(adj)* comune
Common comune
To communicate comunicare
Communication comunicazione *f*
Companion accompagnatore, *m*, (-trice), *f*
Company ditta
To compare confrontare
Compartment scompartimento
Compass bussola
Compassion compassione *f*
Compatriot connazionale *f/m*
Compensation *(for damages)* risarcimento
Competition gara
To complain about lamentarsi di
To complain to someone about something lamentarsi con qd per qc
Complaint reclamo
Completely tutto
Composer compositore/ compositrice

Comprehensive insurance assicurazione *f* di totale copertura
Concert concerto
Concussion commozione *f* cerebrale
Condition stato, condizioni *f pl*
Condition condizione *f*
Condom preservativo, profilattico
Conductor controllore *m*
Confectioner's shop negozio di dolciumi
To confirm confermare
To confiscate sequestrare
To confuse scambiare
To congratulate congratularsi
Congratulations auguri *(m,pl)*, congratulazioni *(f,pl)*
Connection coincidenza
To consent aderire, acconsentire
To consist of essere costituito da
Constipation costipazione *f*, stitichezza
Construction site cantiere edile
Consulate consolato
Consumption consumo
Contact contatto
Contagious contagioso
Contain contenere
Container recipiente *m*
Contemporary contemporaneo
Contents contenuto
Contraceptive anticoncezionale *m*
Contract contratto
Contrary contrario; on the ~ al contrario
Contrary inverso
Convent convento
Conversation conversazione *f*
Converse conversare

Conversion conversione *f*
To convince convincere
Cook cuoco
To cook cucinare
Cookbook libro di cucina
Cookies biscotti *m pl*
Cool fresco
Coolant acqua di raffreddamento
Cooler borsa frigo
Copy copia
Corkscrew cavatappi *m*
Corn mais *m*, granturco
Corner angolo
Corridor corridoio
Corrupt corrotto
To cost costare
Costume jewelry bigiotteria
Cotton cotone *m*
Cotton swab i bastoncini igienici
Cough tosse *f*
Cough syrup sciroppo (contro la tosse)
To count contare
Country paese *m*
Country road strada provinciale
Couple *(people)* coppia
Coupon buono
Course corso; *(meal)* portata; *(food)* piatto, pietanza
Court tribunale *m; (nobility)* corte *f*
Courtyard cortile *m*
Cousin cugino/cugina
Crabs granchi *m pl*
Cramp crampo
Crazy pazzo
Cream crema
Creative creativo
Credit card carta di credito
Crew *(ship)* equipaggio
Crime delitto
To criticize criticare

Cross croce f
To cross attraversare
Cross-country ski track pista di fondo
Crossing passaggio
Crossroad incrocio
Crown corona
Cruise crociera
Crutch gruccia, stampella
To cry piangere
Crystal cristallo
Cucumber cetriolo
Culture cultura
Cumin cumino
Cup tazza
Cupboard armadio
Cupola cupola
Curious curioso
Curlers bigodini m pl
Curling curling m
Curls ricci m pl
Currency divise /valute f pl estere
Currency valuta
Current (elec.) corrente f (elettrica)
Curve curva
Customs dogana
Customs declaration dichiarazione f doganale
Customs duties tariffe f pl doganali
Cut ferita da taglio
To cut tagliare
To cut someone's hair pettinare
Cuttlefish seppia; calamaro
Cycling ciclismo

D

Daily special piatto del giorno
Damage danneggiare
Damage danno
Dance ballo, danza
To dance ballare
Dance band orchestra
Dance theater teatro-danza
Dancer ballerino/a
Dandruff forfora
Danger pericolo
Dangerous pericoloso
To dare osare
Dark scuro
Dark bread pane m nero
Date data
Date of birth data di nascita
Dates datteri m pl
Daughter figlia
Day giorno
Day after tomorrow dopo domani
Day before yesterday l'altro ieri
Day excursion gita di un giorno
Day pass (abbonamento) giornaliero
Day ticket biglietto giornaliero
Day trip marcia di un giorno
Dead morto
Deaf sordo, non udente
Deaf mute sordomuto
Dear caro
Dear (direct address) tesoro
Death morte f
Debt debito
December dicembre
To decide decidere
Deck, cover, blanket coperta
Declaration of value valore m dichiarato

To declare dichiarare; affermare

Decorative arts artigianato

Deep profondo

Defect difetto

Definitive *(adj)* definitivo; definitively *(adv)* definitivamente

Delay ritardo

To delay tardare; ritardare

Delicatessen negozio di specialità gastronomiche

Delicious squisito, gustoso

Demonstration manifestazione *f*

Denatured alcohol spirito industriale

To denounce, report denunciare

Deodorant deodorante *m*

Department reparto

Department store grande magazzino *m*

Departure partenza

Departure; takeoff decollo

Deposit pegno; *(bottle ~)* cauzione *f*

To describe descrivere

Desire voglia

Desperate disperato

Dessert dessert *m*, dolce *m*

Destination *(travel)* meta

To destroy distruggere

Detergent detersivo

Detour deviazione *f*; giro più lungo

To develop sviluppare

Device apparecchio

Diabetes diabete *m*

Diabetic diabetico

Diagnosis diagnosi *f*

To dial *(phone number)* formare il numero, digitare

Diapers pannolini *m pl*

Diarrhea diarrea

To die morire

Diet regime *m*, dieta *f*

Difference differenza

Different *(adj)* diverso; *(adv)* diversamente

Difficult difficile

Digestion digestione *f*

Digital camera macchina fotografica digitale

Dining car vagone *m* ristorante

Dining room sala da pranzo

Dinner cena

Diphtheria difterite *f*

Direct *(adj)* diretto

Direction direzione *f*; messa in scena

Director direttore/direttrice

Dirt sporcizia

Dirty sporco

Disagreeable spiacevole

To disappear sparire

Disappointed deluso

Discount sconto

To discover scoprire

Dish towel canovaccio per asciugare i piatti

Dishes stoviglie *f pl*, piatti *m pl*

Dishwasher lavastoviglie *f*

Dishwashing brush spazzola per le stoviglie

Dishwashing sink lavandino per i piatti

Dishwashing soap detersivo per le stoviglie

To disinfect disinfettare

Disinfectant disinfettante *m*

Display window vetrina

Dispute lite *f*

Distance lontananza

Distant lontano

Distinguished distinto

To distrust something/ someone non fidarsi di qc/qd

To disturb disturbare
To dive nuotare sott'acqua
Divide dividere
Diving gear attrezzatura da sub
Diving mask maschera *f* da sub
Dizziness imbroglio; vertigini *f pl*
Dizzy ho le vertigini
To do fare
Dock banchina
Documentary film documentario
Documents documenti *m pl*
Dog cane *m*
Domestic flight volo nazionale
Donkey asino
Door porta
Double doppio
Down in giù
Downstairs giù, sotto
Downtown centro città
Draft corrente *f* d'aria
Drama dramma *m*, tragedia
To draw disegnare
Drawing disegno
Drawing from a model disegno di nudi
Dream sogno
Dress vestito
Dressing condimento per l'insalata
Drink bevanda
To drink bere
Drinking water acqua potabile
To drive guidare
To drive a car guidare
Driver conducente *m*
Drops gocce
Drugstore farmacia
Drunk ubriaco, brillo
To dry asciugare
Dry secco, asciutto
Dry cleaning lavare/pulire a secco

Dry hair capelli *m pl* secchi
Dryer asciugatrice *f*
Drying rack stendibiancheria *m*
Dumb stupido, scemo
Duration durata
During *(prep.)* durante; *(+ noun)* mentre
During the day di giorno
During the week durante la settimana
Dust polvere *f*
Duty free esente da dazio doganale
Dynasty dinastia

E

Each *(adj)* ogni; *(prn)* ognuno
Ear orecchio
Ear drops gocce *f pl* per gli orecchi
Ear infection otite *f*
Eardrum membrana del timpano
Early presto
Earrings orecchini *m pl*
Earth terra
East est *m*
East of a est di
Easter Pasqua
Easter Monday Lunedì dell'Angelo
Easy facile
To eat mangiare
Edible commestibile
Education educazione *f*
Eel anguilla
Effort sforzo
Eggplant melanzane
Eggs uova

Either... or o ... o ...
Elastic band benda elastica
Electric rate prezzo forfettario per la corrente
Electric stove cucina elettrica
Electric wheelchair carrozzella elettrica
Electrical elettrico
Electrical appliance store elettricista *m*, elettrodomestici
Electrolyte solution soluzione *f* elettrolitica
Elevator elevatore *m;* ascensore *m*
Elsewhere altrove
Embassy ambasciata
Emblem emblema *m*
Emergency caso di emergenza
Emergency exit uscita d'emergenza
Emergency flashers i lampeggiatori d'emergenza
Emergency phone telefono d'emergenza
Emperor/empress imperatore/imperatrice
Employment impiego
Empty vuoto
En route per strada, in viaggio
To encounter incontrare
End fine *f;* Finally alla fine
Endive indivia del Belgio
England Inghilterra
English inglese
To enjoy godere
Enough sufficiente
To enter entrare
Entertainment divertimento
Enthusiastic (about) entusiasta (di)
Entrance ingresso
Entry entrata (in territorio straniero)

Entry code codice *m* per la porta della camera
Envelope busta
Environment ambiente *m*
Epilepsy epilessia
Epoch epoca
Equal uguale
Error errore *m*
Esophagus esofago
Especially particolarmente
Etching acquaforte *f*
EU-citizen cittadino unitario
Euro euro
Europe Europa
European *(adj.)* europeo
European person europeo/europea
Even *(flat)* piano; stesso
Evening sera
Evening dress abito da sera
Every day tutti i giorni
Every hour ogni ora
Everything tutto
Everywhere dappertutto
Exact preciso
Exactly *(time expressions)* proprio
Exaggerated esagerato
Examination esame *m*
To examine esaminare
Example esempio; For example per esempio
Excavations scavi *m pl*
Excellent eccellente
Except for eccetto, tranne
To exchange scambiare
Exchange scambio
Exchange rate corso dei cambi
Excursion gita, escursione *f*
Excuse scusa
To excuse oneself scusarsi
Exercise esercitare
Exercise esercizio

To exert oneself sforzarsi
Exhaust scappamento, marmitta
Exhausted esaurito
Exhibit pezzo d'esposizione
Exit uscita
Exit ramp uscita
To expect aspettarsi
Expenses spese *f pl*
Expensive caro
Exposition mostra, esposizione *f*
Expression espressione *f*
Expressionism espressionismo
Expressly espressamente
Extension cord cavo di prolungamento, prolunga
Extent tratto
To extinguish spegnere
Extra week settimana supplementare
Extraordinary straordinario
Eye drops gocce *f pl* per gli occhi, collirio
Eyes occhi *m pl*

F

Fabric stoffa
Façade facciata
Face faccia
To facilitate render possibile
Fact fatto
Factory fabbrica
Fainting spell svenimento
Fair fiera; leale
Faith, belief fede *f*
Faithful fedele
To fall cadere
False sbagliato
Family famiglia

Family name cognome *m*
Famous famoso
Fan ventilatore *m*
Far lungo; *(distant)* lungo; lontano
Farm fattoria
Farmhouse fattoria
Fashion moda
Fast *(adj)* rapido, veloce; *(adv)* presto, rapidamente, velocemente
Fast lane superstrada
Fasting digiuno
Fat grosso, *(fatty food)* grasso
Fat-free milk latte *m* magro
Father padre *m*
Fatty grasso
Faucet rubinetto
Fault colpa; difetto
Favor favore *m*
Fax fax
Fear paura
To fear temere; To be afraid of aver paura di
February febbraio
To feel sentire
To feel like avere voglia di
Feeling sentimento
Feminine femminile
Fennel finocchio
Ferry traghetto
Festival festival *m*
Fever febbre *f*
Fiancé(e) fidanzato/fidanzata
Field campo
Figs fichi *m pl*
To fill out riempire; compilare
Filling piombatura
Film film *m*
Final cleaning pulizia finale
Finally finalmente
To find trovare
To find oneself trovarsi
Fine multa; ammenda
Finger dito

254

To finish finire
Fire fuọco; incẹndio
Fire alarm segnalatore *m*
  d'incendio
Fire extinguisher estintore *m*
Firemen vịgili *pl* del fuoco,
  pompieri *pl*
First primo/prima
First aid pronto soccorso
First gear prima *f*
First name nome *m*
To fish pescare con l'amo
Fish pesce *m*
Fish bone spina, lisca
Fish market pescherịa
Fish merchant pescivẹndolo
Fishing license licenza di pesca
Fishing rod canna da pesca
Fishing village villạggio di
  pescatori
Fit in forma
Fitness center centro di fitness,
  palestra
Fixed price forfait *m*
Flash attachment flash *m*
Flat piatto, piano; *(land)* pianura
Flat rate prezzo forfettạrio
Flat tire gomma a terra
Flatulence flatulenza
Flea market mercato delle pulci
Flight volo
Floor pavimento; *(story)* piạno
Flotation ring salvagente *m*
Flour farina
To flow scọrrere
Flower fiore *m*
Flower shop fiorạio
Flush sciacquone *m*
Fly *(insect)* mosca
To fly volare
Fog nẹbbia
Fold-out couch divano letto

Folding wheelchair carrozzella
  pieghẹvole
Folk music mụsica popolare
Folklore folclore *m*
Folklore evening serata
  folclorịstica
To follow seguire
Food alimentazione *f*, vitto
Food poisoning intossicazione *f*
  da alimenti
Foot piẹde *m*
Footbridge passerella, pontile *m*
For per; *(conj.)* poiché
To forbid proibire
To force costrịngere
To force oneself sforzarsi
Foreign ẹstero, straniẹro
Foreign country ẹstero
Foreign person straniẹro/a
Foreigner straniero/a
Forest bosco, foresta
To forget dimenticare
Fork forchetta
Form mọdulo
To form formare
Fortress fortezza
Fortunate felice
To forward recapitare
Forward avanti
Fountain fontana
Fraud inganno
Free lịbero; gratis
French francese
Fresh fresco
Friday venerdì
Fried fritto
Friend amico/amica
Friendly gentile
To frighten spaventare
Frightful terrịbile; spaventoso
From *(origin)* da, di; of
  (material) di
From the grill alla griglia

Frost gelo
Fruit frutta *f*
Fruit and vegetable shop fruttivendolo
Full pieno; *(fully occupied)* pieno; pieno, al completo; sazio
Full pension pensione *f* completa
Fun divertimento
To function funzionare
fungus micosi *f*
Fur pelo
Furious arrabbiato
Furniture (piece of) mobile *m*
Fuse valvola (di sicurezza)
Future futuro

G

Gallbladder cistifellea *f*
Gallery galleria (d'arte)
Game partita
Garage garage *m*
Garden giardino
Garlic aglio
Gas bottle bombola di gas
Gas can lattina, tanica
Gas cylinder cartuccia del gas
Gas pedal acceleratore *m*
Gas pump pompa della benzina
Gas range cucina a gas
Gas stove fornello a gas
Gas tank serbatoio
Gate portone *m*
Gauze fascia di garza
Gear marcia
General delivery fermo posta
Generator dinamo *f*

Gentlemen signori
German measles rosolia
To get angry over arrabbiarsi per qc/con qd
To get drunk ubriacarsi
To get gas far benzina
To get lost smarrirsi
To get married sposare
To get off scendere
To get up alzarsi
Gift regalo
Girl ragazza
To give dare
To give a gift regalare
To give back ridare, restituire
Gladly volentieri
Glance sguardo
Glass *(drainage)* bicchiere *m*
Glass painting pittura su vetro, vetrocromia
Gliding volo a vela
Gloves guanti *m pl*
To go andare
To go away andar via
To go back tornare indietro
To go camping campeggiare
To go hiking camminare, fare escursioni
To go out uscire
To go shopping fare la spesa
To go skiing sciare
To go up salire
To go, walk andare
Goal scopo
Goalie portiere *m*
Goat cheese formaggio di capra
God Dio
Gold oro
Golden color oro
Goldsmith's art arte *f* orafa
Golf golf *m*
Golf club *(implement)* mazza da golf; *(association)* circolo golfistico

Good *(adj)* buono
Gothic gotico
Government governo
Gram grammo
Grandfather nonno
Grandmother nonna
Grandson, Granddaughter nipote *m/f*
Grape uva *f*
Graphic art arte *f* grafica
Grave tomba
Gray grigio
Greatness *(extent, spiritual)* grandezza
Greek greco
Green verde
Green beans fagiolini *m pl*
Green card *(insurance card)* carta verde
To greet salutare
Grill griglia
Grippe influenza
Grocery store negozio di generi alimentari
Groin addome *m*
Grotto grotta
Ground suolo; terreno
Ground level a livello del suolo; pianterreno
Group gruppo
To grow crescere
Guarantee garanzia
Guest ospite *m*
To guide guidare
Guide *(for tourists)* guida
Guided Tour visita guidata
Guided tour of the city giro turistico della città
Gum gengiva
Gust of wind raffica di vento
Gymnastics ginnastica

H

Hair capelli *m pl*
Hair band elastico per capelli
Hair dryer fon *m*
Hair gel gel *m* per capelli
Hairdresser parrucchiere *m*
Hairpins mollette *f pl* (per capelli)
Hairspray frizione *f*
Hairstyle pettinatura
Half mezzo
Half metà
Half pension mezzapensione *f*
Ham prosciutto
Hamburger carne *f* macinata
Hand mano *f*
Hand bike bicicletta per disabili
Hand brake freno a mano
Hand cream crema per le mani
To hand over, turn in consegnare
Hand towel asciugamano
Handbag borsa
Handball palla a mano
Handicap accessible idoneo per/a misura degli handicappati
Handicap association associazione *m* handicappati/ svantaggiati
Handicap ID tesserino di riconoscimento per portatori di handicap
Handicap parking posteggio per handicappati
Handicapped toilet bagno *m*/toilette *f* per handicappati
Handle sostegno, maniglia
Handling charges i diritti fissi
Handmade fatto a mano
Handrail corrimano, mancorrente *m*

Hang glider lo sport del deltaplano

To happen succedere

Happy contento, soddisfatto

Happy (about) lieto (di)

Hard duro

Hardware store negozio di ferramenta, mesticheria

Harmful dannoso

Harvest raccolta

Hat cappello

To have avere

To have an accident avere un incidente/infortunio

To have breakfast fare colazione f

To have to dovere

Hay fever raffreddore m da fieno

He lui

Head testa

Headache pills compresse f pl contro il mal di testa

Headaches mal m di testa

Headlight faro

Headphones cuffia

Health food store negozio di prodotti biodinamici

Health insurance cassa malattia

Health insurance card buono per le cure mediche

Healthy sano

To hear sentire

Hearing udito

Hearing impaired sordastro

Heart cuore m

Heart attack attacco cardiaco

Heart-felt cordialmente

Heart trouble i disturbi cardiaci

Heartburn acidità di stomaco

To heat riscaldare

Heat wave ondata di caldo

Heating riscaldamento

Heavy pesante

To heed fare attenzione a; osservare

Heel tacco

Height altezza

helmet casco

Help aiuto

To help oneself servirsi, prendere

To help someone aiutare qd

Hemorrhage emorragia

Her suo

Her (poss. adj.) (la) sua

Herbs erbette

Here qui

Hernia ernia inguinale

Herring aringa; picchetto

To hesitate esitare

High alto

High beams i fari abbaglianti

High point punto culminante

High tide alta marea

Highway autostrada

Hiking map mappa dei sentieri

Hiking trail sentiero (per escursioni)

Hill collina

To hinder impedire

Hip anca

His (poss prn) (il) suo, (la) sua

History storia

To hit colpire

To hitchhike viaggiare in autostop

To hold tenere

Hole buco

Holy santo

Homeland patria

Homemade fatto in casa

Honey miele m

Hood cofano

Hook uncino, gancio

To hope sperare

Horn clacson m

Horse cavallo
Horseback ride cavalcata
Hospital ospedale *m*
Hospitality ospitalità
Host/hostess ospite *m/f*, padrone/padrona di casa
Hot caldo
Hot water acqua calda
Hour ora, ora; a half hour; mezz'ora; a quarter hour un quarto d'ora
House casa
House/building number numero civico
Houseboat house boat *f*
Hovercraft hovercraft *m*
How *(question)* come
To hug abbracciare
Humid afoso
Hunting reserve riserva di caccia
Hurried frettoloso; To be in a hurry aver fretta
To hurry affrettarsi
To hurt far male
Husband marito
Hut capanna; *(alpine)* baita
Hydroplane aliscafo

I

I io
I feel dizzy ho le vertigini
Ice cream ghiaccio
Ice hockey hockey *m* su ghiaccio
Ice skates pattini *m pl* (per ghiaccio)
ID card carta d'identità
Idea idea

If se
Ignition accensione *f*
Ignition key chiave *f* d'accensione
Illness malattia
Immediately subito
Important importante
Impossible impossibile
Impression impressione *f*
Impressionism impressionismo
Impressive impressionante
Improbable improbabile
To improve migliorare
In in, a; in a week fra una settimana
In addition inoltre
In advance in anticipo
In case casomai
In cash in contanti
In front of davanti
In Italian in italiano
In my opinion per me
In the afternoon pomeriggio *m*
In the evening la sera
In the morning di/la mattina *f*
In the short term a breve termine/scadenza
In vain invano
In writing per iscritto
Inappropriate inadatto
Incident contrattempo
Included compreso
Inconsiderate senza riguardo, sconsiderato
To increase *(prices)* aumentare
Indecent indecente
To indemnify *(damages)* risarcire
Indication indicazione *f*
Indigestion indigestione *f*
Infarction infarto
Infection infezione *f*
Inflammable infiammabile

Inflammation infiammazione *f*
Inflatable boat canotto pneumatico
To inform informare; avvertire
Information informazione *f*
Inhabitant abitante *f/m*
Injured person ferito/ ferita
Injury ferita
Inner courtyard cortile *m* interno
Inner tube camera d'aria
Innocent innocente
To inquire informarsi
Inscription iscrizione *f,* epigrafe *f*
Insect insetto
Inside dentro
Insignificant poco importante
To insist on insistere su
Insomnia insonnia
To inspect controllare
Inspector controllore *m*
Instead of invece di
To instruct istruire; *(school)* istruire; *(school)* insegnare
Instruction formazione *f,* istruzione *f*; *(school)* istruzione scolastica
Insulin insulina
Insurance assicurazione *f*
Intelligent intelligente
To intend to avere l'intenzione di, intendere
Interesting interessante
Intermission intervallo
International internazionale
International call comunicazione *f* internazionale
International flight volo internazionale
Interrail interrail *m*
To interrupt interrompere

Intestine intestino
To introduce presentare qd a qd
Introduction presentazione *f*
Invalid invalido/a
Investment *(money)* impianto
To invite invitare
To iron stirare
Island isola
Island tour giro dell'isola
Itinerary itinerario

Jack cric *m*
Jacket giacca
January gennaio
Jaw mascella
Jazz jazz *m*
Jazzercise ginnastica jazz
Jeans jeans *m pl*
Jelly marmellata
Jeweler gioielleria
Jewelry gioielli *m pl*
To jog fare jogging
Jogging pants i calzoni della tuta
Joint articolazione *f*
Joke barzelletta; scherzo
Joy gioia
Juicy succoso
July luglio
To jump saltare
Jumper cables cavo ausiliario per la messa in moto
June giugno
Just the same ciò nonostante, tuttavia

K

To keep custodire; tenere
To keep something in mind tenere a mente qc
Ketchup ketchup *m*
Key chiave *f*
Key return consegna delle chiavi
Kiddy lift impianto di risalita per bambini
Kiddy pool piscina/vasca per bambini
Kidney rene *m*
Kidney disease nefrite *f*
Kidney stone calcolo renale
Kilo chilogrammo
Kilometer chilometro
Kind caro, gentile
King re
Kiss bacio
To kiss baciare
Kitchenette cucinino, cucinotto
Knee ginocchio
Knife coltello
To know sapere; conoscere
To know how sapere
Known noto

L

Lace laccio/stringa per scarpe; pizzo
Ladies signore
Lake lago
Lamb carne *f* d'agnello
Lamp lampada
Land *(opposite of water)* terra

Land trip escursione *f* a terra
Landing atterraggio
Landscape paesaggio
Landscape format formato orizzontale
Language lingua
Laptop notebook *m*
To last durare
Last ultimo/ultima
To last durare
Last Monday lunedì scorso
Lastly alla fine
Late tardi
Late season bassa stagione *f*
Later più tardi
To laugh ridere
Laundromat lavanderia a gettone
Laundry lavanderia; bucato
Laurel alloro
Lawn prato
Laxative lassativo
Lazy pigro
Leaf foglia
To learn *(acquire knowledge)* imparare; venire a sapere
Leather jacket giacca di pelle
Leather shop pelletteria
To leave lasciare, abbandonare; partire
To leave (for) partire (per)
To leave (from) partire (da)
Leek porro
Left sinistro/sinistra
Leg gamba
Lemonade limonata
Lemons limoni *m pl*
Length lunghezza
To lengthen allungare
Lens lente *f*
Lenses lenticchie *f pl*
Letter lettera
Lettuce insalata verde, lattuga

261

License patente *f*

Lie bugia

To lie down sdraiarsi

Life vita

Life jacket giubbetto di salvataggio

Lifeboat scialuppa di salvataggio

Lifeguard bagnino

Lifesaver salvagente *m*

To lift alzare

Light luce *f;* chiaro

To light accendere

Light *(weight)* leggero

Lightbulb lampadina (ad incandescenza)

Light-hearted allegro

Light meter esposimetro

Light switch interruttore *m*

To light, to switch on accendere

Lighter accenditore solido

Lighthouse faro

Lightning fulmine *m*

To like piacere, garbare

Line linea

Linen lino

Lip labbro

Lipstick rossetto

Liquid liquido

Liquor store bottiglieria

List elenco

To listen to someone ascoltare (qd)

Liter litro

Little poco; a ~ un po'

To live vivere; abitare

Live music musica dal vivo

Lively vivace

Liver fegato

Living room soggiorno

Loading area for ski lift stazione *f* a valle

To loan prestare a qd qc

Lobby hall *f*

Local del posto

Local call telefonata urbana

Local train treno locale

Locality località

To lock chiudere (a chiave)

Lock serratura

To lock up chiudere a chiave

To lodge a complaint reclamare

Lodging alloggio

Lonely solitario

Long lungo

Long-distance call interurbana

To look guardare

To look at guardare

To look for cercare

To lose perdere

Loss perdita

Lost and found ufficio oggetti smarriti

Lots of molto

Loud rumoroso

Lousy cattivo

Love amore *m*

To love amare

Low basso

Low beams luci *f pl* anabbaglianti

Low tide bassa marea

Luck felicità

Lucky felice

Luggage lockers deposito bagagli

Lumbago colpo della strega

Lunch pranzo, desinare *m*

Lunch bag cooler piastra refrigerante

Lung polmone *m*

Luxurious lussuoso

M

Machine macchina
Mackerel sgombro
Magazine rivista, rotocalco
Maiden name cognome *m* da ragazza
Mail box cassetta postale
Main course secondo
Main role ruolo principale
Main street strada principale
Main train station stazione *f* centrale
Mainly principalmente
To make fare
Man uomo
Mandarin oranges mandarini *m pl*
Manual controls *(auto)* acceleratore *m* a mano
Map carta geografica
March marzo
Margarine margarina
Market mercato
Marriage nozze *f pl*
Married *(man)* sposato; *(woman)* sposata
Married (to) sposato (con)
Mascara mascara *m*
Masculine maschile
Mass *(religion)* messa
Massage massaggio
Match fiammifero
Material materiale *m*
Mattress materasso
Mauve lilla
May maggio
Me mi, me
Meadow prato
Meal pasto
Meaning significato; senso
Measles morbillo

Meat carne *f*
Mediator mediatore *m*
Medication for the circulatory system farmaco per disturbi circolatori
Medicine medicina, farmaco
Mediterranean Mediterraneo
Medium cotto
To meet incontrare
To meet someone fare la conoscenza di qd
Mellow *(wine)* amabile
Melon melone *m*, popone *m*
Memorial monumento commemorativo
To mend rammendare
Menstruation mestruazione *f*
Menu menù; lista delle vivande
Merry allegro
Meter metro
Microwave microonda
Middle mezzo, centro
Middle Ages Medioevo
Migraine emicrania
Mild mite, dolce
Milk latte *m*
Millimeter millimetro
Mineral water acqua minerale
Mini-bar minibar *m*
Miniature golf minigolf *m*
Minute minuto
Mirror specchio
To miscalculate sbagliare i calcoli
Misfortune sfortuna, disgrazia
To miss the bus perdere l'autobus
Mistake errore
Misunderstanding malinteso
Mixed misto
Model modello
Moderate sobrio
Modern moderno

Moist ụmido
Moment istante *m*
Monastery monastero
Monday lunedì
Money denaro
Money exchange cạmbio
Money order vạglia *m*, assegno
Month mese *m*
Monthly *(adj)* mensile; *(adv)* mensilmente
Monument monumento
Monument protection tutela dei monumenti
Moon luna
More più; ~ than più che, più di
Morning mattino, mattina
Mosaic mosạico
Mosquito zanzara
Motel motẹl *m*
Mother madre *f*
Motor motore *m*
Motorail train treno traghetto
Motorboat motoscafo
Motorcycle belt fạscia coprireni
Mountain montagna; monte *m*
Mountain bike mountain bike *f*
Mountain climbing alpinismo
Mountain village villạggio di montagna
Mouth bocca
Mouth (of river) sbocco, imboccatura
Movie cịnema *m*
Movie actor/actress l'attore *m*/l'attrice *f* di cịnema
Mr. Signore
Mud fango
Muesli müesli *m*
Multicolored a colori, multicolore
Mumps tonsillite *f*; orecchioni *m pl*
Muscle mụscolo

Muscle pull stiramento
Museum musẹo
Music mụsica; listen to ~ ascoltare mụsica
Musical comedy mụsical *m*, commẹdia musicale
Mussels mịtili *m pl*, cozze *f pl*
Mustache baffi *m pl*
Mustard sẹnape *f*, mostarda *f*
Mute muto
Mutton carne *f* di montone
My (il) mio

N

Nail clippers fọrbici *f pl* per le ụnghie
Nail polish smalto
Nail polish remover acetone *m*, solvente *m* per smalto
Naked nudo
Name nome *m*
Napkin tovagliọlo
Narrow stretto
Nasty cattivo
National park parco nazionale
Nationality nazionalità
Nationality sign targa di nazionalità
Natural *(adj)* naturale; ~ly *(adv)* naturalmente
Nature natura
Nature preserve parco nazionale
Nausea nạusea
Near *(location)* vicino a
Necessary necessạrio
Neck collo
Necktie cravatta

To need aver bisogno di
Needle ago
Negative negativo
Neighbor vicino/vicina
Neighborhood quartiere *m*
Nerve nervo
Nervous nervoso
Net rete *f*
Neutral *(gear)* folle *f*
Never mai
New nuovo
New Year Capodanno
News notizia
Newspaper giornale *m*
Newspaper seller giornalaio
Next prossimo/ prossima
Next to vicino a
Next to last penultimo/a
Next year anno prossimo
Nice simpatico; gentile
Night notte *f*
Night table comodino
Nightclub night-club *m*
Ninepins gioco dei birilli
No one nessuno
Noise chiasso; rumore *m*
Non-binding senza impegno
Non-perishable durevole
Non-smoking section scompartimento per non fumatori
None nessuno
Noodles pasta *f*
Noon mezzogiorno
Normal normale
Normally normalmente, di solito
North nord *m*
North of a nord di
Northern del nord
Nose naso
Not non; ~ at all niente affatto
Not yet non ancora
Notepad blocco (di carta)
Nothing niente

To notice notare
Novel romanzo
Novelty novità
November novembre
Now ora
Nowhere in nessun luogo
Nudist beach spiaggia per nudisti
Number numero
Number plate targa
Nun suora
Nurse infermiera
Nutmeg noce *f* moscata
Nuts noci

O

Oar remo
Oatmeal i fiocchi d'avena
Object oggetto
Objective obiettivo
Objective lens obiettivo
Observatory osservatorio astronomico
To observe osservare
Occasion occasione *f*
Occasionally *(adv)* occasionalmente
Occupied occupato
To occur accadere
Occurrence avvenimento
October ottobre
Offense offesa
Offer offrire
To offer porgere
Office ufficio
Official ufficiale
Offside fuorigioco
Often *(adv)* spesso

Oil olio
Oil change cambio dell'olio
Oil painting pittura a olio
Old vecchio; *(from earlier times)* antico
Old city centro storico
Olive oil olio d'oliva
Olives olive
On su, sopra
On Sunday domenica
On the weekend il fine settimana
Once una volta
One *(indefinite pronoun)* si
One colored a tinta unita
Onions cipolle
Only solo, soltanto
Open aperto
To open aprire
Open car vettura pullman
Opera opera
Operation operazione *f*
Operetta operetta
Opinion opinione
Opposite opposto
Optician ottico
Or oppure
Orange arancione
Orange juice succo d'arancia
Oranges arance
Orchestra orchestra; *(theater)* platea
Orchestra conductor direttore/direttrice d'orchestra
Order ordinazione *f*
Original originale *m*
Original version versione *f* originale
Other person (the) l'altro
Our (il) nostro
Outdoor movie cinema *m* all'aperto
Outdoors fuori

Outside fuori di
Over there là, lì
Overnight pernottamento
To owe dovere
Own proprio
Owner proprietario; padrone *m*, oste *m*
Oxygen machine ossigenatore, *m*
Oysters ostriche

P

Pacemaker cardiostimolatore *m*, pacemaker *m*
Pacifier succhietto, tettarella
Pacifier ciuccio, succhietto
To pack *(in suitcase)* mettere in valigia
Package pacchetto
Packaging imballaggio
Packet pacco
Pain pills compresse *f pl* contro il dolore, analgesici *m pl*
To paint dipingere
Painter pittore/pittrice
Painting pittura; quadro; dipinto
Pair paio
Palace palazzo
Pale pallido
Panorama panorama *m*
Pants pantaloni *m pl*, calzoni *m pl*
Panty liners assorbenti *f pl* sottili, proteggi-slip *m pl*
Paper carta
Paper napkins i tovagliolini di carta
Paraglider parapendio

Paralysis paralisi *f*
Paraplegic paraplegico
Parents genitori *(pl)*
Park parco, giardino pubblico
To park parcheggiare
Parking lights luci *f pl* di posizione
Parking space parcheggio
Parsley prezzemolo
Part parte *f*; riga
Pass passaggio; passo
To pass sorpassare; *(time)* passare
Passenger passeggero
Passing through di passaggio
Passport passaporto
Passport control controllo dei passaporti
Past passato
Pastry shop pasticceria
Pâté de foie gras pasticcio di fegato
Path sentiero
Patience pazienza
To pay pagare
To pay in cash pagare in contanti
Payment pagamento
Peach pesco
Pearl perla
Pears pere
Peas piselli *m pl*
Pedal boat patino a pedali, pedalò
Pedestrian pedone *m*
Pedestrian zone zona pedonale
Pediment timpano
Penalty pena
Penalty box area di rigore
Pendant *(jewelry)* ciondolo
Pension pensione *f*
People gente *f*; popolo
Pepper *(pepper)* peperone *m*; *(seasoning)* paprica

Per a, per
Percent percento
Perch *(fish)* pesce *m* persico
Performance rappresentazione *f*, spettacolo
Perfume profumo
Perfume shop profumeria
Perhaps forse
Permanent *(hair)* permanente *f*
Permission permesso
Person persona
Person in a wheelchair disabile *m/f* in sedia a rotelle
Personal personale
Personnel personale *m*
To persuade persuadere
Petroleum petrolio
Pets animali *m pl* domestici
Phone book elenco telefonico
Phone booth cabina telefonica
Phone call telefonata
Phone number numero telefonico
Photo foto(grafia) *f*
To photograph fotografare
Photograph fotografia
Physical handicap handicap *m* fisico, menomazione *f* fisica
To pick cogliere
To pick up prendere, andare a prendere; *(telephone)* rispondere al telefono
Pickpocket borsaiolo, scippatore *m*
Pickup levata
Picture *(photo)* foto *f*
Picture taking fotografare *m*
Piece pezzo; a piece of bread un pezzo di pane
Pilgrimage site luogo di pellegrinaggio
Pill *(contraceptive)* pillola anticoncezionale

267

Pillow guanciale *m*, cuscino

PIN *(secret code)* numero segreto

Pineapple ananas *m*

Ping-pong ping-pong *m*

Pink rosa

Place piazza

To place mettere

Place luogo

Place of birth luogo di nascita

Place setting coperto; posate

Plan piano; progetto

Plant pianta

Plastic bag sacchetto di plastica

Plastic wrap pellicola (per la conservazione dei cibi)

Plate piatto

To play giocare

Play pièce *f* teatrale

To play music fare della musica

Playmate compagno di giochi

Pleasant piacevole

To please piacere

Pleasure piacere *m*, divertimento

Plug spina

Plums prugne

Pneumonia polmonite *f*

Pocket tasca

Pocket book libro tascabile

Pocket knife temperino, coltello tascabile

Point punta

Poison veleno

Poisoning avvelenamento

Poisonous velenoso

Polaroid camera macchina fotografica a sviluppo immediato

Police polizia

Police car auto della polizia

Policeman agente *m f*; vigile/vigilessa

Polio polio(mielite) *f*

Polite cortese

Poor povero

Popular play commedia popolare

Porcelain porcellana

Pork carne *f* di maiale

Pork sausage wurstel *m pl*

Port porto; affrancatura

Portable CD player lettore *m* CD portatile

Portal portale *m*

Portion porzione *f*

Portrait ritratto

Portrait format formato verticale

Positive positivo

Possibility possibilità

Possible possibile

Post office ufficio postale

Postal code CAP (codice di avviamento postale)

Postcard cartolina postale

Poster manifesto

Potatoes patate

Pots and pans vasellame *m*

Pottery arte *f* di vasaio

Pound mezzo chilo

Powder borotalco; *(face)* cipria

Powder snow neve *f* farinosa

Practical pratico

To praise lodare

Prawn gamberetti *m pl*

To pray pregare

Pre-season bassa stagione *f*

Precinct quartiere *m*

Precisely as... as tanto ... quanto

To prefer preferire

Preferably *(adv)* piuttosto

Prefix prefisso

Pregnancy gravidanza

Premiere prima

Premises locale *m*

To prepare preparare

To prescribe prescrivere

Prescription ricetta
Pretty carino
Previously prima
Price prezzo
Price per kilometer prezzo per chilometro
Priest prete *m*
Principal principale
Prison prigione *f*
Private privato
Prize premio
Probable *(adj)* probabile;
  Probably *(adv)* probabilmente
Problem problema *m*
Procession processione *f*
Product prodotto
Profession professione *f*
Profit vincita, guadagno
Program programma *m*
Program booklet opuscolo del programma
Prohibited vietato
Prohibition divieto
To promise promettere
To pronounce pronunciare
Proof prova
Property tenuta
Proposition proposta
Prospectus prospetto
Prosperous benestante
Prosthesis protesi *f*
Protection index fattore *m* protettivo
Protective custody detenzione *f* preventiva
To protest protestare
Provisions provvista
Proxy delega, procura
Public pubblico
To pull tirare
Pullover pullover *m*, maglione *m*
Pulse polso
Pumpkin zucca

To punch *(ticket)* convalidare
Punctual *(adj)* puntuale
Punctually *(adv)* puntualmente
Pus pus *m*
Push spinta
To put mettere
To put down depositare
To put off *(time)* rimandare
To put on *(clothing)* mettersi

Q

Qualified competente
Quality qualità
Quantity quantità; of un mucchio di
Queen regina
Question domanda

R

Rabbit coniglio
Racing bike bicicletta da corsa
Radar control controllo radar
Radiator radiatore *m*
Radio radio *f*
Rag straccio per lavare i piatti
Rail rotaia
Railroad station stazione *f*
Rain pioggia
Rain shower scrosci *m pl* di pioggia
Raincoat impermeabile *m*
Rainy piovoso
Ramp rampa

Ramp access taglio scalato

Rape violenza(carnale), stupro

Rare *(adj)* raro; **Rarely** *(adv)* raramente

Rash eruzione *f* cutanea, esantema *m*

Rather abbastanza

Ravishing incantevole

Raw crudo

Razor *(electric ~)* rasoio

To reach raggiungere

To read leggere

Ready pronto

Real reale; *(authentic)* Vero; **Really** *(adv)* veramente

Rearview mirror specchietto retrovisore

Reason causa; motivo

Receipt ricevuta

To receive ricevere

Receiver ricevitore *m*

Recently recentemente

Reception reception *f*

To recommend raccomandare

To recover *(from illness)* rimettersi; riposarsi

Red rosso

Red wine vino rosso

Reduction riduzione *f*

Refreshment *(food)* rinfresco; *(drink)* bibita

Refreshments rinfreschi

Refrigerator frigorifero

Refuge rifugio

To refuse rifiutare

Region regione *f*, zona

Regional costume costume *m* regionale

Registered letter raccomandata

To regret dispiacere *m;* essere spiacente di

Regular *(adj)* regolare; **Regularly** *(adv)* regolarmente

To regulate regolare

Regulation regolamento

Related to parente di

Relationship relazione *f,* rapporto

Reliable fidato

Religion religione *f*

To remain rimanere

To remain fermarsi

Remains, leftovers resti *m pl*

Remedy rimedio

To remind someone about something ricordare a qd qc

Renaissance rinascimento

Rent affitto, noleggio

To rent affittare

To repair riparare

To repeat ripetere

To replace sostituire

To report denunciare; riferire

Request domanda

To request chiedere di

To require esigere

To resemble assomigliare

Reservation prenotazione *f*

To reserve riservare; *(place)* prenotare

Residence domicilio

To resolve risolvere

To resolve, make up one's mind decidersi

Respiratory difficulties difficoltà di respirazione

Responsible responsabile

To rest riposarsi

Rest riposo

Rest area piazzola di sosta

Result risultato

Return ritorno

To return ritornare; *(money)* rendere

Return trip viaggio di ritorno

Reverse *(gear)* marcia indietro

Reward ricompensa
Rheumatism reumatismi *m pl*
Rice riso
Rich ricco
Ride a bicycle andare in bicicletta
To ride horseback cavalcare
Ridiculous ridicolo
Riding school scuola di equitazione
Right *(direction)* destro/destra; *(correct)* diritto; giusto; *(appropriate)* adatto
Right away subito
Right now proprio ora
Right of way precedenza
Ring anello
Ripe maturo
Risk rischio
River fiume *m*
Riverbank sponda
Road via, strada
Road map carta automobilistica
Roast arrostito
Roasted tostato, arrostito
Rock roccia
Rock and roll rock *m*
Roll panino
Roller blades Rollerblades *m pl*
Roof tetto
Room *(in house)* stanza; camera; sala
Room telephone telefono in camera
Rope corda
Rosemary rosmarino
Rotten guasto; marcio
Round rotondo
Round-trip ticket biglietto di andata e ritorno
To row remare
Rowboat barca a remi

Rubber boots stivali *m pl* di gomma
Ruin rovina
Ruins i reperti archeologici
To run correre
Rupture *(groin)* ernia
Ruptured tendon strappo dei legamenti

S

Sad triste
Safe *(box)* cassaforte *f*
Safety sicurezza; garanzia
Safety pin spillo di sicurezza
Saffron zafferano
Sage salvia
Sailboat barca a vela
Sailing cruise veleggiata, gita in barca a vela
Salad insalata
Salad bar buffet *m* delle insalate
Salami salame *m*
Sale vendita
Salt sale *m*
Saltshaker spargisale *m*, saliera
Salve pomata
Same thing (the) stesso *m*
Sand castle castello di sabbia
Sandals sandali *m pl*
Sandbox recinto con la sabbia
Sanitary facilities servizi igienici *m pl*
Sanitary napkins assorbenti *m pl*
Saturday sabato
Sauce salsa
Saucer piattino
Sauna sauna

271

Sausage salsicce
To save salvare
Savings book libretto di risparmio postale
To say dire
Scar cicatrice *f*
Scarcely appena
Scarf scialle *m;* sciarpa
Schedule orario
School scuola
School children bambini *m pl*
Sciatica sciatica
Scissors forbici *f pl*
To scold sgridare
Screw vite *f*
To scuba dive fare lo snorkeling
Sculptor scultore *m*
Sculpture scultura
Sea mare *m*
Sea conditions moto ondoso
Seagull gabbiano
Seamstress sarta
Seaside resort località marittima
Season stagione *f*
To season condire, drogare
Seat sede *f*
Seat belt cintura di sicurezza
Second secondo/a
Second-hand dealer rigattiere *m*
Secondary road strada provinciale
Secondly secondo
Secret *(adj)* segreto; **Secretly** *(adv)* di nascosto
Security check controllo di sicurezza
Security tax tassa per controlli di sicurezza
See vedere
To see to it that procurare

Seeing-eye dog cane *m* guida per ciechi
To select scegliere
Self service self-service *m*
To sell vendere
To send mandare
Sender mittente *m*
Sensitivity sensibilità del film
Sentence frase *f*
To separate separare
September settembre
Serious serio
To serve servire
Service servizio
Service area stazione *f* di servizio, autogrill *m*
To set mettere
To sew up cucire
Sex sesso
Sexual harassment molestia sessuale
Shadow ombra
Shameless sfacciato
Shampoo shampoo *m*
Shape forma
To share with someone dividere con qd
Shaving brush pennello da barba
Shaving cream schiuma da barba
She ella, lei
Sheep's milk cheese pecorino
Sheet *(paper)* foglio
Shellfish conchiglia
Shinbone tibia
Shirt camicia
Shoe scarpa
Shoe brush spazzola da scarpe
Shoe polish lucido per scarpe
Shoe store negozio di calzature
Shoemaker calzolaio
Short *(measurement)* corto

Short circuit corto circuito
Short feature film a corto metraggio
Shortcut *(travel)* scorciatoia
Shorts pantaloncini *m pl*, shorts *m pl*
Shot iniezione *f*, puntura
Shot record libretto di vaccinazione
Shoulder spalla
Shoulder bag borsa a tracolla
Show show *m*
To show mostrare
Shower doccia
Shower gel gel *m* per la doccia
To shut chiudere
Shutter release scatto
Shuttle bus servizio pulman
Shuttlecock volano
Sick malato
Side parte *f*, lato
Side street strada secondaria
Sideburns basette
Sight vista
Sights cose *f pl* da vedersi, monumenti *m pl*
Sign segno; prova; *(notice)* insegna; *(on door, car)* targa; *(street)* segnale *m*
To sign firmare
Sign language linguaggio mimico/a segni
Signature firma
Signpost segnavia *m*
Silence silenzio
Silent silenzioso
Silk seta
Silk painting pittura in seta
Silver argento
Similar simile
Simple semplice
Since da
Since *(reason)* dato che

To sing cantare
Singer cantante *m/f*
Single singolo
Sink lavabo, lavandino
Sinus infection sinusite *f*
Sister sorella
Sister-in-law cognata
To sit sedere
To sit down sedersi
Situation situazione *f*
Size *(clothing, shoes)* misura
Skateboard skate-board *m*
Skating pattinaggio su ghiaccio
Skating rink pista per pattinaggio su ghiaccio
Ski sci *m*
Ski binding attacco
Ski boots scarponi *m pl* da sci
Ski goggles occhiali *m pl* da sci
Ski instructor maestro/a di sci
Ski lessons corso di sci
Ski lift sciovia
Ski pants pantaloni *m pl* da sci
Ski poles i bastoni da sci
Skin pelle *f*
Skirt gonna
Sky cielo
Sky diving paracadutismo
Sled slitta
To sleep dormire
Sleeping pills sonniferi *m pl*
Sleeve maniche
Slender snello
Slice fetta
Slope salita
Slow *(adj)* lento
Slowly *(adv)* lentamente, piano
Sly furbo
Small piccolo
Smart card tessera
Smell odore *m*
To smell odorare; ~ like sapere di

273

To smoke fumare

Smoked affumicato

Smoker fumatore

Smoking section scompartimento per fumatori

To smuggle fare contrabbando

Smuggling contrabbando

Snack spuntino

Snake serpente *m*

Snapshot istantanea

To snatch strappare

Snore russare

Snorkel respiratore *m* di superficie, snorkel *m*

Snow neve *f*

Soap sapone *m*

Sober non ubriaco

Soccer calcio

Soccer field terreno di gioco

Soccer game partita di calcio

Social services servizio assistenza sociale

Socks calzini *m pl*

Soft morbido

Softly piano, a bassa voce

Solarium solario

Sole sogliola; suola

Solid saldo

Solid ground terraferma

Soloist solista *m/f*

Some alcuni/alcune

Someone qualcuno

Something qualcosa; A little un po' (di)

Sometimes a volte

Son figlio

Song canzone *f;* canto

Soon presto; As soon as possible al più presto possibile

Sore throat mal di gola

Sore throat lozenges pastiglie *f pl* per la gola

To sound suonare

Soup minestra

Soup bowl piatto fondo, scodella

Sour agro

South sud *m*

South of a sud di

Southern del sud *f*

Souvenir shop negozio di souvenir

Space spazio

Spare tire ruota di scorta

To speak parlare

Speaker *(stereo system)* altoparlante *m*

Special speciale

Special diet cibo dietetico

Special issue stamp emissione *f* speciale

Specialty specialità

Spectator spettatore *m*

Speed velocità

To spell sillabare

To spend *(time)* passare; spendere

To spend the night pernottare

Spice spezie

Spicy piccante

Spinach spinaci *m pl*

Spinal column spina dorsale, colonna vertebrale

Splint stecca

Spoon cucchiaio

Sport sport *m*

Sporting goods articoli *m pl* sportivi

Spot macchia

Spot; job posto

Sprained slogato

Spring primavera *f*

Spring sorgente *f*, fonte *f*

Square meter metro quadrato

Stadium stadio

Stage direction regia

Staircase scala

Stamp francobollo; timbro
To stamp affrancare
Stamp machine distributore *m* automatico per francobolli
To stand stare (in piedi)
Star stella
Starter motorino d'avviamento
Starting with da
State stato, paese *m*
Stationery carta da lettere, carta da scrivere
Stationery store cartoleria
Statue statua
Stature statura
Stay soggiorno
To stay trattenersi
To steal rubare
Steamed cotto a vapore
Steamer piroscafo, nave *f* a vapore
Steep ripido
Steering wheel knob manopola sul volante
Step passo; gradino
Steward/stewardess steward *m*, assistente *m/f* di bordo/ hostess *f*
Stick bastone *m*
Still ancora; tranquillo
Still life natura morta
To sting pungere
To stink puzzare
Stir fry piatto al tegame
Stockings calze *f pl*
Stomach stomaco; ventre *m*
Stomachache mal *m* di stomaco
Stone pietra
Stony sassoso
Stop! alt!
Stop *(bus, streetcar, etc.)* fermata
To stop smettere; fermare qc/qd, fermarsi
To stop over in attraccare a

Stopover scalo
To store conservare
Story *(of building)* piano
Stove cucina; fornello
Straight diritto
Straight ahead diritto
Strands colpi *m pl* di sole, méches *f pl*
Strange *(unknown)* sconosciuto
Stranger estraneo/a
Straw cannuccia
Strawberries fragole
Street via, strada
Streetcar tram *m*
Strength forza
Strenuous faticoso
Stretch pants fuseaux *m pl*
String spago
Stroke colpo apoplettico
Stroll passeggiata
Strong forte
Studio studio
To study studiare
Stuffed ripieno
Stupid scemo
Style stile *m*
Subject to customs duties soggetto a dazio doganale
Subtitles sottotitolo
Suburb sobborgo
Subway metropolitana
Suddenly improvvisamente
To suffice bastare
Sugar zucchero
Suit abito
Suitcase valigia
Sum somma
Summer estate *f*
Summit cima
Summit station stazione *f* a monte
Sun sole *m*

275

Sun hat cappello da sole
Sunbathing lawn prato per sdraiarsi
Sunburn scottatura (solare)
Sunday domenica
Sunny soleggiato
Sunroof tetto apribile
Sunscreen protezione *f* solare
Sunstroke colpo di sole
Suntan lotion crema solare
Suntan oil olio solare
Supermarket supermercato
To supervise sorvegliare
Supplement supplemento
Supplementary supplementare, in più
To supply with rifornire di
Suppositories supposta
Sure *(adj)* sicuro; **Surely** *(adv)* certamente
To surf praticare il surfing
Surfboard tavola del wind-surf
Surgeon chirurgo
Surprised sorpreso
Swamp palude *f*
To sweat sudare
Sweet dolce
Sweetener edulcorante *m*, dolcificante, *m*
Sweets dolciumi *m pl*
Swelling gonfiore *m*, tumefazione *f*
To swim nuotare
Swim fins pinne *f pl*
Swimming lessons corso da nuoto
Swindler imbroglione *m*
Swollen gonfio
Swordfish pesce *m* spada
Symphony concert concerto sinfonico
Syringe siringa

T

T-shirt maglietta
Table tavolo
Tablecloth tovaglia
Tablet compressa, pasticca, pillola
Tachometer tachimetro
Taillights fanalino posteriore
Tailor sarto
To take prendere
To take a walk passeggiare
To take an X-ray radiografare
To take away portar via
To take care of occuparsi di
To take one's leave congedarsi, accomiatarsi
To take part (in) partecipare (a)
To take place aver luogo
Tampons tamponi *m pl*
Taste gusto
Taxi driver tassista *m/f*
Taxi stand posteggio di taxi
Tea tè *m*
Teabag bustina di tè
To teach insegnare
Team *(sports)* squadra
Teaspoon cucchiaino
Telegram telegramma *m*
Telephone telefono
To telephone telefonare
Telephoto lens teleobiettivo
Television televisore *m*
Television room stanza della televisione
To tell raccontare
Temperature temperatura
Temple tempio
Temporary provvisorio
Tender tenero
Tennis tennis *m*
Tennis racket racchetta

Tent tenda
Tent pole palo da tenda
Tent rope laccio da tenda
Terminal air terminal *m*
Terra-cotta terracotta
Terrace terrazza
To testify certificare
Tetanus tetano
Than *(comparative)* di, che
To thank ringraziare (qd)
That *(conjunction)* che
That one quello/quella
That's why perciò
To the left a sinistra
To the rear dietro
To the right a destra
Theater teatro
Theater café cabaret *m*
Theater troupe compagnia
teatrale
Theft furto
Them loro *pl*
Then poi
There *(location)* da
There is/are c'è, ci sono
Thermometer termometro
They essi, esse, loro *pl*
Thief ladro
Thin magro; fine; sottile
Thing cosa
To think about pensare a
Third terzo/terza
**Third party, fire, and theft
insurance** assicurazione *f*
parziale per tutti i rischi
This questo/questa
Thriller thriller *m*
Throat gola
Through *(direction)* attraverso
To throw gettare
Thursday giovedì
Thus dunque, allora; così
Thyme timo

Ticket biglietto
Ticket cost prezzo del biglietto
Ticket machine distributore *m*
automatico di biglietti
Ticket window biglietteria,
sportello biglietti
Tied (game) in pareggio; pari
Tights collant *m*, calzamaglia
Time tempo
Timed shutter release
autoscatto
Timely *(adv)* in tempo
Timid timido
Tincture of iodine tintura di
iodio
Tint tingere
Tip suggerimento, consiglio;
mancia
Tire pneumatico
Tire repair kit accessori *m pl*
per la riparazione di forature
Tired stanco
Tissues i fazzoletti di carta
To *(toward things)* a, in, verso
(toward people) da
Toast toast *m*
Toaster tostapane *m*
Tobacco tabacco
Tobacco shop tabaccaio
Today oggi
Toe dito del piede
Together *(adv)* insieme
Toilet paper carta igienica
Toilets toilette *f*, bagno
To tolerate sopportare, tollerare
Toll pedaggio autostradale
Tomatoes pomodori *m pl*
Tomb monumento sepolcrale
Tone *(sound)* suono; *(color)* tono,
tonalità
Tongue lingua
Tonsils tonsille *f pl*
Too anche

Too bad! Che peccato!

Too much troppo

Tool utensile *m*, attrezzo

Tooth dente *m*

Toothache mal *m* di denti

Toothbrush spazzolino da denti

Toothpaste dentifricio

Toothpick stuzzicadenti *m*

Total *(adj)* intero; **Totally** *(adv)* interamente; tutto

To touch toccare

Tough duro

Tour gita, giro

Touring bike bicicletta da trekking

Tourist turista *m/f*

Tourist guide guida turistica, cicerone *m*

Tourist office ente *m* per il turismo

To tow rimorchiare, trainare

Tow truck carro attrezzi

Toward *(direction, time)* verso

Tower torre *f*

Towing cable cavo da rimorchio

Towing service autosoccorso

Town hall municipio

Toy store negozio di giocattoli

Toys giocattoli *m pl*

Track binario

Track and field atletica leggera

Traffic traffico

Traffic jam ingorgo

Traffic light semaforo

Tragedy tragedia

Trailer roulotte *f*

Train treno

Tranquilizer calmante *m*

Transfer rimessa, trasferimento

Transfusion fleboclisi *f*

To translate tradurre

Transmission *(engine)* cambio

Transportation service servizio di trasporto

Trash immondizia; spazzatura

Trash bag sacco delle immondizie

To travel viaggiare

Travel agency agenzia di viaggi

Travel bag borsa da viaggio

Travel group comitiva

Travel guide guida *m*

Traveler viaggiatore/viaggiatrice

Traveler's check assegno turistico, traveller's chèque *m*

To treat trattare, curare

Tree albero

Trip viaggio

Tripod treppiedi *m*

True vero

Trunk *(of car)* bagagliaio

Trust fiducia

To try tentare; *(food)* tentare; assaggiare

Tuesday martedì

Tumor tumore *m*

Tuna fish tonno

Tunnel tunnel *m*, galleria

Turbid torbido

To turn around ritornare, tornare indietro

Turquoise turchese

Tweezers pinzetta

Type specie *f*

Typhus tifo

Typical (of) tipico, caratteristico (per)

U

Ugly brutto

Ulcer ulcera
Umbrella ombrello
Unaccustomed insolito
Unbearable insopportabile
Unbelievable incredibile
Unconscious privo di sensi
Uncooked ham prosciutto crudo
Undecided indeciso
Under sotto di
Underpants mutande *f pl;* slip *m*
Underpass sottopassaggio
Undershirt maglietta, canottiera
To understand capire
Underwater camera macchina fotografica subacquea
Underwear biancheria intima
Unemployed disoccupato
Unfortunately purtroppo
Uninhabited disabitato
United States Stati Uniti
University università
Unmarried *(man)* celibe; *(woman)* nubile
Unpleasant spiacevole
Until fino a; So far finora
Unwillingly di mala voglia
Upstairs sopra, sù
Upwards in su
Urgent urgente
Urinal gabinetto alla turca/vespasiano
Urine urina
Us *(dir. obj.)* ci, noi; *(ind. obj.)* ci, a noi
To use adoperare, usare
Usual usuale
Usual solito, abituale
Usually di solito

V

Vacation vacanze *pl;* ferie *f pl*
Vacation house casa per le vacanze
Vacation resort centro vacanze
Vaccination vaccinazione *f*
Valid valido
Valley valle *f*
Valuables oggetti *m pl* di valore
To value stimare
Value valore *m*
Variable variabile
Variety show varietà *m*
Vase vaso
Vault volta
Veal carne *f* di vitello
Vegetables verdura
Vegetarian vegetariano
Vehicle identification number numero del vagone
Vending machine distributore *m* automatico
Very molto
Vice-versa viceversa
Vicinity dintorni *m pl;* in the ~ of nei dintorni di
Video camera videocamera
Video cassette videocassetta
Video film videofilm *m*
Video recorder videoregistratore *m*
View vista
View vista
Viewfinder mirino
Viewpoint belvedere *m*
Villa villa
Village villaggio, paese *m*
Vinegar aceto
Vineyard vigneto, vigna
Violet viola
Virus virus *m*

Visa visto
Vision impaired menomato nella vista
To visit visitare
Visit vịsita
To visit someone andare a trovare qd
Visiting hours orạrio di vịsita
Voice voce *f*
Volcano vulcano
Volleyball pallavolo *f*
Volt volt *m*
Voltage voltạggio

Wading pool piscina/vasca per bambini
To wait aspettare
To wait in line fare la fila
Waiter camerịere *m*
Waiter/waitress camerịere/camerịera
Waiting room sala d'aspetto; soggiọrno *m*
To wake up svegliarsi
Walk passeggiạta
Wall parete *f*; muro
Wall socket presa di corrente
Wallet portamonete *m*
Warm caldo
To warn (about) avvertire (di)
Warning triangle triạngolo
To wash lavare
Washcloth guanto di spugna
Washing machine lavatrice *f*
Washroom stanzino da bagno
Wasp vespa

Wastebasket bidone *m* delle immondịzie
Watch out! attenzione!
To watch (over) stare attento (a)
Watchmaker orologiạio
Water ạcqua
Water can tạnica dell'ạcqua
Water consumption consumo d'ạcqua
Water glass bicchịere *m* da ạcqua
Water skiing sci *m pl* nautici
Water wings bracciali *m pl* salvagente, braccioli *m pl*
Watercolor acquerello; ~ painting, pittura di acquerello
Waterfall cascata
Watt *(elec.)* watt *m*
Wave far segno
Way; modo
We noi
Weak dẹbole
To wear portạre
Weather forecast previsioni *f pl* metereolọgiche
Weather report bollettino meteorolọgico
Wednesday mercoledì
Week settimana
Week pass abbonamento settimanale
Weekend rate forfait *m* per il fine settimana
Weekly *(adj)* settimanale; *(adv)* settimanalmente
Weekly menu abbonamento settimanale
To weigh pesare
Weight peso
Welcome benvenuto
To welcome ricẹvere
Well *(adv)* bene

Well done ben cotto
West ovest _m_
West of a ovest di
Western western _m_
Wet bagnato
Wet suit muta _f_ in neoprene
What cosa, che cosa, che; What
  kind of...? quale, che... ?
Wheel ruota
Wheelchair carrozzella, sedia a
  rotelle
Wheelchair accessible
  adatto/idoneo per carrozzelle
When quando
White bianco
White bread pane _m_ bianco
White wine vino bianco
Whooping cough pertosse _f_
Why perché
Wide largo, ampio
Widow vedova
Widower vedovo
Wife moglie _f_
Wig parrucca
Wild _(animal, person)_ selvaggio;
  (plant) selvatico
To win vincere
Wind vento
Wind speed intensità del vento
Windbreaker giacca a vento
Window finestra
Window seat posto al finestrino
Windshield parabrezza _m_
Windshield wiper tergicristallo
Wine vino
Wine glass bicchiere _m_ da vino
Wine shop fiaschetteria, enoteca
Wing ala
Winter inverno
Winter tires pneumatici _m pl_ da
  neve
Wire filo

Wire transfer vaglia _m_
  telegrafico
Wisdom tooth dente _m_ del
  giudizio
To wish desiderare
To wish, want volere
With con
Without senza
Woman donna; _(direct address,_
  before name) signora
To wonder (about)
  meravigliarsi di
Wonderful magnifico;
  meraviglioso
Wood legno
Wood sculpture intaglio
Woodcut silografia
Wool lana
Wool blanket coperta di lana
Wool jacket giacca di lana, golf
  _m_
Word parola
Work lavoro
To work lavorare
World mondo
Worm verme _m_
To worry preoccuparsi
To worry about preoccuparsi di
Worthless senza valore
To wound ferire
Wound ferita
To wrap _(in paper)_ incartare
Wristwatch orologio da polso
To write scrivere
Writing calligrafia

X

X-ray radiografia

Y

Year anno
To yell gridare
Yellow giallo
Yes (indeed)! certo, sì
Yesterday ieri
Yoga yoga *m*
Yogurt iogurt *m*
You tu, lei, voi; *(indir. obj.)* ti, a te; *(dir. obj.)* vi, voi; *(indir. obj.)* vi, a voi

Young giovane
Young lady signorina
Young person minorenne *(m,f)*
Your (il) vostro
Yours truly (il) tuo

Z

Zoo zoo *m*